DK Children's ENCYCLOPEDIA

DK
Children's
ENCYCLOPEDIA
The book that explains everything

Penguin
Random
House

Senior editor Lizzie Davey
Senior designers Joanne Clark, Jim Green
Editorial Anwesha Dutta, Satu Fox, Marie Greenwood,
Jolyon Goddard, Radhika Haswani, Deborah Lock,
Ishani Nandi, Sam Priddy, Allison Singer, Kathleen Teece,
Shambavi Thatte, Megan Weal, Amina Youssef
US editorial Karyn Gerhard, Shannon Beatty
Design Ann Cannings, Rhea Gaughan, Rashika Kachroo,
Shipra Jain, Anthony Limerick, Fiona Macdonald, Nidhi Mehra,
Bettina Myklebust Stovne, Seepiya Sahni, Victoria Short,
Lucy Sims, Mohd Zishan
Educational consultants Jacqueline Harris,
Christina Catone
DTP designers Vijay Kandwal, Vikram Singh
Jacket designer Amy Keast
Jacket coordinator Francesca Young
Picture researcher Sakshi Saluja
Managing editors Laura Gilbert, Alka Thakur Hazarika
Managing art editors Diane Peyton Jones, Romi Chakraborty
Production manager Pankaj Sharma
Pre-production producer Nikoleta Parasaki
Producer Isabell Schart
Art director Martin Wilson
Publisher Sarah Larter
Publishing director Sophie Mitchell
Design director Philip Ormerod

First American Edition, 2017
Published in the United States by DK Publishing
345 Hudson Street, New York, New York 10014

Copyright © 2017 Dorling Kindersley Limited
DK, a Division of Penguin Random House LLC
17 18 19 20 21 10 9 8 7 6 5 4 3 2 1
001-298820-Oct/2017

A catalog record for this book is available from the Library of Congress.
ISBN 978-1-4654-6207-7

DK books are available at special discounts when purchased in bulk for sales
promotions, premiums, fund-raising, or educational use. For details, contact:
DK Publishing Special Markets, 345 Hudson Street, New York, New York 10014
SpecialSales@dk.com

Printed and bound in Hong Kong

All images © Dorling Kindersley Limited
For further information see: www.dkimages.com

A WORLD OF IDEAS:
SEE ALL THERE IS TO KNOW

www.dk.com

Experts

Simon Adams has written and contributed to more than 80 books on a wide range of topics: from history to the arts and politics.

Peter Bond has written 12 books and contributed to, or edited, many more. He also writes for the European Space Agency and is consultant editor for IHS Jane's Space Systems & Industry. He was formerly a press officer for the Royal Astronomical Society.

Dr. Marina Brozovic is a physicist at NASA's Jet Propulsion Laboratory. She has written many research papers, and works on asteroids, satellites of the giant planets, and was involved in the New Horizons mission to Pluto.

Peter Chrisp is an author of children's history books, with over 80 titles to his name. He specializes in ancient Rome, ancient Greece, and myths and legends.

Emily Dodd is a screenwriter for the CBeebies science television show *Nina and the Neurons*. She is passionate about science, wildlife, and storytelling, and is an author of fiction and nonfiction books.

James Floyd Kelly is a writer from Atlanta, Georgia. He has written over 35 books on a range of subjects that include 3-D printing, robotics, and coding.

E.T. Fox is an author and historian, with particular expertise in the areas of British and Atlantic maritime history and piracy, among others. He is a lecturer, has published books and articles, and has advised on numerous television productions.

Kirsten Geekie is a film programmer and writer specializing in short films and cinema for young people. She is the Film Programming Manager at Into Film, co-curator of the Into Film Festival, and was the lead writer of the *Children's Book of the Movies*.

Cat Hickey is the learning manager at ZSL Whipsnade Zoo. She has worked in zoos for eight years and spent a year working as a research scientist in Madagascar, collecting data on lemurs.

Dr. Emily Hunt is a professor of engineering at West Texas A&M University. She has a background in mechanical engineering, with a particular interest in innovative nanotechnology.

Phil Hunt has written, edited, and acted as consultant on a wide range of travel and transportation illustrated reference books and magazines for adults and children.

Sawako Irie has taught the Japanese language at the University of Sheffield and has run training programs at SOAS University of London. Currently, she provides Japanese cultural and language services.

Klint Janulis is a former US Army Special Forces operator, medic, and primitive skills survival instructor. He provides expert information to the UK television show *10000 BC* and is currently completing an archeological Doctoral program at Oxford University.

Rupert Matthews has written more than 170 books about history. He writes for newspapers and magazines, and is a public speaker at events and in schools.

Sean McArdle was a headteacher and primary school educator, specializing in math. He has written and contributed to many publications and mathematics websites.

Dr. Angela McDonald is an Egyptologist based at the Centre for Open Studies at the University of Glasgow. She has a PhD from Oxford University, and is an expert on Egyptian texts. She led tours to Egypt for many years, and has published books and articles on ancient Egypt.

Bill McGuire is an academic, broadcaster, and popular science and fiction writer. He is currently Professor Emeritus of Geophysical and Climate Hazards at University College London.

Marcus Weeks is a musician and author. As well as contributing to numerous reference books, he has written several books on philosophy, psychology, and music.

Contents

How this book works

Ever wonder what a planet is? Do you know the difference between frogs and toads? Every page in this encyclopedia is packed with fun facts and amazing photographs. Dive right in or jump to a page that catches your eye to discover all about our wonderful world. The helpful tips here will guide you through using this book.

Alphabetical pages

The book's pages are arranged alphabetically. You can look up topics using the contents list, which starts on page four, or flip through the pages in whichever order you like.

See also

If you enjoy reading a page, you can use the "see also" box to find similar pages in the book and see where they are. This lets you make links across topics and subject areas and create your own journey through the encyclopedia.

In the "see also" box, "p." stands for page and "pp." for pages.

Follow the suggestions in the "see also" box to get to related topics elsewhere in the book.

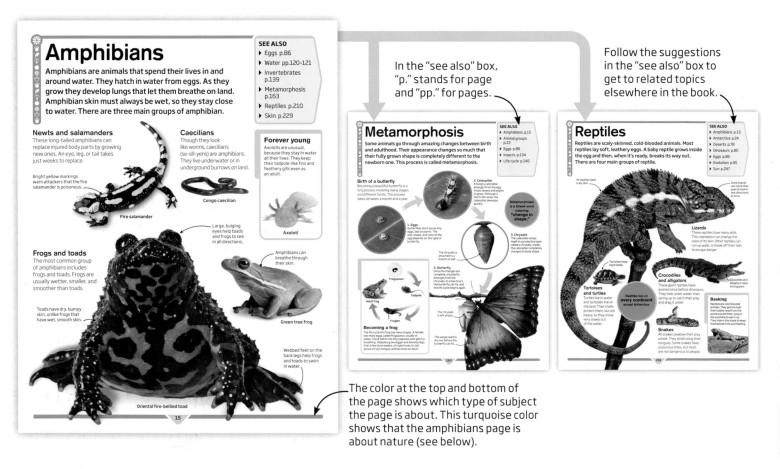

The color at the top and bottom of the page shows which type of subject the page is about. This turquoise color shows that the amphibians page is about nature (see below).

Subject areas

The encyclopedia covers nine different subject areas. Each one has its own color, which is shown at the top and bottom of the page.

Art   People   History   Earth   Nature   Science   Technology   Space   Human body

The story of...

These pages bring together information from the different subjects, to get you thinking about things from lots of different angles. These pages are not arranged alphabetically.

Reference

The reference section contains useful lists, diagrams, and tables. For example, there is a map of the world, and there are lists of great artists, scientists, and writers.

Glossary

The glossary is a list of some of the more difficult words used in the book. If you would like an explanation of what a word means, you can look for it in the glossary.

Index

The index lists alphabetically everything covered in the book, along with its page number. If there is anything you want to know about, you can look it up here.

Africa

Africa is a very hot continent, and a lot of the landscape is made up of deserts and dry plains. Its central region is covered in rain forest. This continent was home to the first people on Earth millions of years ago.

SEE ALSO
- Ancient Egypt p.17
- Conservation p.72
- Deserts p.78
- Early humans p.82
- Language p.144
- World p.275

The Tuareg live in the desert. They wear traditional blue robes.

Tamarisk tree

Temple of Zeus

Pyramids

Bedouin camel train

Bedouin people use camels to move goods across the Sahara Desert.

Addax

Tuareg people

The horns of this rare antelope can grow to 47 in (120 cm) long.

Jerboa

Zebra

African elephant

Benin bronzes

Okapi

Lion

Bonobo

Diamonds

African animals

Africa is home to many types of animals. Large areas have been set up where they can roam freely and safely. Tourists go to watch them in the wild.

Mount Kilimanjaro

Acacia tree

Lemurs live on the island of Madagascar.

Grey parrot

Leopard

Lemur

About Africa

Population: 1.216 billion

Highest point: Mount Kilimanjaro

Lowest point: Lake Assal

Biggest desert: Sahara Desert

Longest river: Nile

Giraffes are the world's tallest animals, with males reaching 18 ft (5.5 m).

African elephants are the heaviest land animals.

Giraffe

Victoria Falls

Fossils of human ancestors

Table Mountain

Ancient pyramids

The pyramids in Egypt were built 4,500 years ago. Inside are the tombs of Egyptian rulers called pharaohs.

The pyramids are made of millions of stone blocks that were cut and dragged into place.

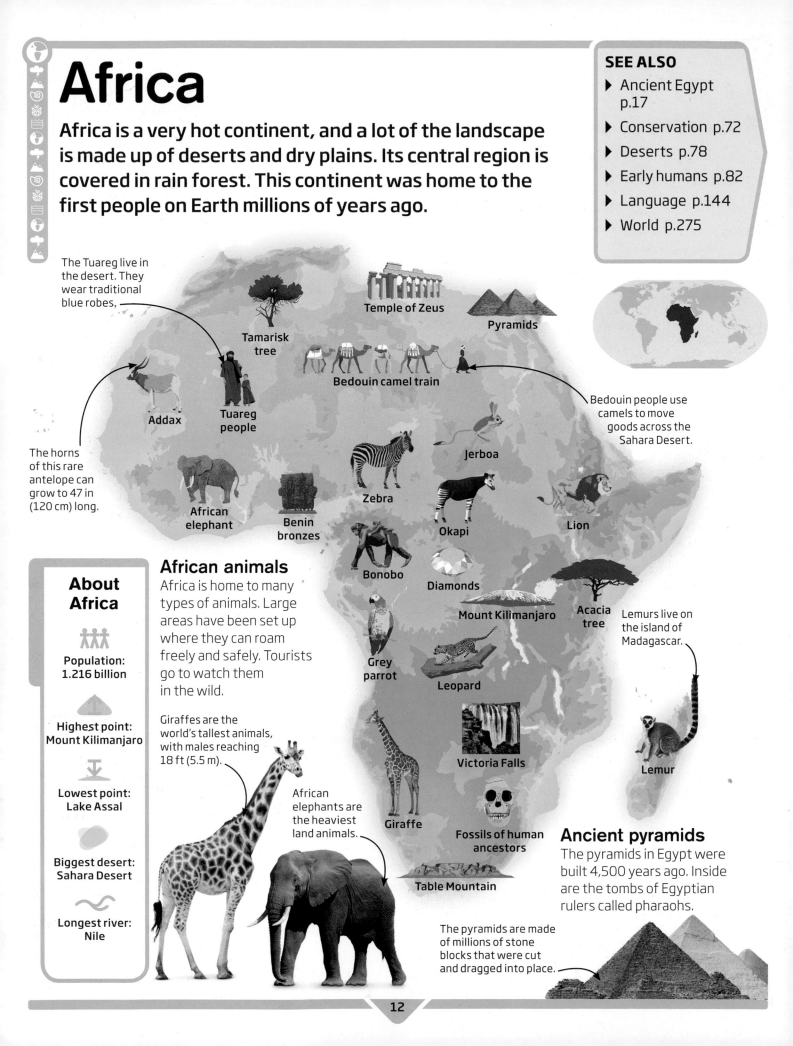

Aircraft

Aircraft are types of transportation that let us travel through air. They take people on vacations and are also used by fire crews, doctors, and farmers. Types of aircraft include planes, helicopters, and hot air balloons.

SEE ALSO
▶ Atmosphere p.33
▶ Birds p.39
▶ Forces p.108
▶ Gravity p.125
▶ Transportation pp.258–259

Plane

The Airbus A380 is the world's largest passenger plane. It can carry more than 800 people on two decks and fly nonstop from the US to Australia.

This 79 ft (24 m) high tail section has a flap called a rudder that steers the aircraft.

Ailerons are flaps on each wing that move up and down to turn the aircraft.

This part of the tail helps to keep the aircraft flying straight.

The cockpit is where the pilot and copilot fly the aircraft.

The A380 is powered by four huge jet engines, each as long as a family car.

Helicopter

A helicopter uses fast-spinning blades, called rotors, to fly through the air. These rotor blades raise the helicopter and move it forward. Smaller rotors on the tail keep the craft straight.

Main rotor blades

Tail rotor

Cockpit

Landing skis

How aircraft fly

The green arrows show the four pushes and pulls, or forces, acting on an aircraft during flight. The weight of gravity pulls it down, lift raises it up, thrust moves it forward, and drag pulls it back. The pilot uses the controls to manage these forces to take off, fly, and land safely.

Gravity

Drag

Thrust

Lift

American West

Between the years of 1840 and 1900, many people living in the eastern United States moved west to find adventure and start new lives. Some, called settlers, set up farms and cattle ranches. Others dug mines in search of gold.

SEE ALSO
▶ Gold pp.200–201
▶ Native Americans p.179
▶ North America p.184
▶ Transportation pp.258–259
▶ Trains p.260

Wagon train

Settlers traveled west in groups of wagons called wagon trains. They took with them everything they needed to make their new homes.

Wagons were pulled by horses or oxen. They carried people, supplies, and farming equipment.

A wagon train could have up to 250 wagons.

Native American wars

Wars were fought between the settlers and the local Native American tribes. Despite winning some battles, the tribes ultimately lost the wars and their land.

Painting of Custer's Last Stand, a Native American victory

Early railroads

People built railroads into the American West in the years from 1869 to 1893. The railroads brought in lots of farmers and settlers, and carried out goods to be sold in cities.

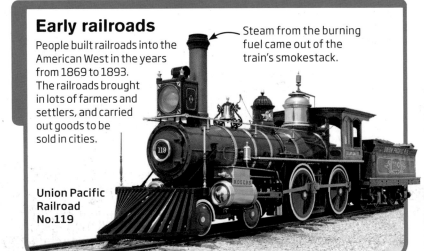

Steam from the burning fuel came out of the train's smokestack.

Union Pacific Railroad No.119

Amphibians

Amphibians are animals that spend their lives in and around water. They hatch in water from eggs. As they grow they develop lungs that let them breathe on land. Amphibian skin must always be wet, so they stay close to water. There are three main groups of amphibian.

SEE ALSO

▶ Eggs p.86
▶ Water pp.120–121
▶ Invertebrates p.139
▶ Metamorphosis p.163
▶ Reptiles p.210
▶ Skin p.229

Newts and salamanders

These long-tailed amphibians can replace injured body parts by growing new ones. An eye, leg, or tail takes just weeks to replace.

Bright yellow markings warn attackers that the fire salamander is poisonous.

Fire salamander

Caecilians

Though they look like worms, caecilians (se-sill-yens) are amphibians. They live underwater or in underground burrows on land.

Congo caecilian

Forever young

Axolotls are unusual, because they stay in water all their lives. They keep their tadpole-like fins and feathery gills even as an adult.

Axolotl

Frogs and toads

The most common group of amphibians includes frogs and toads. Frogs are usually wetter, smaller, and smoother than toads.

Toads have dry, bumpy skin, unlike frogs that have wet, smooth skin.

Large, bulging eyes help toads and frogs to see in all directions.

Amphibians can breathe through their skin.

Green tree frog

Webbed feet on the back legs help frogs and toads to swim in water.

Oriental fire-bellied toad

Ancient China

Chinese culture is thousands of years old. By 200 BCE, China was united under a family of emperors called the Han Dynasty from the city of Hanzhong. China produced many new inventions that spread to the rest of the world.

SEE ALSO
▶ Eating pp.104–105
▶ Inventions pp.136–137
▶ Exploration pp.180–181
▶ Trade p.257
▶ Writing p.280

This silk costume was worn by a woman in a Chinese opera.

Inventions
The Chinese first made silk clothes about 5,500 years ago. They also invented paper, gunpowder, printing, mechanical clocks, the compass, porcelain, and umbrellas.

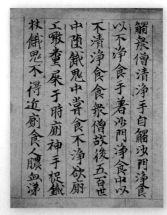

Writing
Chinese writing dates to about 1400 BCE. Each of the 4,000 symbols represents a word or part of a word. The text is read from top to bottom and right to left.

The Great Wall
Chinese emperors built strong walls to keep out northern tribes. The Great Wall of China is 5,500 miles (8,850 km) long and 500 years old.

The wall has 25,000 watchtowers. Soldiers used them to look out for the enemy.

Hilltop walls were easier to defend.

The top of the wall is wide enough for soldiers to march along.

Rice-growing
Rice was first grown in China about 10,000 years ago. It is still farmed today. Rice grows in flooded fields, such as these terraces.

Ancient Egypt

Thousands of years ago, between 7000 BCE and 395 CE, Egypt was led by powerful rulers called pharaohs. The Egyptian people farmed the land next to the Nile river and built amazing monuments for their pharaoh and the gods.

SEE ALSO
- Buildings p.48
- Governments p.123
- Life cycle p.146
- Rivers p.211
- Ships p.224
- Weather p.271

Nile River

The Nile was very important in Egyptian life. Farmers grew food along the river's banks and people used it to travel up and down the whole country.

The Sphinx of Giza (a lion statue with a man's head) guards the pyramids.

Every year, rain causes the river to flood, watering the land and all its crops.

Trading ships sailed the Red Sea, bringing back exotic treasures.

● Giza

People fished in the waters of the Nile.

Some pharaohs were buried in the Valley of the Kings.

● Luxor

Pharaoh Ramses II carved two great temples out of rock at Abu Simbel. He made himself one of the gods worshipped inside.

Houses were built of mud-bricks, baked in the sun.

Abu Simbel ●

Egyptian society

The Pharaoh ran Egypt with the help of rich people called noblemen. Everyone else in Egyptian society worked very hard for them.

Pharaoh

Noblemen

Farmers and other workers

Pyramids

The pyramids were tombs built to protect the pharaoh when he died. They were filled with treasure for the pharoah to use in the afterlife. The largest pyramid is nearly 460 ft (140 m) tall.

The mummy was put in a painted wooden mummy case.

Words were written with picture signs, called hieroglyphs.

Living forever

The Egyptians turned their bodies into mummies when they died. The body was dried out using salt, then wrapped in bandages. This way, they hoped they would live forever.

Ancient Greece

The ancient Greeks were among the most creative people in history. They were great builders and artists who invented theater, politics, history, writing, science, and sports. Some of the words they created are still used today. Greek civilization was at its best between 510 and 323 BCE.

SEE ALSO

▶ Ancient Rome p.20
▶ Buildings p.48
▶ Crafts p.75
▶ Religion p.208
▶ Games pp.240–241
▶ Sports p.239

Parthenon

The most famous Greek temple is the Parthenon in Athens. It was built for the goddess Athena, protector of the city.

The Parthenon stands on the Acropolis, a hill overlooking Athens.

The Parthenon was built with white marble.

There were 46 main columns.

Greek pottery

Greek vases were often painted with scenes from myths. This vase shows one of 12 labors, or tasks, carried out by the mythical hero Hercules.

Vases like this were all-purpose containers, for oil, wine, honey, or other foods.

Olympics

The Greeks held the first athletic competitions, such as the Olympic Games. This lifelike statue shows someone throwing a round weight, called a discus.

Gods and goddesses

The Greeks worshipped dozens of gods. Here are six of the most important ones, who are all members of the same family.

Zeus, king of the gods

Aphrodite, goddess of love

Apollo, god of music

Poseidon, god of the sea

Artemis, goddess of hunting

Hades, god of the Underworld

Ancient India

Great cities were built in India 5,000 years ago. This marked the start of a unique civilization. In the years 1526-1857, India was united as the Mughal Empire. The Mughals made scientific breakthroughs and beautiful works of art.

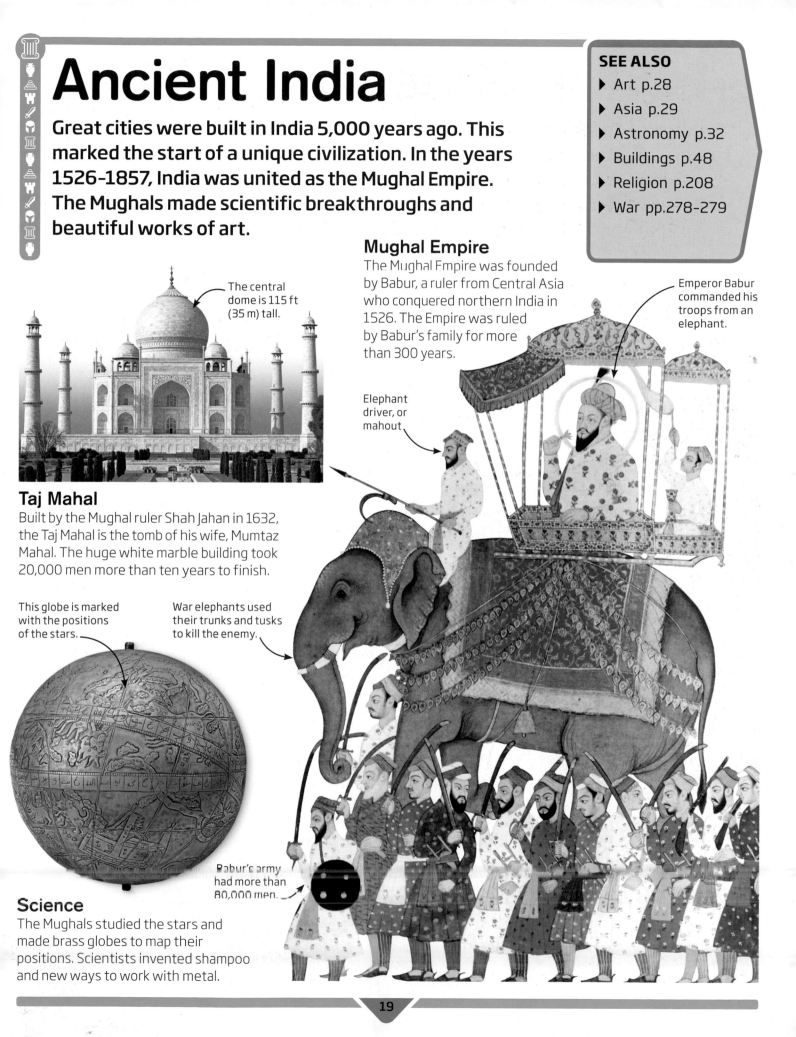

The central dome is 115 ft (35 m) tall.

Taj Mahal
Built by the Mughal ruler Shah Jahan in 1632, the Taj Mahal is the tomb of his wife, Mumtaz Mahal. The huge white marble building took 20,000 men more than ten years to finish.

Mughal Empire
The Mughal Empire was founded by Babur, a ruler from Central Asia who conquered northern India in 1526. The Empire was ruled by Babur's family for more than 300 years.

Emperor Babur commanded his troops from an elephant.

Elephant driver, or mahout

This globe is marked with the positions of the stars.

War elephants used their trunks and tusks to kill the enemy.

Babur's army had more than 80,000 men.

Science
The Mughals studied the stars and made brass globes to map their positions. Scientists invented shampoo and new ways to work with metal.

Ancient Rome

About 2,000 years ago, the ancient Romans ruled a great empire, including all the lands around the Mediterranean Sea. The Roman Empire was well organized, and it lasted for hundreds of years.

SEE ALSO
▶ Buildings p.48
▶ Europe p.94
▶ Governments p.123
▶ Law p.145
▶ Maps p.155
▶ Slavery p.230
▶ War pp.278–279

Roman society

Within the empire, there were different groups of people, with different rights. Citizens had more rights than non-citizens, and slaves had no rights at all.

Emperor
The ruler of the empire, who was all-powerful.

Citizen
Only citizens were able to vote and become government officials.

Freed person
A former slave, freed by their owner.

Slave
A person owned as property.

Only **Roman citizens** and above were allowed to wear **togas.**

Roman Empire

The Roman Empire started as just one city, Rome, in what is now Italy. Over time it grew across Europe.

Roman soldiers

The Romans conquered their empire using well-trained armies, called Legions. This is a centurion, an officer in charge of 80 legionnaires (foot soldiers).

Centurions wore a helmet crest.

Armor was made from metal links called chain mail.

Shin guards

Roman buildings

The Romans were expert builders, and many of their buildings still stand. This is the Pont du Gard, an aqueduct that carried water to Nîmes, a Roman city in France.

Animal families

Animals live in many different types of family groups. Some animals live in big groups, called colonies. They work together to bring up their babies. Other animals form male and female pairs. Family groups help animals to survive.

SEE ALSO
▶ Animal groups p.22
▶ Animal homes p.23
▶ Birds p.39
▶ Insects p.134
▶ Mammals p.154
▶ Homes pp.244–245

Pair
After mating, a pair of emperor penguins take turns looking after the egg and then feeding the baby. They live with up to 5,000 other penguins.

Herd
Zebras move around in large groups, called herds. When babies are born, the large numbers help protect them from other animals' attacks.

Colony
Ant families can be very large. The queen is the leader of the colony and lays the eggs. The other ants work to protect and feed the colony.

Small family
After giving birth, a female river otter cares for her pups for two to three years until they are ready to hunt and look after themselves.

Animal groups

Animals can be divided into groups, depending on their body features. Animals that look and act in similar ways are grouped together. This is called classification.

SEE ALSO
▶ Animal families p.21
▶ Fish p.101
▶ Insects p.134
▶ Invertebrates p.139
▶ Spiders p.238
▶ Vertebrates p.266

The green band shows which animal groups are vertebrates.

Amphibians
These animals have wet skin. They live in or near water. The babies hatch from eggs, and change body shape to become adults.

Birds
Birds have feathers, which keep them warm and help most to fly. They have beaks to catch or pick up food.

Invertebrates
There are many groups of invertebrates, including insects, slugs, spiders, and shellfish.

Animal groups
Animals are divided into two main groups. Vertebrates have spines, invertebrates don't. There are more groups inside these two main groups.

Fish
Fish live in water. They are covered in bony plates, called scales, and have special organs called gills for breathing.

Reptiles
Reptiles have scaly skin. They are cold-blooded, which means they must warm up in the sun before they can move.

Mammals
Mammals have fur or hair on their bodies. They feed their babies on milk made by the mothers.

Animal homes

Animals need homes for shelter and to keep their young safe. Animal homes are built in many different places and in all shapes and sizes. Some animals work together to build large structures. Others move every night, making new homes as they go.

SEE ALSO
▸ Animal groups p.22
▸ Birds p.39
▸ Insects p.134
▸ Mammals p.154
▸ Homes pp.244–245
▸ Work p.274

Weaver bird nest

Male weaver birds loop leaves and grass together to build their nests. The entrance is at the bottom to stop other animals from getting in.

Termite mound

Termites work together to build large mounds. The chimney shape of the mound helps to keep the termites inside cool.

Soldier termites protect the mound from ants.

Turrets are built for different entrances and exits.

The termite workers store grass in the outer areas.

The queen termite lives in the center of the colony.

Termite mounds can reach more than **6 ft (2 m) high!**

New mud and sticks are added each year.

Beaver lodge

Beavers build their homes from branches and mud. The entrance is underwater, to stop other animals from finding it.

Antarctica

Antarctica is the fifth largest and most southern continent. It is very cold and windy. Most of the land is buried under huge ice sheets, which stretch far out into the sea. In winter, it can be as cold as -130°F (-90°C), and windspeeds during storms can reach an incredible 200 mph (320 kph).

SEE ALSO
▸ Arctic p.25
▸ Birds p.39
▸ Changing world pp.50–51
▸ Climate change p.60
▸ Explorers p.96
▸ Glaciers p.122

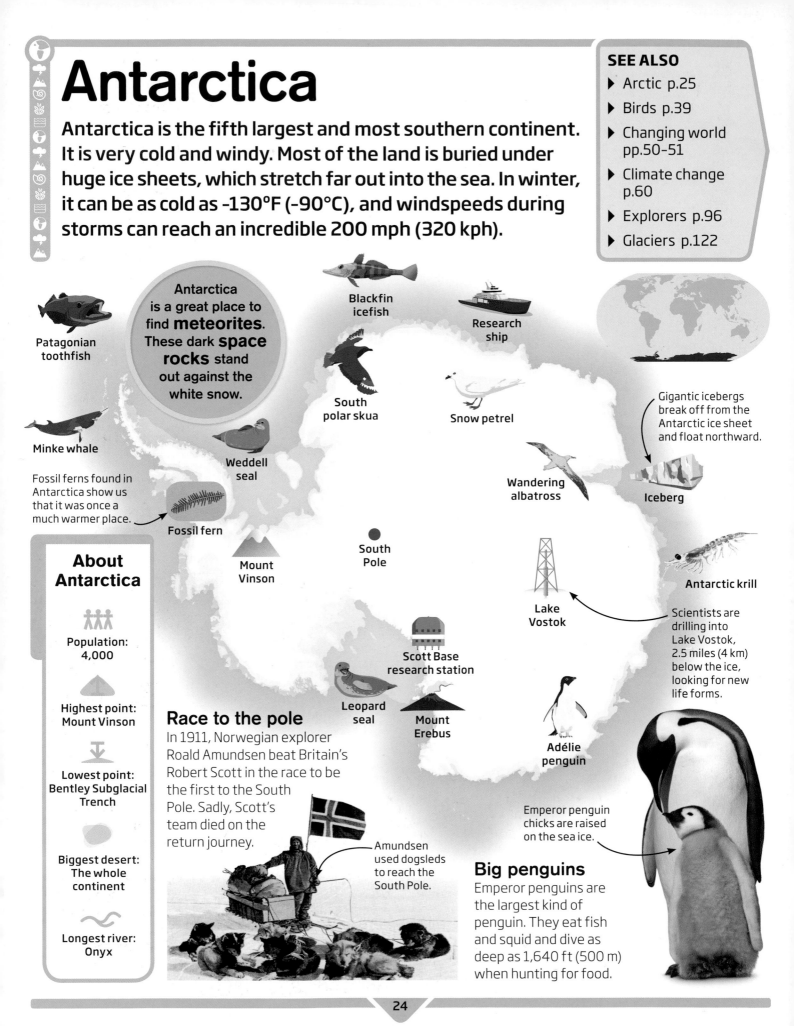

Patagonian toothfish

Antarctica is a great place to find **meteorites**. These dark **space rocks** stand out against the white snow.

Blackfin icefish

Research ship

Minke whale

Fossil ferns found in Antarctica show us that it was once a much warmer place.

Weddell seal

South polar skua

Snow petrel

Fossil fern

Wandering albatross

Gigantic icebergs break off from the Antarctic ice sheet and float northward.

Iceberg

Mount Vinson

South Pole

Lake Vostok

Antarctic krill

Scientists are drilling into Lake Vostok, 2.5 miles (4 km) below the ice, looking for new life forms.

Scott Base research station

Leopard seal

Mount Erebus

Adélie penguin

About Antarctica

Population: 4,000

Highest point: Mount Vinson

Lowest point: Bentley Subglacial Trench

Biggest desert: The whole continent

Longest river: Onyx

Race to the pole

In 1911, Norwegian explorer Roald Amundsen beat Britain's Robert Scott in the race to be the first to the South Pole. Sadly, Scott's team died on the return journey.

Amundsen used dogsleds to reach the South Pole.

Emperor penguin chicks are raised on the sea ice.

Big penguins

Emperor penguins are the largest kind of penguin. They eat fish and squid and dive as deep as 1,640 ft (500 m) when hunting for food.

Arctic

The Arctic is a cold region that surrounds the North Pole. It is mostly sea, which is frozen for much of the year, but it also includes most of Greenland and the northernmost parts of North America, Europe, and Asia.

SEE ALSO

▶ Antarctica p.24
▶ Climate change p.60
▶ Oceans and seas p.187
▶ Polar habitats p.197
▶ World p.275

Chilly circle

The Arctic Circle is about twice the size of the US. The animals that live there need to be able to survive in the cold. Land animals have thick fur or fluffy feathers, and sea animals have a thick layer of fat.

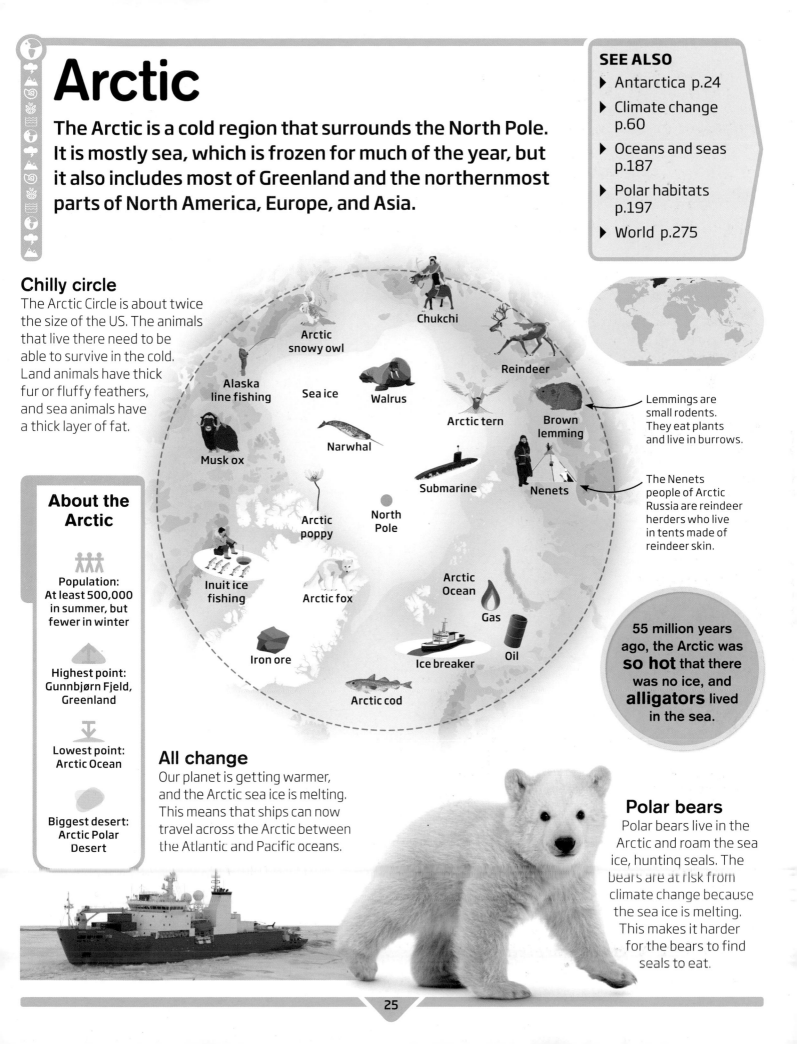

Chukchi

Arctic snowy owl

Reindeer

Alaska line fishing

Sea ice

Walrus

Arctic tern

Brown lemming

Lemmings are small rodents. They eat plants and live in burrows.

Musk ox

Narwhal

Submarine

Nenets

The Nenets people of Arctic Russia are reindeer herders who live in tents made of reindeer skin.

Arctic poppy

North Pole

About the Arctic

Population: At least 500,000 in summer, but fewer in winter

Highest point: Gunnbjørn Fjeld, Greenland

Lowest point: Arctic Ocean

Biggest desert: Arctic Polar Desert

Inuit ice fishing

Arctic fox

Arctic Ocean

Gas

Iron ore

Ice breaker

Oil

Arctic cod

55 million years ago, the Arctic was **so hot** that there was no ice, and **alligators** lived in the sea.

All change

Our planet is getting warmer, and the Arctic sea ice is melting. This means that ships can now travel across the Arctic between the Atlantic and Pacific oceans.

Polar bears

Polar bears live in the Arctic and roam the sea ice, hunting seals. The bears are at risk from climate change because the sea ice is melting. This makes it harder for the bears to find seals to eat.

Color

Our world is full of beautiful colors. The colors we see around us are actually different types of light bouncing off objects and into our eyes. Colors also have meanings. For example, a red light means "stop" in traffic, and a white flag means "surrender" in war.

Paint

Artists make paint by mixing something called a pigment with water. A pigment is a material that changes the color of reflected light by absorbing some colors and reflecting other colors.

Artists mix paint on a palette.

Rainbow colors

White light is made from all the colors of the rainbow–red, orange, yellow, green, blue, indigo, and violet. When white light from the sun passes through rain, it can refract (split) to make a rainbow.

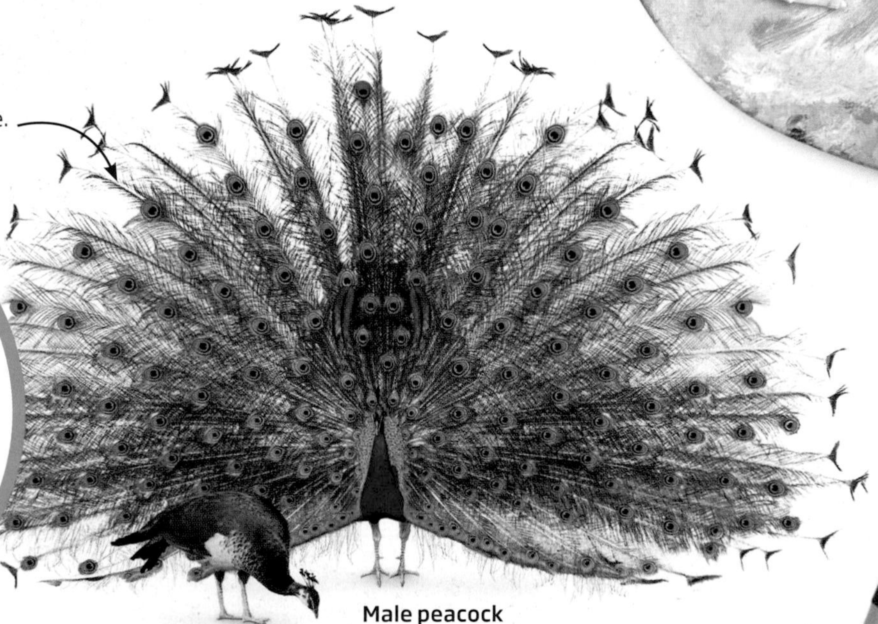

The male peacock is brightly colored compared to the female.

Animal colors

Male birds are often colorful to attract female birds. Some animals use bright colors as a warning, and some can change color. Others use their coloring to blend in with their surroundings.

Male peacock

Female peacock

All the colors of light except for green are absorbed by the leaf.

Green light reflects into our eyes.

Eye

The green light is not absorbed and bounces off the leaf.

Reflecting colors

A plant looks green because green light reflects off it into our eyes. The other colors of light from the sun are absorbed by the plant's leaves.

Yellow (Primary)

Yellow and red make orange.

Yellow and blue make green.

Blue (Primary)

Red (Primary)

Blue and red make purple.

Silk dress from 1750

Fashion

All around the world, different styles and colors are used in clothing to help people express themselves. Fashion changes over time. Clothes are very different now from those worn 250 years ago.

Mixing colors

Primary paint colors can be mixed to make secondary colors. The primary colors are red, yellow, and blue. Secondary colors can also be mixed to make new colors—for example, mixing orange and green makes brown.

Art

When you create a picture or sculpture, you are making art. Art can show something from real life or the imagination, and is made of different materials. Throughout history, people have drawn or painted pictures of the world around them. Art helps us show our feelings about the world and creates beautiful objects to look at.

SEE ALSO
- Ancient Rome p.20
- Color pp.26–27
- Buildings p.48
- Crafts p.75
- Photography p.190
- Stone Age p.243

Painting

Painters use an object such as a brush loaded with colored paint to create an image on paper, board, or canvas. Paintings can be detailed or simply show lines and shapes.

Bedroom in Arles by Vincent van Gogh, 1888

Landscape at Ceret by Juan Gris, 1911

Stone Age handprints at Cueva de las Manos

Cave painting
The first paintings were made on cave walls around 40,000 years ago. They showed handprints, people, and animals.

Lifelike painting
Many paintings show lifelike images from the world. This could be an indoor or an outdoor view, a person, or an object.

Abstract painting
Abstract art uses colors and shapes to show amazing pictures that aren't lifelike, but could show something real.

Sculpture

Sculptors work in clay, wood, stone, metal, or other materials to create objects. These might show people or abstract shapes.

Sculpture of a man, from ancient Rome.

Dancer Adjusting her Shoe by Degas, c.1890

The Great Wave by Hokusai, c.1831

Drawing
Artists use pencils, colored crayons, chalk, charcoal, and ink to draw beautiful images on paper. Drawing is quicker than painting, so it is a good way of recording real-life scenes.

Printing
Pictures can be cut out of a material such as wood and covered in ink or paint. The ink or paint on the cutout picture is then transferred onto paper, to create a print.

Asia

The biggest continent on Earth is Asia. More than 60 percent of the world's population live here. Asia has many landscapes, from snow-capped mountains and sun-scorched deserts to lush rain forests and sandy beaches.

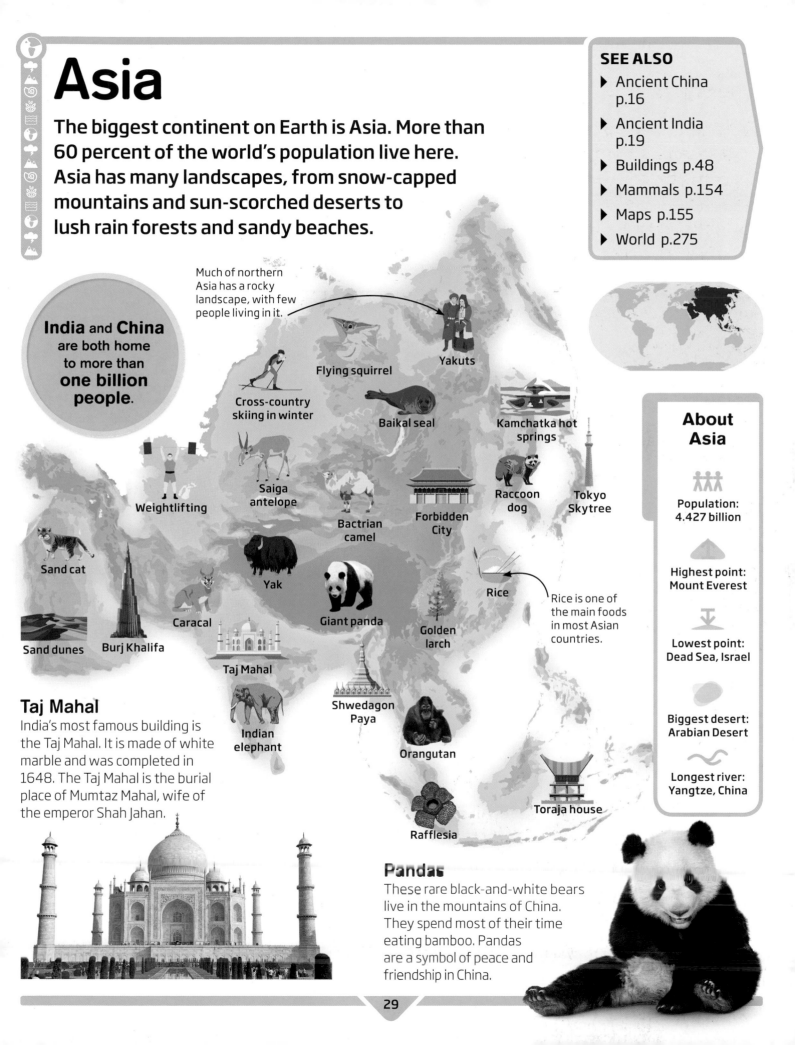

India and **China** are both home to more than **one billion people**.

Much of northern Asia has a rocky landscape, with few people living in it.

Yakuts

Flying squirrel

Cross-country skiing in winter

Baikal seal

Kamchatka hot springs

Weightlifting

Saiga antelope

Bactrian camel

Forbidden City

Raccoon dog

Tokyo Skytree

Sand cat

Yak

Giant panda

Golden larch

Rice

Rice is one of the main foods in most Asian countries.

Caracal

Sand dunes

Burj Khalifa

Taj Mahal

Indian elephant

Shwedagon Paya

Orangutan

Rafflesia

Toraja house

About Asia

Population: 4.427 billion

Highest point: Mount Everest

Lowest point: Dead Sea, Israel

Biggest desert: Arabian Desert

Longest river: Yangtze, China

Taj Mahal

India's most famous building is the Taj Mahal. It is made of white marble and was completed in 1648. The Taj Mahal is the burial place of Mumtaz Mahal, wife of the emperor Shah Jahan.

Pandas

These rare black-and-white bears live in the mountains of China. They spend most of their time eating bamboo. Pandas are a symbol of peace and friendship in China.

Asteroids

Asteroids are rocky or metallic objects that travel around the sun. They formed at the same time as the planets. Most asteroids are covered in craters, or dents, from where they have smashed into each other.

Asteroid shapes

Most asteroids have uneven shapes, but the biggest asteroids are round. The biggest asteroids are also called dwarf planets.

The craters on an asteroid's surface are made by bumping into smaller asteroids.

The asteroid **Toutatis** is **3 miles (5 km) long.**

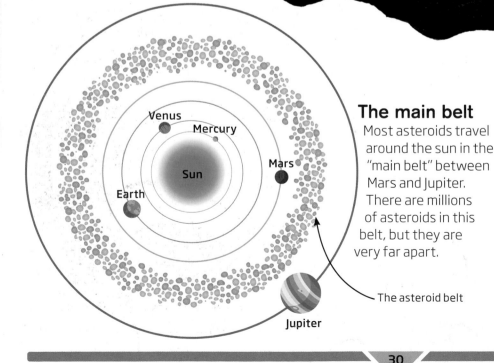

Scientists think Toutatis is made of two separate pieces held together by gravity.

It takes Toutatis four years to travel around the sun.

The main belt

Most asteroids travel around the sun in the "main belt" between Mars and Jupiter. There are millions of asteroids in this belt, but they are very far apart.

Venus
Mercury
Sun
Mars
Earth
The asteroid belt
Jupiter

Asteroid mining

Scientists think that in the future people will mine asteroids for their metals, minerals, and water. Spaceships may stop off on asteroids as they travel around the solar system.

Astronauts

Astronauts are people who are specially trained to take part in missions in space. They help us learn more about the universe we live in. Fewer than 600 people have been into space, and only 12 have walked on the moon.

SEE ALSO
▶ Explorers p.96
▶ Moon p.171
▶ Exploration pp.180–181
▶ Solar system p.233
▶ Space travel p.237
▶ Universe p.263

The helmet visor has a special filter that shields sunlight, as it can be extremely bright in space.

A camera records what the astronaut is seeing.

Tools can be attached to the front of the spacesuit.

The suit is made of many layers of fabric that keep the astronaut safe and warm.

NASA

The backpack holds oxygen supplies for breathing.

Solar panels

The International Space Station

The International Space Station is a permanent base for astronauts. The station is 250 miles (400 km) above the Earth. It can house six astronauts at a time.

In 1961, Russian space explorer **Yuri Gagarin** became the first human to go into space.

Becoming an astronaut

It takes many years of work to become an astronaut. Astronauts have to learn many new skills. They also train hard to make sure they are fit and healthy.

Astronauts train underwater because they float weightlessly, like in space.

Astronaut suit

Space can be both very hot and very cold. To keep themselves safe, astronauts wear special suits with helmets, gloves, boots, and an air supply.

Astronomy

Astronomy is the science of studying space. The first astronomers looked at the night sky with just their eyes. Modern astronomers use binoculars and telescopes to look at things too far away to be seen with the naked eye. They look at space to learn about our planet and the universe around it.

SEE ALSO
▶ Earth p.83
▶ Light p.147
▶ Science p.217
▶ The sciences pp.218-219
▶ Sun p.247
▶ Universe p.263

Telescope

Telescopes collect light and magnify images of distant objects. They are made of specially shaped glass surfaces called mirrors and lenses, which can bounce (reflect) or bend (refract) rays of light.

Rays of light enter the telescope's tube.

The "eyepiece" has a small lens that magnifies the image.

A mirror reflects light towards the eye.

Light is reflected off this curved mirror.

The **biggest telescope** on Earth is the Gran Telescopio Canarias in Spain. It has a mirror **34 ft** (10 m) wide!

Galileo Galilei

Galileo Galilei (1564-1642) was the first scientist to use a telescope to study space objects. However, his findings weren't always accepted by other people. He was put in prison for saying that the sun, as opposed to the Earth, was at the center of the solar system.

Earth in space

Until the 16th century, people believed that the Earth was at the center of the solar system. We now know this is not true.

Sun   Earth   Moon

People used to believe that the sun and moon moved around the Earth.

Now we know that the moon moves around the Earth, which moves around the sun.

Atmosphere

An atmosphere is a blanket layer of gases that surrounds a planet or moon. The Earth's atmosphere gives us the air we breathe. It also keeps our planet warm, blocks harmful rays from the sun, and stops space rocks from hitting us.

Earth's atmosphere

The Earth's atmosphere has five layers, each of a different thickness. The atmosphere gets thinner as it gets higher and closer to space.

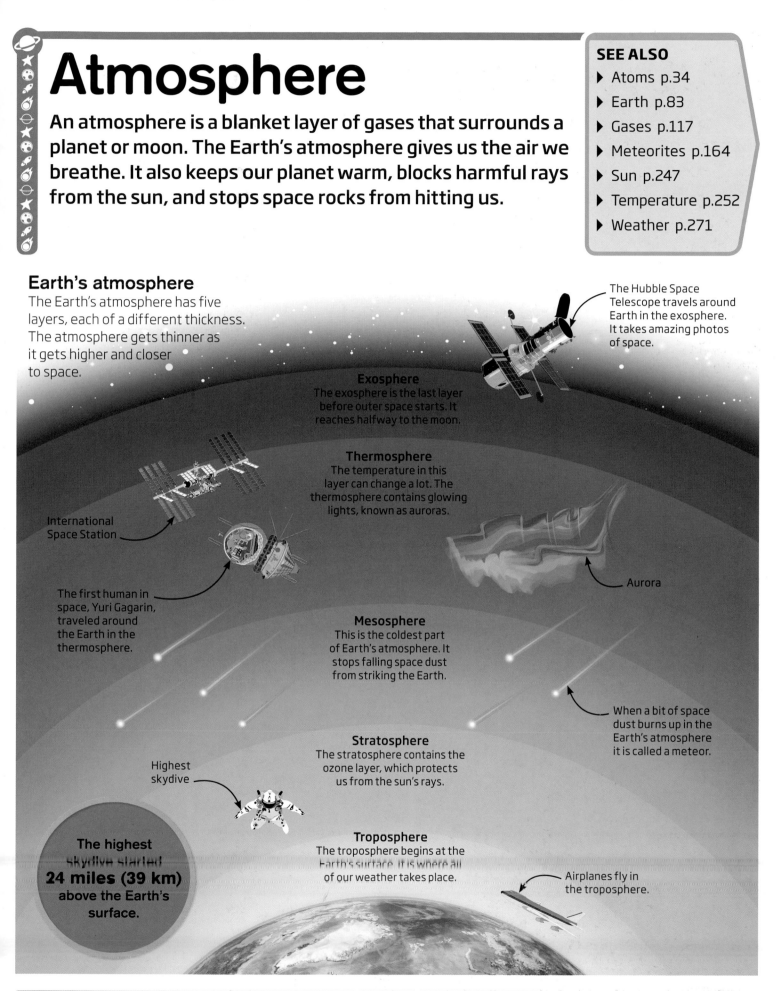

The Hubble Space Telescope travels around Earth in the exosphere. It takes amazing photos of space.

Exosphere
The exosphere is the last layer before outer space starts. It reaches halfway to the moon.

Thermosphere
The temperature in this layer can change a lot. The thermosphere contains glowing lights, known as auroras.

International Space Station

Aurora

The first human in space, Yuri Gagarin, traveled around the Earth in the thermosphere.

Mesosphere
This is the coldest part of Earth's atmosphere. It stops falling space dust from striking the Earth.

When a bit of space dust burns up in the Earth's atmosphere it is called a meteor.

Stratosphere
The stratosphere contains the ozone layer, which protects us from the sun's rays.

Highest skydive

The highest skydive started **24 miles (39 km)** above the Earth's surface.

Troposphere
The troposphere begins at the Earth's surface. It is where all of our weather takes place.

Airplanes fly in the troposphere.

Atoms

Atoms are tiny, round building blocks that build everything in the universe. They are so small we can't see them and are mostly made of empty space. Humans, cars, stars, and everything else around us are all made from tiny atoms.

SEE ALSO
▶ Carbon cycle p.49
▶ Changing states p.57
▶ Chemistry p.58
▶ Elements p.90
▶ Solar system p.233

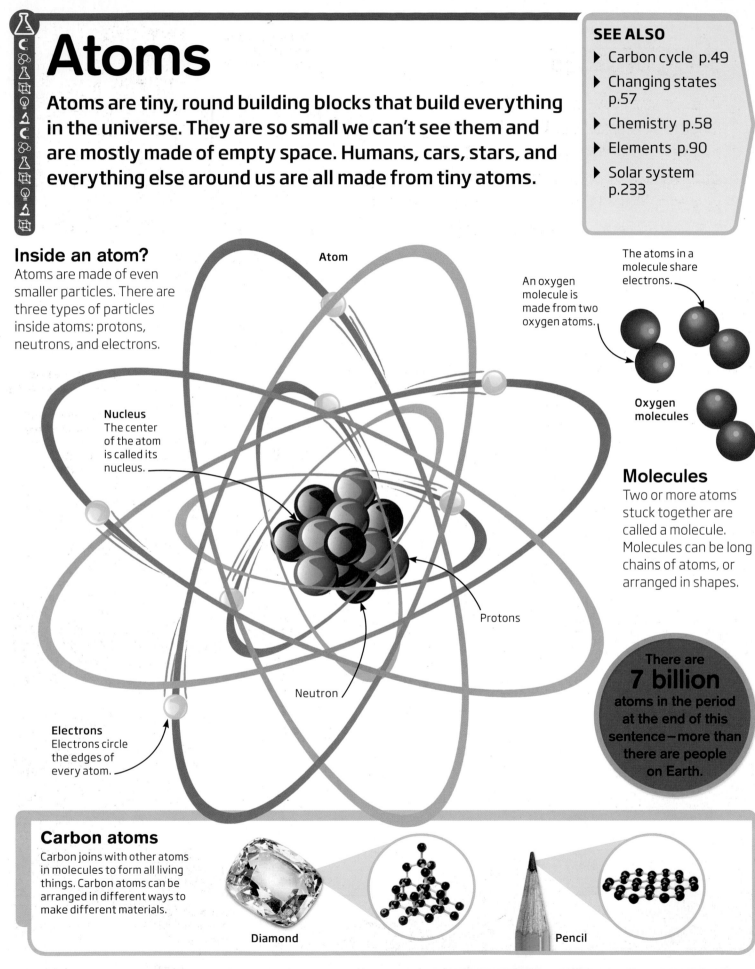

Inside an atom?

Atoms are made of even smaller particles. There are three types of particles inside atoms: protons, neutrons, and electrons.

Atom

The atoms in a molecule share electrons.

An oxygen molecule is made from two oxygen atoms.

Oxygen molecules

Nucleus
The center of the atom is called its nucleus.

Molecules

Two or more atoms stuck together are called a molecule. Molecules can be long chains of atoms, or arranged in shapes.

Protons

Neutron

There are **7 billion** atoms in the period at the end of this sentence – more than there are people on Earth.

Electrons
Electrons circle the edges of every atom.

Carbon atoms

Carbon joins with other atoms in molecules to form all living things. Carbon atoms can be arranged in different ways to make different materials.

Diamond

Pencil

Aztecs

The Aztecs were a people who lived in Central America. They had a huge empire between 1400 and 1519 CE, during which time they built great stone cities. Farmers produced corn and avocados, and bred turkeys.

The turquoise stone symbolized the breath of the gods.

SEE ALSO
▶ Buildings p.48
▶ Crafts p.75
▶ Farming p.98
▶ Incas p.132
▶ Maya p.158
▶ Religion p.208

Mask

The Aztecs used masks in religious ceremonies or to display in temples. This wooden mask is covered with pieces of a precious blue-green stone called turquoise.

Aztec city

At the center of each city stood a group of temples. Most temples were set on top of enormous stepped pyramids that could be more than 197 ft (60 m) tall.

Priests sacrificed animals and humans using knives of flint.

Many pyramids had twin temples on top.

Pyramids and palaces were made of stone.

Only priests and those who were to be sacrificed climbed the pyramid.

Markets were held once a week.

Boats were used for transporting goods.

Crowds sang during sacrifices.

Most cities were built beside lakes or rivers.

Merchants traveled huge distances to sell their goods.

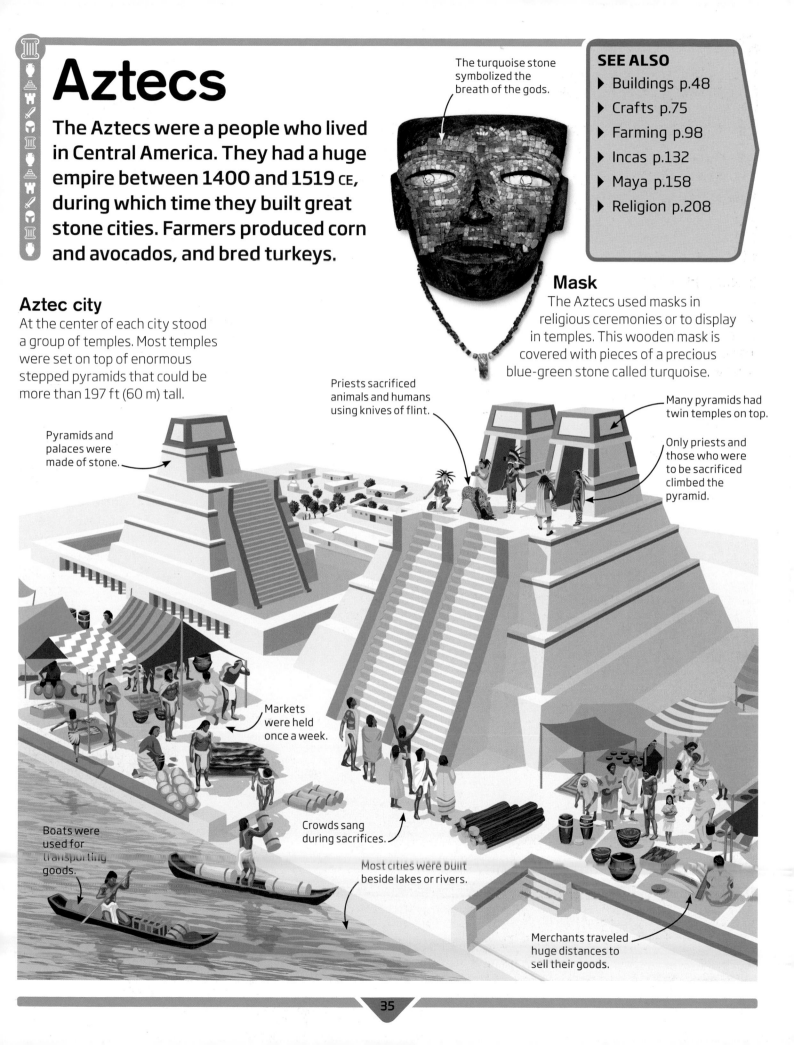

Bicycles

A bicycle is a two-wheeled vehicle. There are many types of bicycles. Some are for cycling on the road, others for riding up and down mountains, and others for racing around a track. Cyclists wear helmets to protect their heads.

SEE ALSO

▶ Inventions
pp.136–137

▶ Metals p.162

▶ Sports p.239

▶ Games
pp.240–241

▶ Transportation
pp.258–259

How a bicycle works

To move a bicycle forward, a cyclist pushes down on the pedals. These move a chain connected to the rear wheel. The bike is steered with a set of handlebars, which have brake levers to help the rider to slow down.

The hard outer covering and spongy inner material of bicycle helmets protect riders' heads if they fall.

The right lever applies the front brake, and the left lever applies the rear brake.

This racing bike has very thin tires for extra speed.

The curved handlebars on this bike allow the rider to crouch down for an easier ride.

The derailleur is a part of the bike that moves the chain to a different cog for going up or down hills.

Bicycle wheels

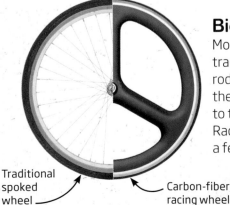

Most bicycle wheels have traditional spokes (wire rods) that join the hub at the center of the wheel to the rim at the edge. Racing wheels have just a few large spokes.

Traditional spoked wheel

Carbon-fiber racing wheel

Cycle racing

In the fastest type of bike racing, riders compete on bicycles without brakes or gears. They ride on sloped tracks in arenas called velodromes. Other types of races take place on mountain tracks and on roads. The most famous of these races is the 2,175 mile (3,500 km) Tour de France.

Big Bang

Scientists believe that the universe began in a dramatic event called the Big Bang, 13.8 billion years ago. The universe was tiny at the start, but it has been expanding ever since.

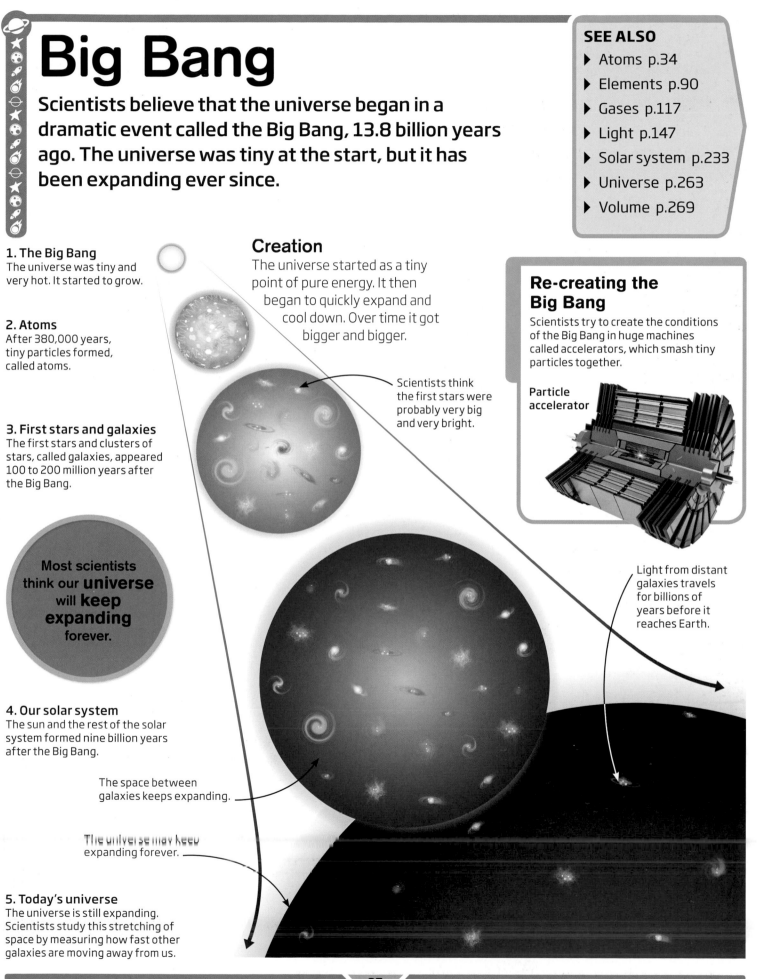

1. The Big Bang
The universe was tiny and very hot. It started to grow.

2. Atoms
After 380,000 years, tiny particles formed, called atoms.

3. First stars and galaxies
The first stars and clusters of stars, called galaxies, appeared 100 to 200 million years after the Big Bang.

Most scientists think our **universe** will **keep expanding** forever.

4. Our solar system
The sun and the rest of the solar system formed nine billion years after the Big Bang.

The space between galaxies keeps expanding.

The universe may keep expanding forever.

5. Today's universe
The universe is still expanding. Scientists study this stretching of space by measuring how fast other galaxies are moving away from us.

Creation
The universe started as a tiny point of pure energy. It then began to quickly expand and cool down. Over time it got bigger and bigger.

Scientists think the first stars were probably very big and very bright.

Re-creating the Big Bang
Scientists try to create the conditions of the Big Bang in huge machines called accelerators, which smash tiny particles together.

Particle accelerator

Light from distant galaxies travels for billions of years before it reaches Earth.

Biology

Biology is the science of living things. It studies how plants and animals interact with each other and their surroundings. It includes grouping and labeling living things and investigating how they live.

SEE ALSO
▶ Cells p.56
▶ Evolution p.95
▶ Food p.106
▶ Food chains p.107
▶ Habitats p.126
▶ Human body p.130
▶ Plants p.194

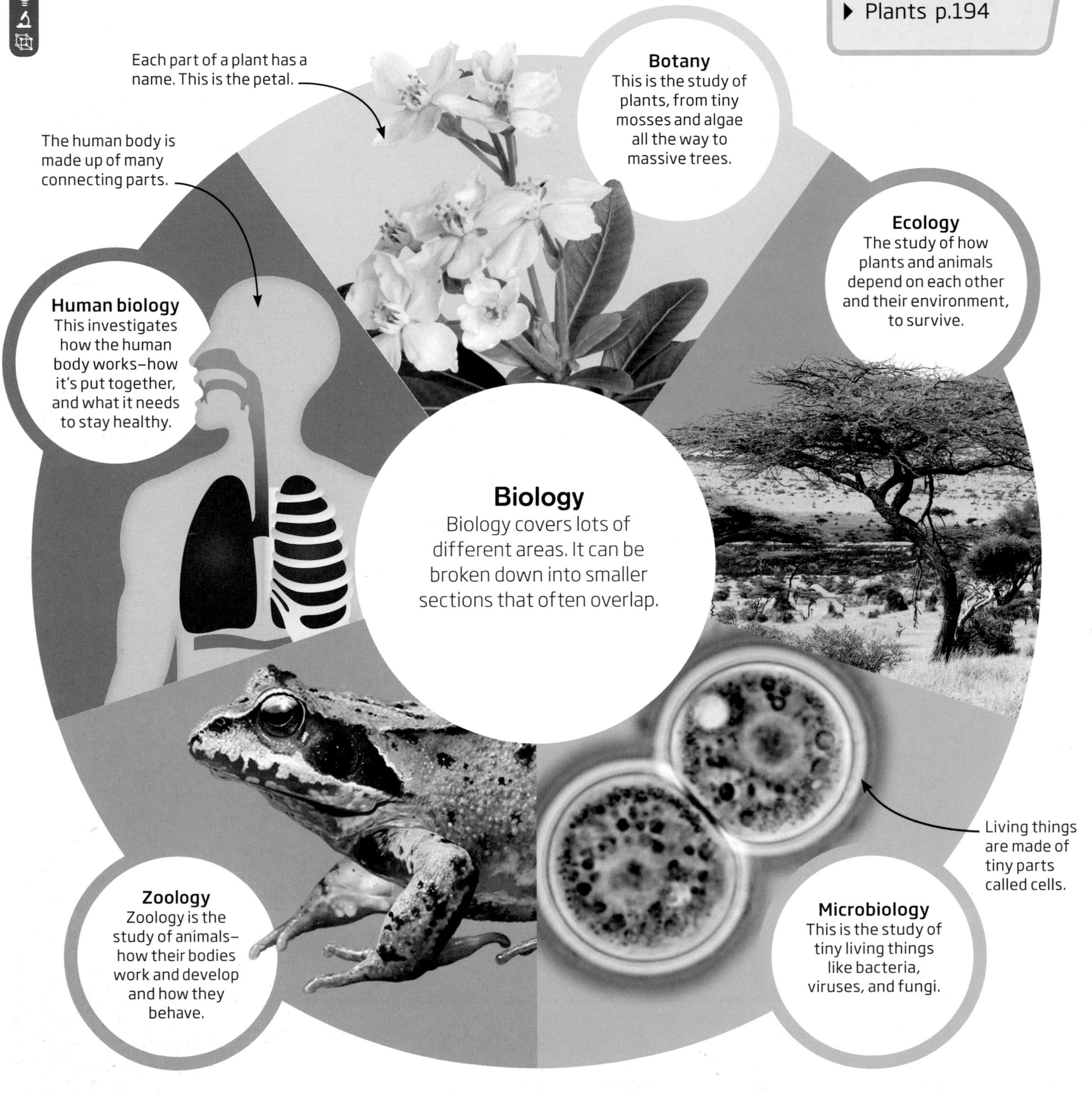

Each part of a plant has a name. This is the petal.

The human body is made up of many connecting parts.

Botany
This is the study of plants, from tiny mosses and algae all the way to massive trees.

Ecology
The study of how plants and animals depend on each other and their environment, to survive.

Human biology
This investigates how the human body works—how it's put together, and what it needs to stay healthy.

Biology
Biology covers lots of different areas. It can be broken down into smaller sections that often overlap.

Living things are made of tiny parts called cells.

Zoology
Zoology is the study of animals—how their bodies work and develop and how they behave.

Microbiology
This is the study of tiny living things like bacteria, viruses, and fungi.

Birds

Birds are animals that have feathers and beaks. They lay hard eggs, which their chicks hatch out of. Most birds can fly, and they are found all over the world.

SEE ALSO
- Aircraft p.13
- Animal groups p.22
- Dinosaurs p.80
- Eggs p.86
- Fruit and seeds p.115
- Rain forest p.204

Brightly colored feathers stand out among the trees.

Short beak to pick up nuts and seeds.

Yellow warbler

Hooked beak for picking food.

Macaw

Songbirds

Most birds in the world are part of a huge family called songbirds. Each type of songbird has its own special song.

Parrots

These tropical birds are colorful and often very noisy. They are strong fliers and eat fruit, nuts, and seeds.

Strong claws to move along branches.

Long tail feathers help with steering.

Curved beak tears food.

Birds of prey

Birds of prey hunt for their food. They have sharp beaks, fly fast, and grab food, such as fish, with their feet.

Large wings help to fly high.

Bald eagle

There are almost **10,000** different kinds of birds.

Long, curved bill used to find food.

Wading birds

These long-legged birds wade around in the mud. They search for small animals, such as crabs, in the water to eat.

Webbed feet for walking in water.

Scarlet ibis

Swimming birds

Not all birds can fly. Penguins swim underwater instead. Their feathers are waterproof, and they use their wings to steer.

Emperor penguin

Black holes

Black holes are the universe's most mysterious objects. They form when a star much more massive than the sun runs out of fuel. It explodes as a "supernova," then collapses under its own gravity, creating a black hole.

The enormous gravity of a black hole distorts space and time.

The edge of a black hole is called an event horizon.

Invisible monster

We can't see black holes, as even light gets trapped by their gravity. However, many are surrounded by hot discs of gas and dust, which give off high-energy radiation that can be seen using special telescopes.

Black holes can **collide** with other black holes and **get larger.**

The center of a black hole is called a singularity.

Supermassive black hole

The most massive black holes are found at the center of galaxies such as the Milky Way. They may form when massive clouds of gas collapse.

Spaghettification

Things that fall into black holes are stretched out, or "spaghettified." An imaginary astronaut would feel a stronger pull on one end of their body than the other, stretching them apart.

Body cells

Body parts are made up of tiny things called cells. Cells have important jobs to do, like sending messages, turning food into energy, and fighting off germs. Every cell has a particular job to do to keep the body healthy.

SEE ALSO
▶ Cells p.56
▶ Genes p.119
▶ Human body p.130
▶ Microscopic life p.165
▶ Sickness p.225
▶ Skin p.229

Inside a cell
All our body cells have an outer shell with a liquid inside. In the very center of the cell is a core, called the nucleus.

Nucleus
The nucleus is the control center of the cell. It contains instructions called genes.

Cell membrane
The membrane is the edge of the cell. It allows things to move in and out.

Mitochondria
These tiny structures release energy to power the cell.

Cytoplasm
Cytoplasm is a liquid inside the cell where chemicals mix together to bring the cell to life.

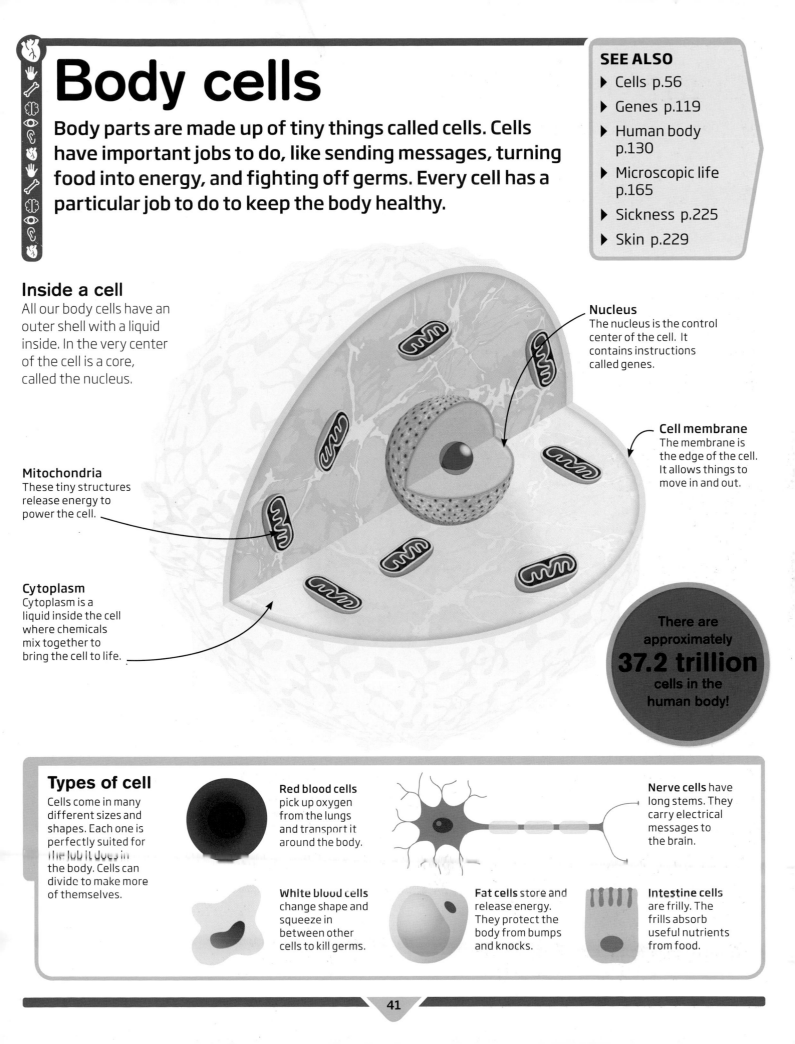

There are approximately **37.2 trillion** cells in the human body!

Types of cell
Cells come in many different sizes and shapes. Each one is perfectly suited for the job it does in the body. Cells can divide to make more of themselves.

Red blood cells pick up oxygen from the lungs and transport it around the body.

White blood cells change shape and squeeze in between other cells to kill germs.

Nerve cells have long stems. They carry electrical messages to the brain.

Fat cells store and release energy. They protect the body from bumps and knocks.

Intestine cells are frilly. The frills absorb useful nutrients from food.

Storytelling

Storytelling is the activity of telling or writing stories. They can be real or made up, can be of any length, and can be about any subject. People have always told stories to entertain each other or to inform people about, and make sense of, their world.

Animal stories
Many stories feature animals as their main characters. These animals speak and dress like real people, although they often live in animal homes. Br'er Rabbit is a character from the South.

Br'er Rabbit wears human clothes.

Br'er Rabbit

Oral history
Because early people couldn't read or write, they passed on stories by telling them to each other. The storyteller often acted out bits of the story. People still tell stories in this way today.

Storytelling in a library

In ancient India, people recited all

10,600

verses of the sacred hymn book, *Rigveda*, from memory.

What is a story?
A story is a fictional (made-up) account of imaginary or real events and people. A story has a beginning, a middle, and an end. The Chinese story of Pangu explains the creation of the Earth.

Beginning
In the beginning, there was chaos. Out of chaos came an egg, and out of this egg hatched Pangu, the first creature.

Middle
As Pangu grew up, he created the Earth and the sky, and stood between them to force them slowly apart.

End
When Pangu died, his breath became the wind, his voice became thunder, and his bones became valuable minerals.

Poetry

Poetry is a type of literature. It often has short, rhyming lines joined together in verses. A poem uses words very carefully to suggest different meanings or ideas. It can be any length and about any subject.

Beowulf is a very long poem about an ancient hero.

Fairy tales

A fairy tale is a story that contains magic and characters such as fairies, witches, goblins, or giants. Fairy tales tell the story of good versus evil, and usually have a happy ending. *Sleeping Beauty, Aladdin*, and *The Boy Who Cried Wolf* are all examples of fairy tales.

In the fairy tale *Aladdin*, a genie magically appears from a lamp.

Magical lamp

Novels

A novel is a long story about people and their lives. Novels can be set in imaginary or real worlds, and can take place at any point in time. There are many different types of novel. For example, a historical novel would be set in the past and teach about history.

With more than **8,000 pages,** the world's longest novel is *Men of Goodwill* by French author Jules Romains.

Children's stories from around the world

Filming *Romeo and Juliet*

Films

Films are a visual form of stories. Actors perform the story in a real-life setting. The actors speak the lines of the story and try to make the film as realistic and lifelike as possible.

Books

Books are collections of written words put together to tell stories or give you information. Before books were invented, people shared stories by remembering and telling them to each other. Millions of books have been created since paper was invented, and many are now read on electronic devices such as tablets.

SEE ALSO
- Storytelling pp.42–43
- Inventions pp.136–137
- Language p.144
- Materials p.157
- Writing p.280

Early books

Books have been written and decorated by hand for thousands of years. Pages were often made from parchment, which is the thinned skin of an animal. These books took a long time to make.

> J.K. Rowling's first Harry Potter book has sold more than **100 million** copies since 1997.

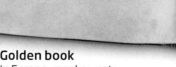

Medieval prayer book

Golden book
In Europe, monks wrote the first books in Latin. They decorated them with real gold.

Printing

In around 1440 in Germany, Johannes Gutenberg invented the printing press. He carved single letters onto metal blocks, then put them together as words, and printed them onto pages.

1900s printing press

Fiction

A book of fiction is a story in which the author writes about imaginary people and events. Fiction books can also be called novels.

Non-fiction

A non-fiction book contains facts about the real world. Dictionaries, atlases, cookbooks, and books about history and animals are all examples of non-fiction books.

Brain

The brain controls the whole body. Every time we think, feel, or move, the brain is at work. It even keeps working when we're asleep. The brain is the most complicated organ in the living world.

SEE ALSO
▶ Body cells p.41
▶ Feelings p.99
▶ Human body p.130
▶ Robots p.212
▶ Sight p.226
▶ Sleep p.231

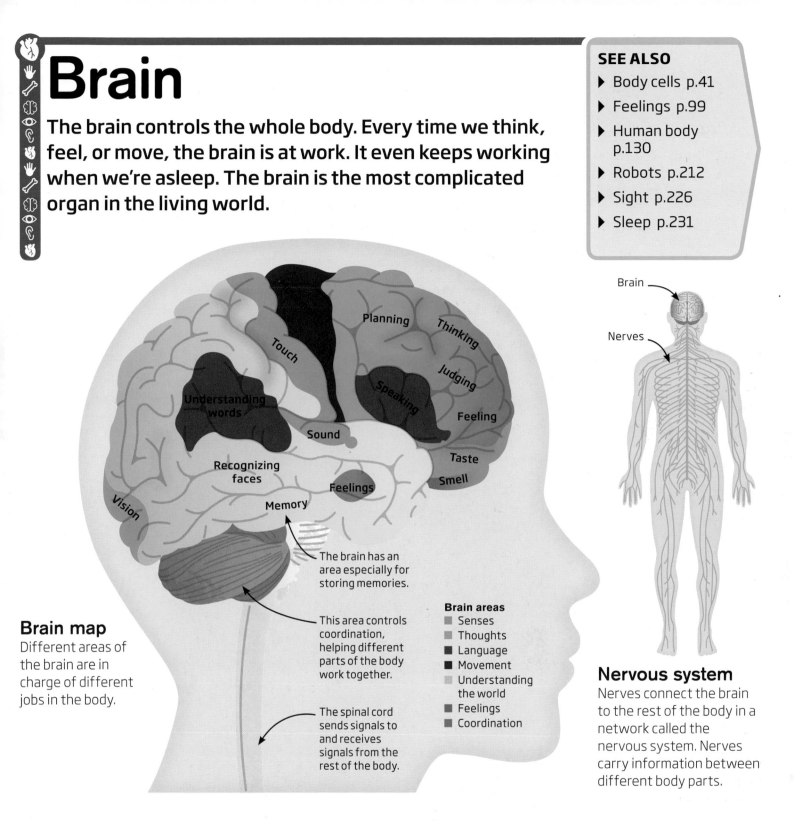

Planning

Thinking

Touch

Judging

Speaking

Understanding words

Feeling

Sound

Taste

Recognizing faces

Smell

Feelings

Vision

Memory

The brain has an area especially for storing memories.

This area controls coordination, helping different parts of the body work together.

Brain areas
- Senses
- Thoughts
- Language
- Movement
- Understanding the world
- Feelings
- Coordination

The spinal cord sends signals to and receives signals from the rest of the body.

Brain map
Different areas of the brain are in charge of different jobs in the body.

Nervous system
Nerves connect the brain to the rest of the body in a network called the nervous system. Nerves carry information between different body parts.

Brain

Nerves

Thinking
The brain is made up of tiny cells called nerves, or neurons. They look like little trees. When we think, tiny electrical and chemical signals move quickly through the cells

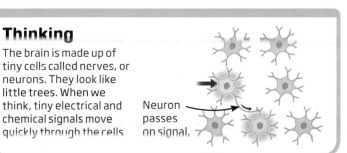

Neuron passes on signal.

Acting alone
The brain does some things without us having to think. For example, it keeps our hearts pumping blood around our bodies at the right speed and controls our breathing.

Bridges

Bridges are structures that carry people and vehicles over obstacles. They are usually built over rivers, valleys, and roads. Bridges are designed to hold heavy loads and survive bad weather.

SEE ALSO
- Cars p.52
- Engineering p.91
- Materials p.157
- Rivers p.211
- Storms p.243
- Transportation pp.258–259

Bridge types

Engineers design different types of bridges depending on the size of the gap to be crossed, the type of land around it, and the weight of the crossing traffic.

Suspension bridges

A suspension bridge can carry heavy loads. Steel cables are anchored to strong supportive towers, spreading the weight.

The wires used for the cables on the **Golden Gate Bridge** could go around the Earth three times.

Cables provide support from above.

Tall towers at each end of the bridge are anchored deep in the ground.

Golden Gate Bridge, San Francisco, CA

Road or walkway made from strong concrete.

Arch
Arch bridges are usually made of stones cut into exactly the right wedge shapes to form an arch.

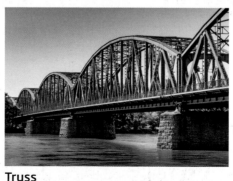

Truss
A truss bridge is built from triangles called trusses. Triangles are the strongest shapes, so this bridge can carry heavy weights.

Beam
A beam bridge is the most simple design. All the weight is placed directly on top. It is built to be stiff and not bend.

Bronze Age

The Bronze Age is a period of history after the Stone Age and before the Iron Age. It began about 5,500 years ago when societies first learned to make a metal called bronze. Bronze is a mix of the metals tin and copper. Combined, these metals are stronger than they would be alone.

SEE ALSO
▶ Buildings p.48
▶ Crafts p.75
▶ Iron Age p.140
▶ Metals p.162
▶ Stone Age p.243
▶ Trade p.257
▶ Writing p.280

Bronze Age bracelets

Bronze weapons were used by the first armies during the Bronze Age.

Bronze Age spear tip

Early writing

The first written language was invented in the Bronze Age. It was called cuneiform. Writers used pointed reeds called styluses to make marks in soft clay tablets, which then hardened.

Bronze Age cuneiform tablet from Iraq

Bronze

Using bronze tools allowed societies to clear more land for farming, and to grow, store, and trade more food and goods. Bronze was also used to make weapons and jewelry.

People traded more with other societies during the Bronze Age. Some traders used their money to buy bronze jewelry.

Settlements

During the Bronze Age, people lived together in large groups for the first time. Settlements were bigger than earlier villages had been. There were even towns and cities.

These buildings in Germany are copies of Bronze Age houses.

The houses have wooden frames and are built on stilts.

Buildings

A building is a solid structure fixed in one place. It has walls and a roof to shelter us from the weather. The shape of the building depends on its purpose. Buildings can be many different things, including hospitals, schools, and houses.

SEE ALSO

▶ Ancient Greece p.18

▶ Ancient India p.19

▶ Bridges p.46

▶ Castles p.53

▶ Engineering p.91

▶ Factories p.97

Types of buildings

Many towns and cities have a mix of buildings from across history. These buildings have different designs and are made from a variety of materials.

Older buildings, like this cathedral, are less tall but are often designed to look very impressive.

The world's **tallest building**, the Burj Khalifa in Dubai, is 2,716 ft (828 m) tall—which is more than 100 houses tall.

Skyscrapers are tall buildings with many floors. They are used as offices or apartments.

Modern buildings are often made of glass. Glass is strong and lets in lots of light.

Stone has been used for building for thousands of years, because it is strong and lasts a long time.

London skyline

Construction

Machines are used to put up large buildings. Foundations are dug deep into the ground to stop the building from falling down. Cranes lift heavy building materials such as steel beams and panes of glass for windows.

Carbon cycle

Without the element called carbon, our world would be frozen and lifeless. Carbon constantly moves between living things, the atmosphere, the oceans, and the Earth below us. This movement is known as the carbon cycle.

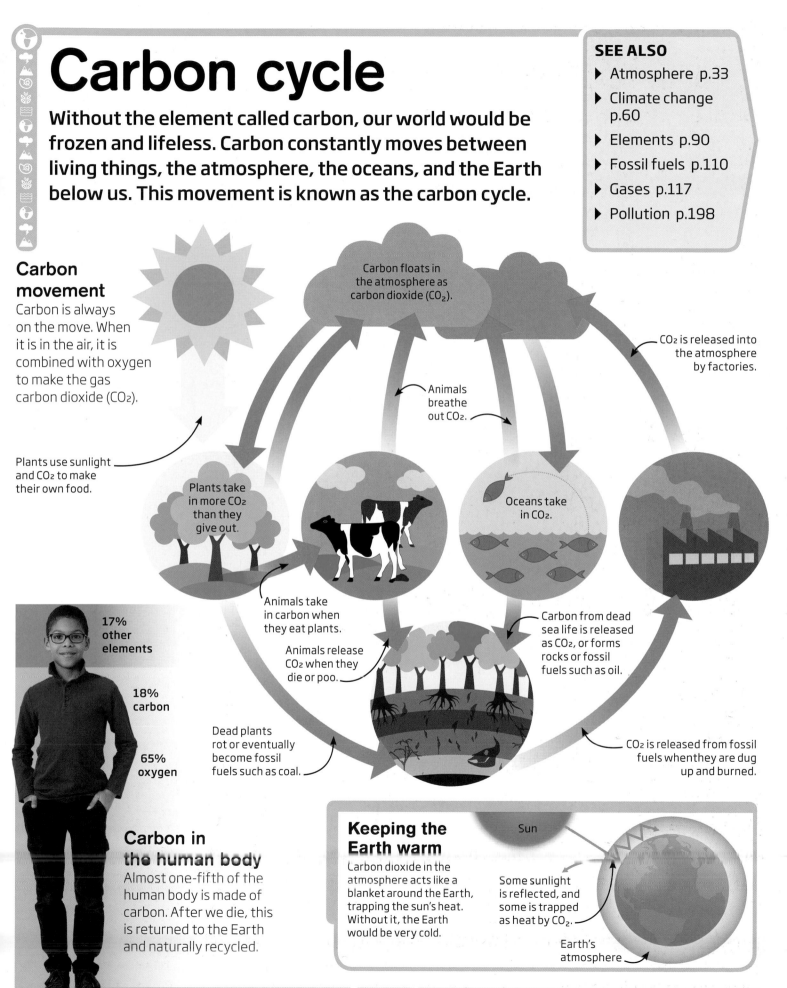

Carbon movement

Carbon is always on the move. When it is in the air, it is combined with oxygen to make the gas carbon dioxide (CO_2).

Plants use sunlight and CO_2 to make their own food.

Carbon floats in the atmosphere as carbon dioxide (CO_2).

CO_2 is released into the atmosphere by factories.

Animals breathe out CO_2.

Plants take in more CO_2 than they give out.

Oceans take in CO_2.

Animals take in carbon when they eat plants.

Animals release CO_2 when they die or poo.

Carbon from dead sea life is released as CO_2, or forms rocks or fossil fuels such as oil.

Dead plants rot or eventually become fossil fuels such as coal.

CO_2 is released from fossil fuels when they are dug up and burned.

17% other elements

18% carbon

65% oxygen

Carbon in the human body

Almost one-fifth of the human body is made of carbon. After we die, this is returned to the Earth and naturally recycled.

Keeping the Earth warm

Carbon dioxide in the atmosphere acts like a blanket around the Earth, trapping the sun's heat. Without it, the Earth would be very cold.

Sun

Some sunlight is reflected, and some is trapped as heat by CO_2.

Earth's atmosphere

Changing world

Since it formed, the Earth has been covered with molten lava, bombarded by rocks from space, and blanketed in ice. In 4.5 billion years, the Earth has changed from a hot, lifeless planet into a watery home, full of life.

Earth is born
Our planet was formed when rocks orbiting the sun crashed into each other and stuck together. The early Earth had a poisonous atmosphere and a volcanic landscape with lots of craters.

The formation of the Earth

On the move
Earth's land is split up into huge chunks called continents. Throughout Earth's history, the continents have shifted around. Today, there are seven continents, but they have not always looked the way they do today.

Mountains are created when **continents move** and hit each other.

The continents were grouped together in a "supercontinent" called Pangaea.

250 million years ago

120 million years ago

Marrella, a life form from 540 million years ago.

Life begins
At first, nothing lived on Earth. The earliest life forms appeared 4,600 million years ago. Over time, more species developed. Now there are millions of different types of life, and over 7.5 billion people.

Pangaea split in two, forming Laurasia in the north and Gondwana in the south.

Under ice

For much of the last two million years, huge ice sheets covered large parts of Northern Europe and North America. We are currently living in a warmer period.

The Andes mountains formed 45 million years ago.

Changing surface

The Earth's surface changes constantly. As continents crash together or move apart, mountain ranges are forced up, then worn down. Rainforests become icy wastelands, oceans expand and shrink, and glaciers turn into deserts.

Mammoths lived during the last ice age.

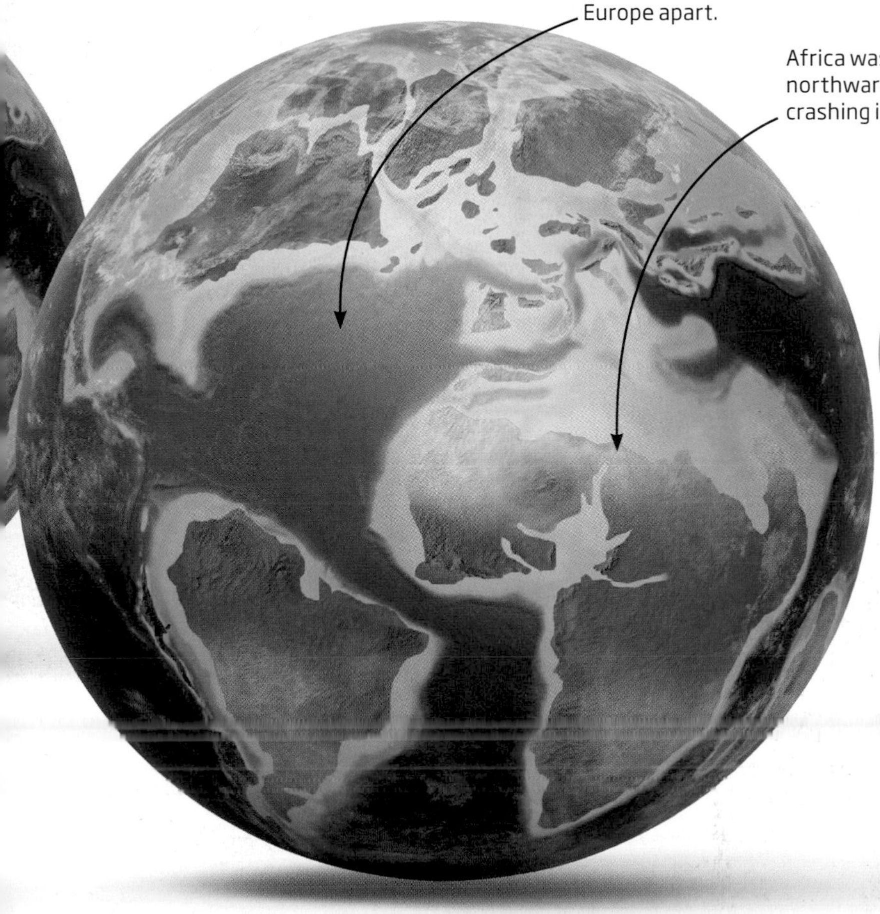

The Atlantic Ocean was opening, pushing North America and Europe apart.

Africa was moving northward, on its way to crashing into Europe.

If the sea level today was as high as it was 500 million years ago, London, New York, and Sydney would all be **underwater**.

Climate change

Humans have a direct impact on Earth's climate. We burn fossil fuels such as coal, oil, and gas to make power. This releases dangerous gases into the air, making Earth hotter.

80 million years ago

Burning fossil fuels

Cars

Cars are vehicles that travel on roads. The shape and size of a car depends on its use, such as for a family or for racing. Cars are powered by engines. Engines can be powered by fuel such as gasoline or diesel, or by using electricity.

SEE ALSO
▶ Electricity p.87
▶ Engines p.92
▶ Fossil fuels p.110
▶ Inventions pp.136–137
▶ Sports p.239
▶ Transportation pp.258–259

Parts of a car

All cars have a strong metal frame called a chassis. Attached to this are all the other parts, such as the engine and wheels.

The engine is powered by burning gasoline or diesel.

The battery provides electricity to start the car and to power the lights.

This shaft takes power from the engine to the axle.

The axle spins to move the wheels forward or backward.

The front wheels are turned by the driver's steering wheel.

Formula 1

Some of the world's fastest cars take part in a racing competition called Formula 1. They compete on special tracks and around some city streets. The cars have long, low shapes to help them go super fast.

1998 Ferrari F300 F1

Electric car

Today, many cars are powered by electricity. Fuel-powered cars release harmful gases into the air, but electric cars don't. The battery in an electric car is powered up at a charging point.

52

Castles

Most castles were built between 1000 and 1500 CE. They had homes and workshops inside their walls. Kings and wealthy people built castles as protection from enemy attack. Once cannons were invented, they were no longer safe. Many fell apart over time, but some are still standing.

SEE ALSO

▶ Buildings p.48

▶ Engineering p.91

▶ Europe p.94

▶ Imperial Japan p.131

▶ Knights p.142

▶ Homes pp.244–245

Stone castles

Later castles in Europe had stone walls and towers. The biggest ones could hold hundreds of soldiers. Smaller stone castles were home to just a single family and its servants.

The bailey was an open space inside the castle with areas for growing food.

The largest tower in the castle was called the keep.

Stone walls were difficult for attackers to climb.

Sheep and other livestock were kept safe in the castle.

The drawbridge could be lifted to keep the enemy out of the castle.

Some castles had a water-filled moat around them for extra protection.

People kept watch for the enemy from tall towers.

Early castles

Hundreds of "motte and bailey" castles were built from 1020–1200. They had two parts—a mound of earth (motte) topped by a tower, and a courtyard (bailey).

Many castles were built on hilltops so they had a clear view of everything around them.

Himeji Castle in south Japan is called "the white heron" as its peaks look like wings flapping.

Japanese fortress

Castles in Japan were designed with towers built of both wood and stone. The central tower was used as the main hideout if the castle was attacked.

Cats

The cat family are all meat-eaters. They have sharp teeth that let them slice up their food. Cats are very fast, with strong bodies that let them run, jump, and even swim.

SEE ALSO
▶ Dogs p.81
▶ Food chains p.107
▶ Habitats p.126
▶ Pets pp.152–153
▶ Sight p.226
▶ Vertebrates p.266

Small wild cats

Most wild cats are much smaller than lions. The colors of their fur help them to be camouflaged, or hidden, in their habitat.

Cat tongues are covered in **sharp hairs**. They are used to clean meat off a bone and to **wash their fur.**

Cats have good hearing.

Whiskers help cats sense their surroundings.

Chartreux

Pet cats

Cats were one of the first animals that humans tamed from the wild to become pets, around 12,000 years ago.

Big cats

The largest types of cat are known as "big cats." They include lions, tigers, leopards, and jaguars. These are the only cats that are able to roar.

Male lions have longer hair over their shoulders, called manes.

Lion

Lynx

Night vision

Cats hunt at dawn and dusk. Their eyes are good at seeing when there is not much light. Their eyesight is six times better than a human's.

Leopard

Caves

Caves are large natural holes in the ground. They are usually formed when rock is hollowed out by running water over millions of years. Prehistoric humans used caves for shelter, and some people still live in caves today. They are also home to lots of animals, including bats.

SEE ALSO

▶ Animal homes p.23

▶ Erosion p.93

▶ Glaciers p.122

▶ Rocks and minerals p.214

▶ Homes pp.244–245

Cave network

Caves form when rainwater dissolves the soft limestone rock in the ground. They often contain fantastic rock features, such as stalactites and stalagmites.

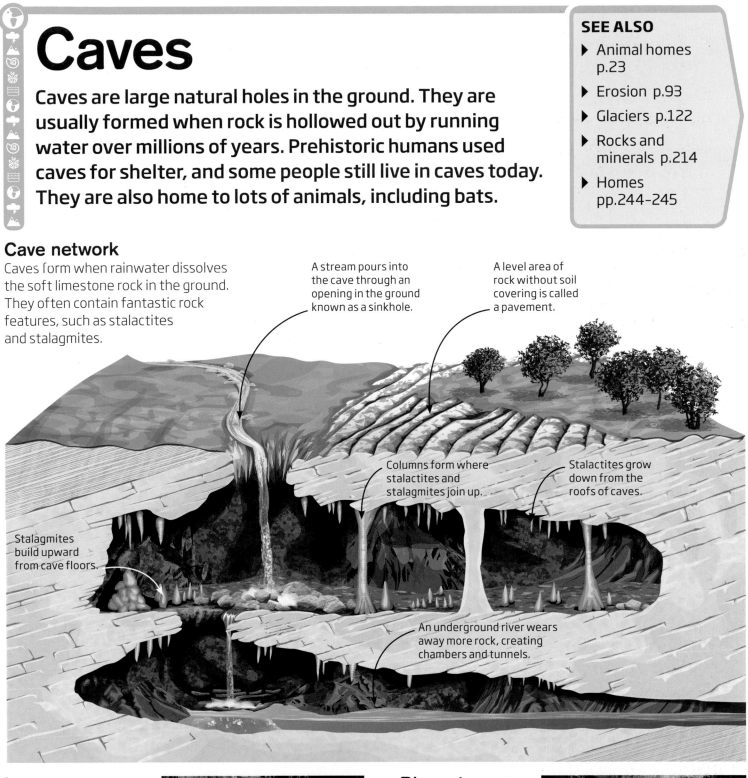

A stream pours into the cave through an opening in the ground known as a sinkhole.

A level area of rock without soil covering is called a pavement.

Columns form where stalactites and stalagmites join up.

Stalactites grow down from the roofs of caves.

Stalagmites build upward from cave floors.

An underground river wears away more rock, creating chambers and tunnels.

Ice caves

Glaciers are rivers of ice that move very slowly. Some glaciers have caves inside them. They are made by streams of water tunneling through the glacier.

This ice cave is inside a glacier in Iceland.

Biggest cave

The 40-story-high Hang Son Doong cave in Vietnam is the world's biggest cave. Inside, it has a river, a forest, and even its own clouds!

A river flows through part of the huge cave.

Cells

Living things are made from tiny parts that stick together, called cells. Cells come in different shapes and sizes depending on the job they do. They can divide and make copies of themselves.

SEE ALSO
▸ Body cells p.41
▸ Genes p.119
▸ Heart p.128
▸ Photosynthesis p.191
▸ Plants p.194
▸ Sickness p.225

Plant cell

Plant cells can collect air and make their own food from sunlight. They have a strong cell wall, which gives the plant strong stems and leaves.

Cell wall
The strong outer wall gives the cell and plant their shape.

Cytoplasm
This is the liquid inside the cell that everything else floats in. Chemicals mix together here.

Cell membrane
The cell membrane is a barrier that keeps the cytoplasm inside the cell.

Nucleus
The nucleus controls the cell and contains instructions called genes.

Bacteria

Bacteria are living things made from just one cell. They can divide to make copies of themselves. This is how germs spread and make us sick.

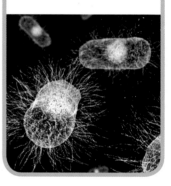

Mitochondrion
This is where energy from sugar is released to power the different parts of the cell.

Chloroplast
Chloroplasts collect sunlight and use air and water to make food.

Vacuole
The vacuole is a storage bubble filled with liquid food, water, or waste.

Animal cell

Animal cells use oxygen to break down sugar and make energy. Animals get sugar from the food they eat, while oxygen gets to the cells through the blood.

Cell membrane

Cytoplasm

Nucleus

Mitochondrion

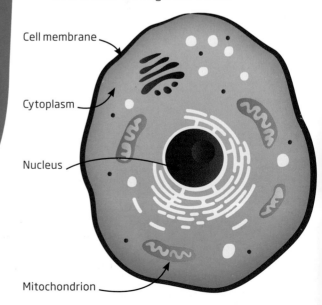

Changing states

Most materials can change between being solid, liquid, or gas, depending on their temperature and how tightly packed they are. Substances such as water can change from one state to another and then back again.

SEE ALSO
▶ Atoms p.34
▶ Gases p.117
▶ Water p.120-121
▶ Liquids p.148
▶ Solids p.234
▶ Temperature p.252

Different states

All substances are made from tiny particles that are arranged in different ways depending on whether they are solid, liquid, or gas.

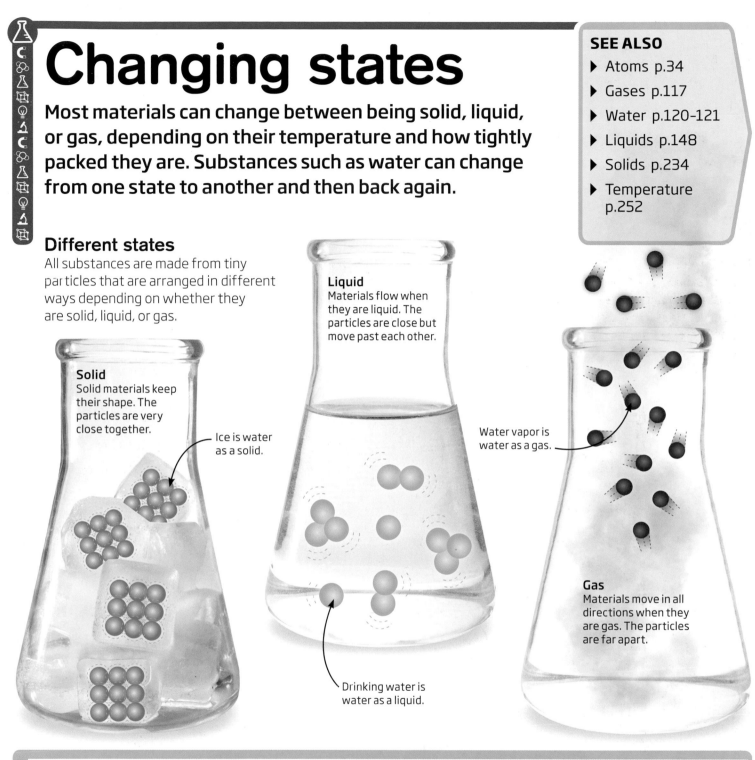

Liquid
Materials flow when they are liquid. The particles are close but move past each other.

Solid
Solid materials keep their shape. The particles are very close together.

Ice is water as a solid.

Water vapor is water as a gas.

Drinking water is water as a liquid.

Gas
Materials move in all directions when they are gas. The particles are far apart.

Shifting states

The same material can change from being solid to liquid and from liquid to gas when it is heated, and back again as it cools. These changes are called melting, solidifying, evaporating, and condensing.

Melting When we heat a solid, it melts and changes to a liquid.

Solidifying When a liquid like this lava cools, it becomes solid.

Evaporating When a liquid changes into a gas, it evaporates as steam.

Condensing When water turns from a gas back into a liquid form, this is condensing.

Chemistry

Chemistry is a science that looks at the smallest ingredients of everything, called elements. It studies how elements react when we mix them together, and how tiny particles in materials are arranged and can be rearranged.

SEE ALSO
▶ Atoms p.34
▶ Body cells p.41
▶ Elements p.90
▶ Engineering p.91
▶ Changing states p.57
▶ Materials p.157

Building blocks

Everything around us is made from tiny parts called atoms. Atoms join to each other and other types of atoms to make arrangements called molecules. These basic building blocks are what chemistry investigates.

An atom is mostly empty space. If an atom was the **size of a football stadium**, the nucleus would be the size of a marble.

Particles called electrons move around the outside.

1. Atoms
Atoms are so small we can't see them and they're mostly empty space. They have even smaller particles inside. The type of atom depends on the number of particles inside it.

The center is called the nucleus. It contains particles called protons and neutrons.

2. Elements
Materials that that have only one type of atom are known as elements. Elements have just one ingredient—themselves. Antimony, plutonium, and gold are all elements.

Gold

Antimony

Plutonium

Chemical reaction

When two or more elements come together to make a new compound, it is called a chemical reaction. Reactions can fizz, burn, or even explode when new compounds are made.

Iron and oxygen react to form rust.

3. Compounds
Elements that have joined together are called compounds. For example, water is a compound made from the elements oxygen and hydrogen.

Oxygen and hydrogen combined make the compound water.

Circuits

A circuit is when an object that uses electricity is connected with wires to a power source. Circuits in our homes connect lights and appliances, like the fridge or television, to electricity.

SEE ALSO
▶ Computers p.71
▶ Electricity p.87
▶ Light p.147
▶ Measuring p. 159
▶ Television p.251

How circuits work

When a circuit is a complete loop with no gaps, electricity can flow around it. We use symbols to represent the different parts of the circuit.

Electricity travels through metal wires.

Wires are covered in plastic to stop electricity escaping.

Battery "cell"

Batteries are power sources that hold electricity. Electricity can flow around the circuit when we connect it to both ends of a battery.

Switch

Electricity only flows around the circuit when the switch closes and is switched on. Once the switch is opened, the circuit breaks.

Light bulbs

Electricity makes the light bulb switch on and light up. Objects in a circuit that need electricity to work are called components.

Crocodile clips connect circuit wires to objects.

The flow of electricity around the circuit is called the **current**.

Circuit boards

Computers have tiny boards in them called circuit boards. Circuit boards have lots of wires connected up to tiny components to make the computer work.

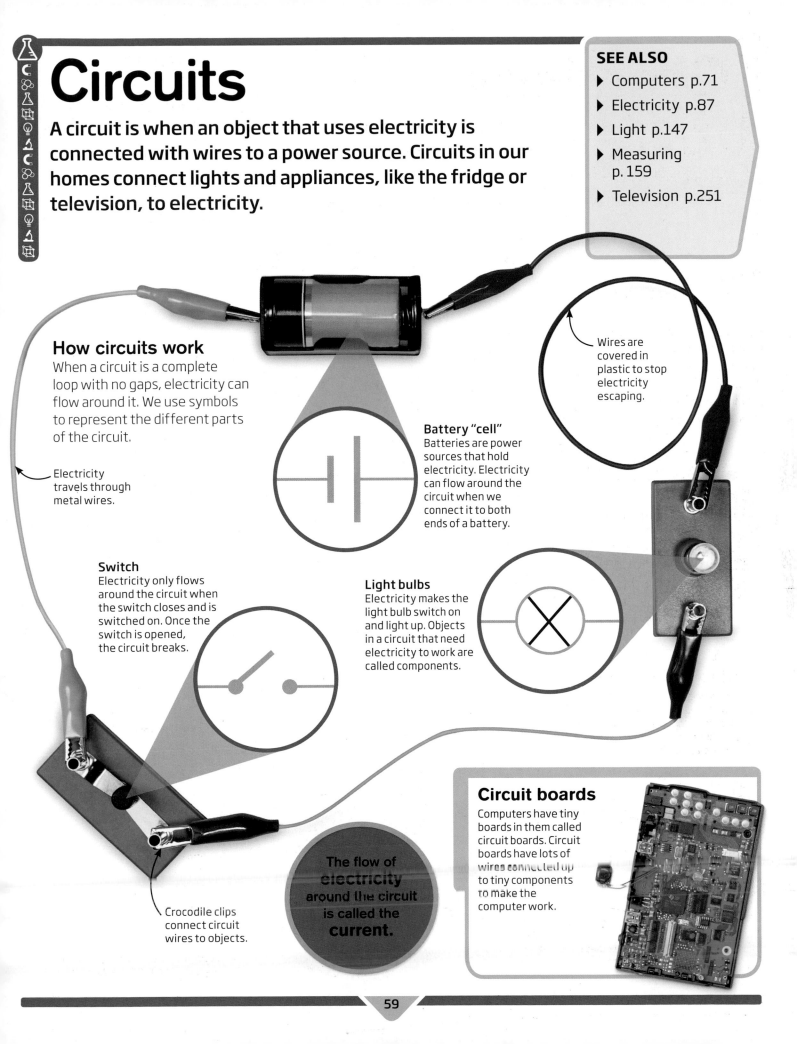

Climate change

Climate is the average weather for an area. The way we live is changing the Earth's climate. It is becoming warmer. This change is causing extreme weather conditions, such as long periods of little rainfall, called droughts, and huge storms. Many countries are now trying to stop climate change.

More than **39 billion tons** (35 billion metric tons) of **CO₂** is released **every year.**

What is the cause?

Power stations, factories, and cars pump gigantic amounts of the gas carbon dioxide (CO_2) into the atmosphere. This gas acts like a blanket, trapping the sun's heat and warming our planet.

Exhaust fumes from road traffic are one of the biggest causes of climate change.

How is the climate changing?

Climate change is making our summers hotter. Floods, droughts, and powerful storms are becoming more common. The ice in cold parts of the world is melting, which is making sea levels rise.

Flooding in New Orleans, Louisiana

What can we do?

We need to reduce the amount of fuels we burn that release CO_2. We can do this by using sources of energy that do not produce CO_2, such as sunlight, wind, and water.

Solar panels make energy from sunlight and do not release harmful gases.

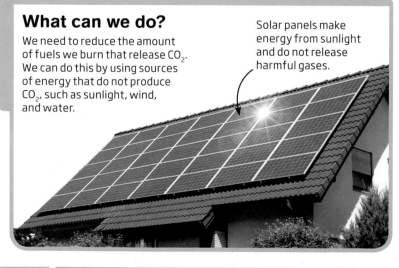

Clocks

A clock is a device used to keep track of time. Ancient civilizations measured time by falling sand, flowing water, or the position of the sun. Modern clocks are either digital or have clockwork mechanisms.

SEE ALSO
▶ Machines p.150
▶ Measuring p.159
▶ Numbers p.185
▶ The sciences pp.218–219
▶ Sun p.247
▶ Time zones p.255

How does a clock work?

Clocks make regular movements for measuring time. They do this using machinery known as clockwork. The clock face has moving hands that show the hours, minutes, and seconds.

Gears

Gears are wheels that lock together. In a clock, they make the hands turn at different speeds.

Pendulum

Each swing of the pendulum turns the gears one click, usually once a second.

Clock face

This part of the clock shows the time, in hours, minutes, and seconds.

Minute hand

The long minute hand makes a full turn around the clock every hour.

Hour hand

The short hour hand makes a complete turn around the clock every 12 hours.

Second hand

This long, thin hand makes a complete rotation of the clock every minute.

Then and now

In the past, people had sundials, which showed the time of day using shadows cast by the sun. Modern digital clocks show time as numbers.

Sundial

Digital clock

Counterweight

This weight stores energy so the clock can work without a battery.

The first **pendulum clock** was made by Dutch scientist Christiaan Huygens in 1656.

The **story** of...

Clothing

Over time, the things we wear have changed a lot. The clothes that people wear often reflect where they live, what jobs they do, and how much money they have. Clothes are generally made from woven materials such as cotton, wool, or silk, with special designs. They are often worn for show, but can also be practical or even worn for fun.

First clothes
The first people wore clothes made of animal skins to keep out the cold and wet. They later discovered how to clip the wool off a sheep's back and spin it into a thread that could be woven to make material.

This long, embroidered dress is made of silk.

The **Roman Emperor Nero** wore a **purple toga** and punished anyone else who wore purple with **death**.

A toga wraps around the body and is thrown over the left shoulder.

Roman clothes
The main item of clothing for ancient Romans was a simple tunic. For special occasions, men wore a long piece of cloth called a toga on top of their tunic. Women wore a woollen shawl called a palla.

Court finery
In the royal courts of Europe in the 1500s and 1600s, men and women wore special, expensive clothing. The women wore long, embroidered dresses, while the men wore padded jackets with short trousers and silk stockings.

A long cotton or silk sari is wrapped around the waist.

Traditional costume

Around the world, people wear clothes that are unique to their country. For traditional events, Indian women wear saris, while Japanese women wear long, decorated kimonos with wide sleeves. A kimono is tied at the back with an *obi*, or sash.

Kimono

A padded jacket, called a doublet.

Hats were designed to match the rest of the outfit.

A New Look skirt was full and long, with a small waist.

Weaving

The cotton, silk, wool, or linen material used to make clothes is woven on a loom. Different colored threads can be used to make patterns, such as checks or stripes.

Loom

A suit is often worn with a shirt and tie.

The New Look

During World War II (1939–45), material for new clothes was in short supply. In reaction to this, fashion designer Christian Dior introduced in Paris in 1947 a "New Look" for women. The full skirts were shorter and became fashionable around the world.

Smart suit

All around the world, businessmen and women wear a suit of a jacket and matching pants. The suit was developed in Europe during the 1800s and is a practical uniform for work and other formal occasions.

Clouds

Clouds are made of tiny droplets of water or ice. They form when air that contains water rises and cools. As well as making rain, snow, and hail, clouds help control our planet's temperature.

SEE ALSO
▶ Gases p.117
▶ Water pp.120–121
▶ Storms p.246
▶ Temperature p.252
▶ Water cycle p.270
▶ Weather p. 271

Types of cloud
There are many different types of cloud. Some float very high up, while others hug the ground. Clouds may look white and fluffy or dark and stormy.

High-level clouds

Cirrus
These wispy clouds form very high up in the air.

Cirrocumulus
Cirrostratus clouds sometimes break up to form these little clouds.

Altostratus
These clouds form a thin sheet across the sky.

Medium-level clouds

Cirrostratus
These thin clouds are made of tiny ice crystals.

Altocumulus
These clouds are broken into segments, or "cloudlets."

Stratus
These flat sheets of cloud can be white or gray.

Low-level clouds

Stratocumulus
These big clouds form a lumpy layer in the sky.

Cumulonimbus
Towering and huge, cumulonimbus clouds are often seen during thunderstorms.

Nimbostratus
Tall and gray, these clouds bring hours of rain or snow.

Cumulus
These fluffy heaps of cloud are often seen on sunny, breezy days.

Temperature control
Clouds reflect the sun's heat, stopping the Earth from getting too hot. They also trap heat below them, so a cloudy night is warmer than a clear one.

Clouds reflect heat from the sun.

Clouds trap heat reflected from the Earth.

Cloud or UFO?
Clouds that do not move can form in the sheltered air behind areas of high ground, such as mountains. They are shaped like saucers or lenses and have been mistaken for unidentified flying objects (UFOs)!

Coding

Computers follow instructions from special programs. These instructions are known as code, and writing them is called coding. Code can be written in many different coding languages.

SEE ALSO
▶ Codes p.66–67
▶ Communication p.69
▶ Computers p.71
▶ Internet p.138
▶ Language p.144
▶ School pp.272–273

Computer languages

Programming languages tell computers what to do. This example shows a text-based language called Python.

```
Python 3.5.2 (v3.5.2:4def2a2901a5, Jun 26 2016,
10:47:25)
[GCC 4.2.1 (Apple Inc. build 5666) (dot 3)] on
Darwin
Type "copyright", "credits" or "license()" for
more information.
>>>
```

```
print ( 'Hello World!')
```

Hello World!

The first programmer was **Lady Ada Lovelace** (1815–1852).

Input
Instructions are typed into a text window. These instructions tell the computer to show, "Hello World!"

Output
When the program is run, it follows the typed instructions. Here, the computer screen shows, "Hello World!"

Learning to code

Some computer languages are easier to learn than others. Scratch uses colorful blocks of code that you can arrange to make your own games.

Output
The blocks control the actions of the characters here, on the "Stage."

Input
In Scratch, coding is done by putting together instruction blocks.

The **story** of...

Codes

Codes are words, letters, and numbers that are used to represent other words, letters, and numbers. People used codes to communicate with each other, or to keep things secret. Others, such as DNA, are just instructions.

Morse Code
Morse Code represents letters and numbers as dots and dashes. It was used to send messages through wires before telephones were invented.

Morse Code tapping machine

The ancient Egyptians used **hieroglyphics** as a **writing system** to record their history.

Writing with pictures
The ancient Egyptians used drawings to communicate, instead of written words. These symbols are called hieroglyphics. Hieroglyphics were not understood by modern people until a stone was discovered with a translation of hieroglyphics into Greek, allowing the "code" to be worked out.

Programming
Computers need instructions to operate. These are created by programmers, who use combinations of symbols and words. Programming is often called coding.

1000101110
0101010
0110101110
010010
10111000
0 1011
0101010
01101011100011
010010 001010   010110
101 1001011 0101101010101

Bonjour
Boh-zhoo, French

您好
Nee-how, Mandarin

Hello
English

こんにちは
Konnichiwa, Japanese

Languages
The different languages humans speak are types of code. Until you learn a foreign language, hearing someone using it to speak or reading their writing will make little sense to you.

здравствуйте
Zdrast-wui-tyeh, Russian

Merhaba
Mehr-hah-bah, Turkish

Holá
Oh-lah, Spanish

নমস্কার
Nômoshkar, Bengali

Jambo
Ja-m-boh, Swahili

Codes in war

One of the most common uses for codes is to keep secrets, especially during wartime. When commanders give orders to their armies, they need those orders to be kept secret from the enemy. Code breakers try to crack the codes and learn enemy secrets.

This system of writing from ancient Greece is still not understood.

Linear A tablet

The **Enigma Code** was broken by a machine called a **"bombe,"** created by **Alan Turing**.

Unbroken codes

Some languages remain a mystery–their writings have been discovered but never translated. It is likely that we will never know what they mean.

Messages typed here were encoded by special wheels.

DNA strand

DNA

DNA–short for Deoxyribonucleic acid–is found inside the cells of all living things, including plants and animals. It contains a genetic code on how the living thing will form.

The Enigma machine was used by Germany during World War II.

Comets

Comets are objects in the solar system made of ice, dust, and rock. They have a hard core and long tails of gas and dust. Every now and again they appear within sight of Earth, before disappearing into deep space.

SEE ALSO
- Asteroids p.30
- Gases p.117
- Gravity p.125
- Meteorites p.164
- Solar system p.233
- Sun p.247

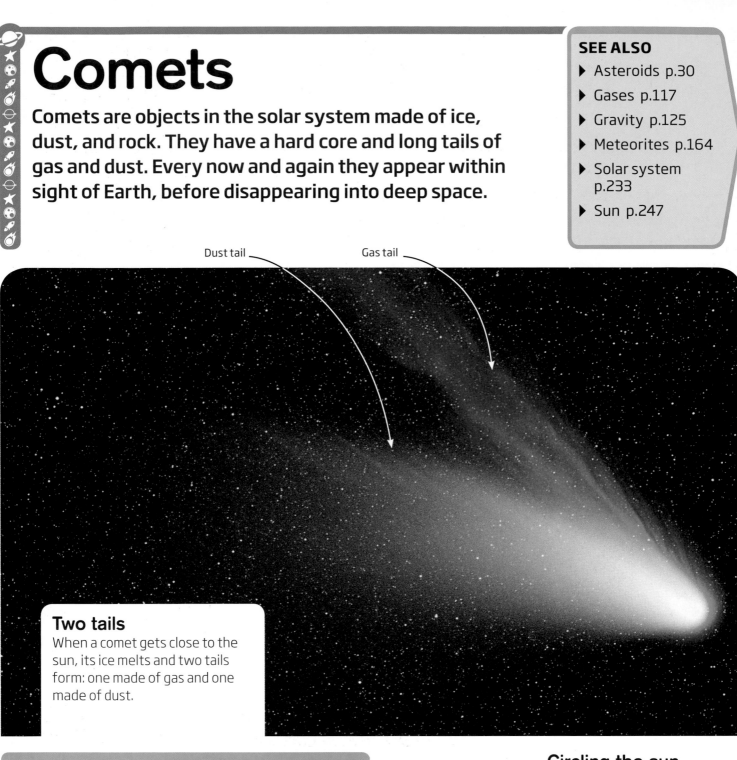

Dust tail

Gas tail

Two tails
When a comet gets close to the sun, its ice melts and two tails form: one made of gas and one made of dust.

Halley's Comet
Halley's Comet makes one full circle around the sun every 75 years, and it has been recorded by historians for more than 2,000 years. The Bayeux Tapestry, which tells the story of the Battle of Hastings, shows it moving across the sky in the year 1066.

Circling the sun
Comets move around the sun. Their tails always point away from the sun, but in slightly different directions. The tails get longer as the comet gets closer to the sun.

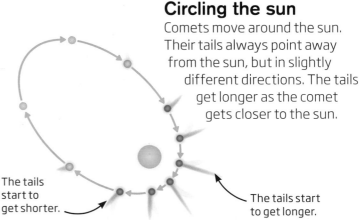

The tails start to get shorter.

The tails start to get longer.

Communication

The different ways people keep in touch are all forms of communication. People have many ways of communicating, such as talking to each other or writing letters. Most modern communication other than talking is done using mobile phones.

SEE ALSO
▶ Codes pp.66-67
▶ Computers p.71
▶ Internet p.138
▶ Satellites p.215
▶ Games pp.240-241
▶ Telephones p.250

Mobile phones

Mobile phones are very useful, as they let people communicate in many different ways.

Video calling
This type of call lets you see the person you are speaking to.

Email
Email lets us send written messages. It is much faster than sending a letter through the mail.

Gaming
People can chat and talk to one another while they play games.

Photo messaging
Photos can be taken and then shared with other people.

Internet
The internet lets people find out information very quickly.

Phone
Using a phone lets you talk to others around the world.

Texting
Texts are short written messages. Texting is a popular way to communicate.

Past and future

People have always found clever ways to communicate. The first humans drew pictures for each other on cave walls. Modern communication is becoming more high tech.

Telegraph
In the early 1800s, messages were sent in a series of dots and dashes (called Morse Code) over a thin wire.

HoloLens
This is a computer you can wear. It displays 3-D objects that the wearer can interact with.

Compass

A compass is a simple instrument that helps people find their way around by showing directions. It is usually round and contains a freely rotating, magnetic needle that always points north-south. This lets you work out other directions.

SEE ALSO

▶ Ancient China p.16

▶ Inside Earth p.135

▶ Magnets p.151

▶ Maps p.155

▶ Navigation p.182

How to use a compass

When using a compass, lay it flat and then turn it until the north end of the needle is above north on its base. Now you know which direction is north, you can find the other directions.

Direction hand

This hand can be turned to mark the direction that you want to travel toward.

Compass rose

The base of the compass shows all the different directions and is known as the compass rose.

Directions

The main directions are north (N), east (E), south (S), and west (W). They are called the cardinal directions.

Finer directions

Between the four cardinal directions are more precise ones, such as northeast (NE) and southwest (SW).

Needle

The magnetic needle detects Earth's magnetic field and lines up with north-south. The end of the needle pointing to north is usually colored or marked.

A compass on a phone shows which direction the phone is pointing in.

Directions can be written as angles. For example, southwest is 225°.

Walking compass

A walking compass has a see-through back so that it can be used on top of a map. This lets you work out where you are and which direction you want to go in.

21st-century compass

Many of today's phones contain a device called a magnetometer. It detects the Earth's magnetic field and lets you use your phone as a compass.

Computers

Computers are machines that store information and can be programmed to perform tasks. Many show information on a screen, such as on a mobile phone or a laptop. Others are hidden inside objects to make them work.

SEE ALSO
▶ Coding p.65
▶ Codes pp.66–67
▶ Communication p.69
▶ Internet p.138
▶ Machines p.150
▶ Robots p.212

How computers work

Computers are programmed in code to perform different tasks. This is called software. The programs are stored and run by the parts, or hardware, of the computer.

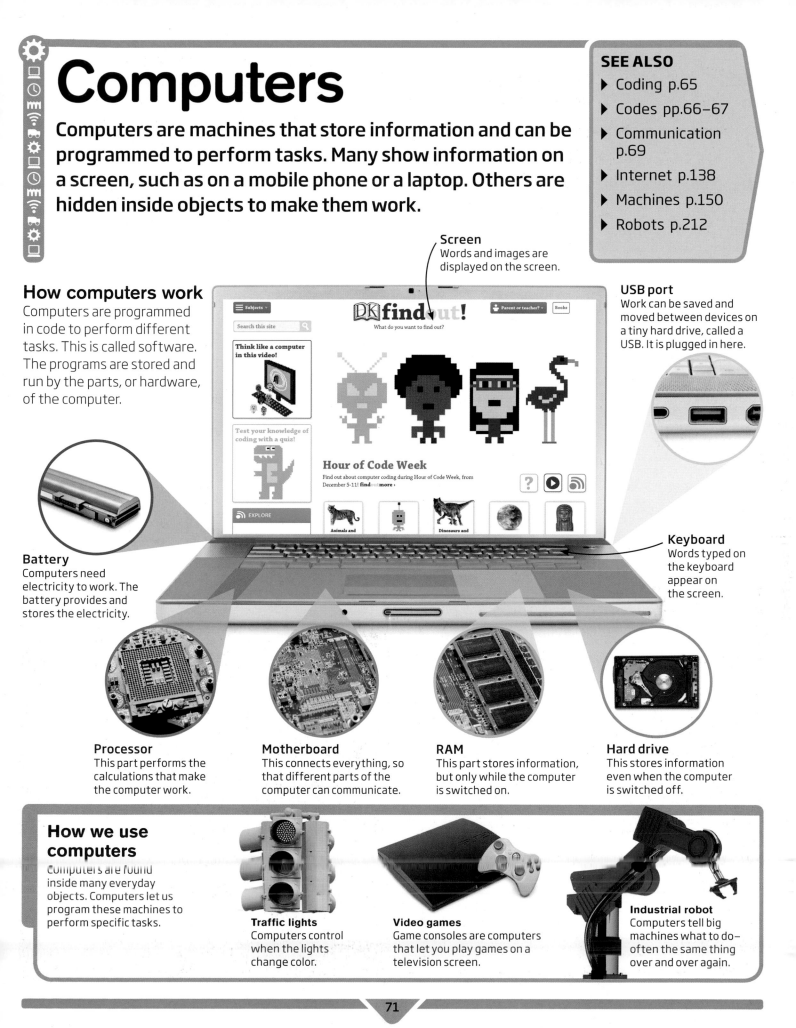

Screen
Words and images are displayed on the screen.

USB port
Work can be saved and moved between devices on a tiny hard drive, called a USB. It is plugged in here.

Keyboard
Words typed on the keyboard appear on the screen.

Battery
Computers need electricity to work. The battery provides and stores the electricity.

Processor
This part performs the calculations that make the computer work.

Motherboard
This connects everything, so that different parts of the computer can communicate.

RAM
This part stores information, but only while the computer is switched on.

Hard drive
This stores information even when the computer is switched off.

How we use computers

Computers are found inside many everyday objects. Computers let us program these machines to perform specific tasks.

Traffic lights
Computers control when the lights change color.

Video games
Game consoles are computers that let you play games on a television screen.

Industrial robot
Computers tell big machines what to do–often the same thing over and over again.

Conservation

Conservation is the protection of habitats and the plants and animals that live in them. This is important because human activity, such as cutting down trees and throwing away garbage, destroys animal homes.

Habitats
Animals live in areas we call habitats. When people damage habitats, they threaten many animals and plants. Wildlife reserves protect habitats and the animals that live in them.

Forests
People cut down trees for wood and to make space for farms. Some wood is used to make paper. Recycling paper helps save trees.

In danger
Many animals are in danger of dying out. When a type of animal has completely died out, we say it is extinct. National parks and laws try to stop animals from becoming extinct.

Under threat
Here are some of the ways humans have affected animals and their habitats, or homes. We can help protect animals by making small changes in our everyday lives.

Pollution
Pollution happens when people release dirty or harmful substances into the world around them. It can kill wildlife. Reusing and recycling things reduces the amount we throw away.

Fishing
People have caught so many fish from the sea that many species are becoming rare. We can now choose to eat farmed fish instead, leaving wild fish alone.

Constellations

Ancient civilizations looked at the night sky and grouped stars into patterns or constellations to represent heroes, creatures, and objects. As the Earth moves, the constellations appear to move across the sky. The stars are all at different distances from the Earth.

SEE ALSO

▶ Ancient Greece p.18

▶ Galaxies p.116

▶ Myths and legends p.178

▶ Navigation p.182

▶ Seasons p.221

▶ Stars p.242

Modern constellations

Astronomers today look at 88 constellations. Some can be seen from both the north and south parts of the world, others from only one or the other.

This star is called Menkent, meaning "shoulder of the Centaur."

This star is called Mizar.

Ursa Major
Also known as the Big Dipper, Ursa Major ("great bear") can only be seen from the northern half of Earth.

Betelgeuse is a red supergiant star.

Centaurus
This constellation represents a half-man, half-horse creature from Greek myth. It is only visible from the southern half of Earth.

Navigation

Ancient sailors used the constellations to find where they were. By looking at the pattern of stars they could work out where they were on Earth. One key signpost was Polaris, the North Star.

Orion's belt

Orion
The hunter, Orion, is one of the most well-known constellations. Three bright stars line up to make Orion's belt.

Over thousands of years, stars shift and **constellations change their shape.**

Coral reefs

Coral reefs are underwater structures where many plants and animals live. They are made by tiny animals called corals that grow hard shells. When they die, the shells remain and new corals grow on top of them. Some coral reefs can grow very big.

Coral reef

Coral reefs cover only a tiny part of the ocean, but are home to nearly a quarter of all ocean life. The reefs are full of food for sea creatures.

Great Barrier Reef

This reef is home to more than 1,500 different types of fish. It is the longest reef in the world and is found off the east coast of Australia.

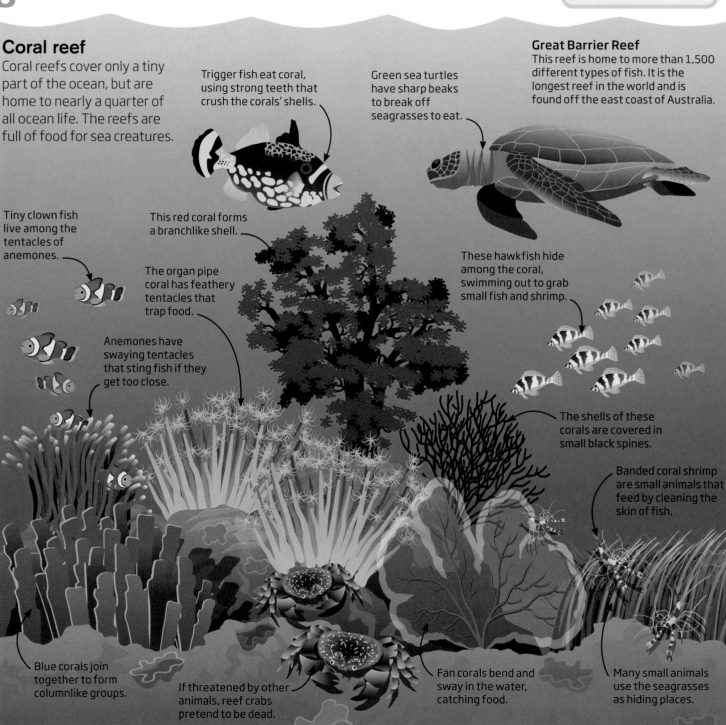

Trigger fish eat coral, using strong teeth that crush the corals' shells.

Green sea turtles have sharp beaks to break off seagrasses to eat.

Tiny clown fish live among the tentacles of anemones.

This red coral forms a branchlike shell.

The organ pipe coral has feathery tentacles that trap food.

Anemones have swaying tentacles that sting fish if they get too close.

These hawkfish hide among the coral, swimming out to grab small fish and shrimp.

The shells of these corals are covered in small black spines.

Banded coral shrimp are small animals that feed by cleaning the skin of fish.

Blue corals join together to form columnlike groups.

If threatened by other animals, reef crabs pretend to be dead.

Fan corals bend and sway in the water, catching food.

Many small animals use the seagrasses as hiding places.

Crafts

A craft is something done by hand, often with a lot of skill. People have always used natural and artificial materials, such as clay or glass, to make things. Craft objects can be for everyday use, such as plates for eating, or for decoration, such as jewelry.

SEE ALSO

▶ Ancient Rome p.20

▶ Art p.28

▶ Books p.44

▶ Clothing pp.62-63

▶ Inventions pp.136-137

Pottery

Potters use clay from the ground to make things such as plates, bowls, cups, and vases. They shape the clay, then put it in a special oven called a kiln to heat it up and make it hard.

Glass Roman jug

African wooden figure

Woodcarving

Woodworkers shape wood into different things. They can make furniture, bowls, and other useful or decorative items.

Glasswork

When sand is heated to a very high temperature, it becomes liquid glass. This can be shaped and cooled into solid objects such as jugs.

Beads are made in different sizes and shapes.

Red terra-cotta clay

Ancient Egyptian vase

Native American woven rug

Weaving

Weavers bring together wool, silk, or cotton threads to make material. This can be used for many things, such as clothes, rugs, and wall decorations.

Beading

Materials such as glass can be made into beads. Beads can be threaded onto string to make jewelry, or sewn onto clothing.

Ancient Middle-Eastern beads

Dance

Moving your body in time to a beat is called dancing. People dance to music to enjoy themselves, to be close to their friends, and to show their skills. Dances can be very formal with set movements to follow, or much more casual and relaxed.

SEE ALSO
▶ Clothing pp.62-63
▶ Music pp.176-177
▶ Festivals pp.206-207
▶ Religion p.208
▶ Sports p.239
▶ Theater p. 253

Fans used in dance

Arms above the head

Elegant arm positions

Feet lift high off the ground

Traditional dance
Many countries or regions have their own dances, called traditional dances. Korean fan dancing involves making shapes with fans.

Tribal dance
Many African tribal dances follow drum beats and have strong rhythms. The historical dances of tribes can include whole crowds.

Religious dance
Some people in the Islamic religion dance by spinning around in circles. This is called Sufi whirling and helps them feel closer to God.

Bollywood dance
Bollywood films from India are famous for their dance routines. Often, the whole cast perform exciting dances with precise arm movements and footwork.

Precise hand shapes

Acrobatic moves

Complicated footwork

Ballet
Ballet is a formal dance style with graceful and strong moves. Ballet dancers use a series of precise steps, leaps, and lifts.

Pointed toes

Street dance
Street dance often involves dancers making up their own moves to hip-hop music. They usually do flips and spins.

Latin dance
Latin dance began in Latin America. Dances such as the tango involve two people dancing close together, as if they are in love.

Day and night

Day and night are times of light and darkness that occur because the Earth spins, or rotates. One full day-and-night cycle is called a "day" for short. The half of the spinning Earth that faces the sun has daylight, and the half facing away from the sun is in darkness.

What makes day and night?

As the Earth spins round, parts of it move in and out of the sun's light. The light parts are in day and the dark parts are in night.

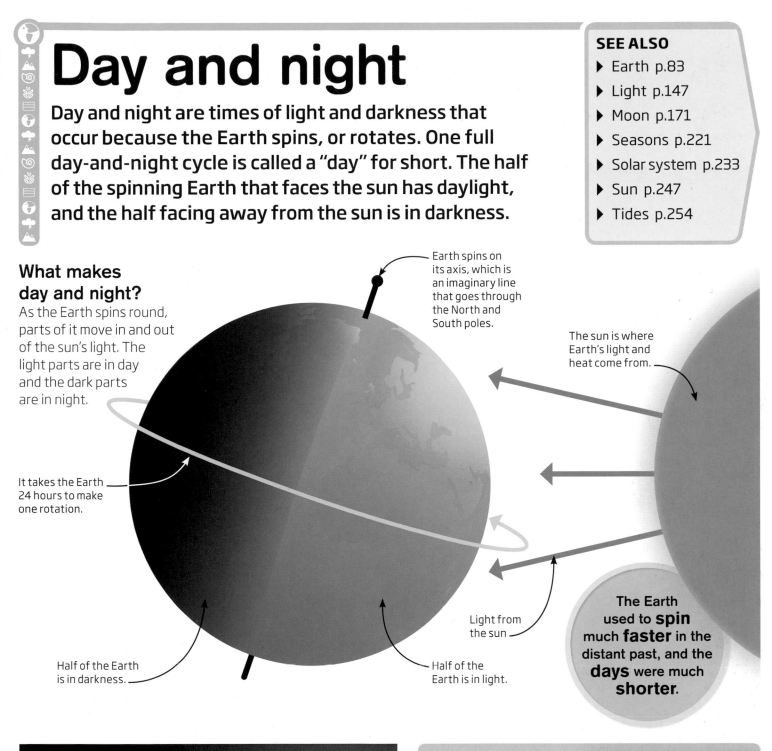

Earth spins on its axis, which is an imaginary line that goes through the North and South poles.

The sun is where Earth's light and heat come from.

It takes the Earth 24 hours to make one rotation.

Light from the sun

Half of the Earth is in darkness.

Half of the Earth is in light.

The Earth used to **spin** much **faster** in the distant past, and the **days** were much **shorter**.

Moving sun

The sun appears to move across the sky during the day as the Earth spins around it. It rises in the east and sets in the west. In the summer, the sun is higher in the sky than in the winter.

Eclipses

The moon circles the Earth. Occasionally, it blocks our view of the sun during the day, and the sky darkens for a few minutes. This event is called a solar eclipse. If the moon blocks all of the sun, it is called a total eclipse, and stars can be seen in the sky.

Total eclipse

Deserts

The world's driest areas are deserts. They have less than 10 in (25 cm) of rain a year. Deserts can be sandy, rocky, or even icy. Most deserts have hot days and cold nights. Some animals survive here by getting water from plants or by only moving around after sunset.

Desert living

Animals and plants living in deserts must be able to survive with little water. In hot deserts, animals are active at night. During the day, they retreat under the sand to stay out of the hot sun.

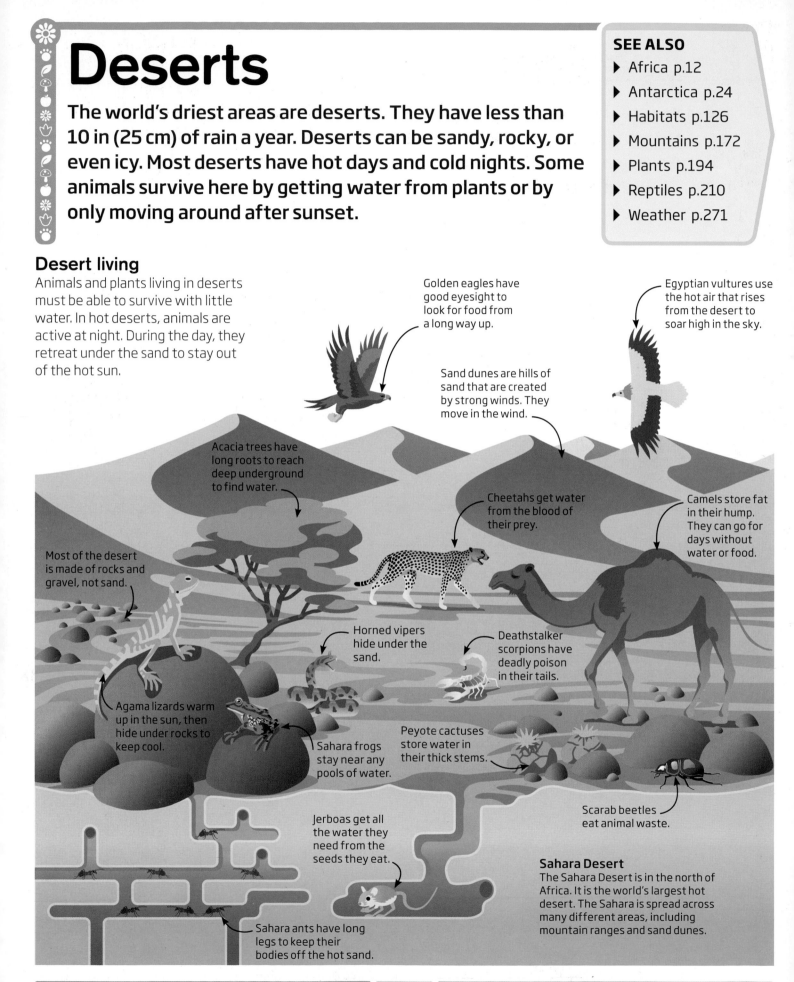

Golden eagles have good eyesight to look for food from a long way up.

Egyptian vultures use the hot air that rises from the desert to soar high in the sky.

Sand dunes are hills of sand that are created by strong winds. They move in the wind.

Acacia trees have long roots to reach deep underground to find water.

Cheetahs get water from the blood of their prey.

Camels store fat in their hump. They can go for days without water or food.

Most of the desert is made of rocks and gravel, not sand.

Horned vipers hide under the sand.

Deathstalker scorpions have deadly poison in their tails.

Agama lizards warm up in the sun, then hide under rocks to keep cool.

Sahara frogs stay near any pools of water.

Peyote cactuses store water in their thick stems.

Scarab beetles eat animal waste.

Jerboas get all the water they need from the seeds they eat.

Sahara ants have long legs to keep their bodies off the hot sand.

Sahara Desert

The Sahara Desert is in the north of Africa. It is the world's largest hot desert. The Sahara is spread across many different areas, including mountain ranges and sand dunes.

Digestion

Digestion is when we eat food and it gets broken down and used by our bodies to give us the energy we need to move and stay healthy. Your digestive system starts with your mouth and ends at your bottom.

SEE ALSO
▶ Food p.106
▶ Eating pp.104–105
▶ Human body p.130
▶ Lungs p.149
▶ Taste p.249

Esophagus

Food journey
Once it has been swallowed, food passes into the stomach. From here, it moves through the intestines and is then pushed out of the body.

Stomach
Inside the stomach, liquid chemicals are added to the food and churned around.

Small intestine
After passing through the stomach, the mushed-up food liquid travels through the small intestine.

A large meal takes **one to three days** to pass through the digestive system.

Digestive system

Large intestine
The waste parts of food stay in the large intestine until they are pushed out as poo.

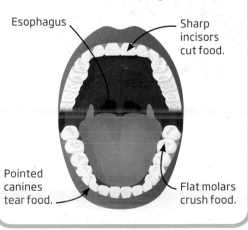

In the mouth
When we chew, food is broken and mixed with saliva. Different teeth do different jobs. When the chewed food is swallowed, it goes down a tube called the esophagus.

Esophagus

Sharp incisors cut food.

Pointed canines tear food.

Flat molars crush food.

Dinosaurs

Dinosaurs are reptiles that lived on Earth for 160 million years, about 225 million years ago. Some were fierce meat eaters, others gentle plant eaters. Scientists have learned about dinosaurs from studying the fossils left behind when the dinosaurs died.

SEE ALSO
▶ Asteroids p.30
▶ Birds p.39
▶ Fossils p.111
▶ Prehistoric life p.202
▶ Reptiles p.210
▶ Rocks and minerals p.214

Ceratopsians

Ceratopsians were plant-eating dinosaurs. They had a protective frill around their head.

Triceratops's frill was used to protect the neck during fights.

The horns were used for defending itself against other dinosaurs.

Dinosaur fossils

The remains of dinosaurs have been preserved in rock. Some even show the dinosaur's last meal still inside them.

Archaeopteryx fossil

Dinosaur remains have been found on **every continent,** including Antarctica.

The sharp beak was used for tearing pieces off tough plants.

A long neck let Brachiosaurus reach leaves at the top of tall trees.

The legs had to be strong, as Triceratops weighed the same as four cars.

Triceratops
(try-SER-uh-tops)

Tyrannosaurus rex
(TIE-ran-oh-SORE-us rex)

Sharp teeth let T. rex tear meat off bones.

Theropods

Theropods were fierce meat-eating dinosaurs. They lived in what is now North America.

The long tail was used for balance.

Sauropods

Sauropods were enormous plant-eating dinosaurs. They had to eat all the time to fuel their huge bodies.

Brachiosaurus
(brack-ee-oh-SORE-us)

Dogs

Dogs are meat-eaters with sharp teeth and excellent senses. They include wild jackals, foxes, and wolves, as well as the tame dogs we keep as pets in our homes. Wild dogs hunt for food or eat animals that have already died.

SEE ALSO
▶ Animal families p.21
▶ Cats p.54
▶ Deserts p.78
▶ Hearing p.127
▶ Pets pp.152–153
▶ Work p.274

Pet dogs

There are lots of different types of dogs. Some are friendly and make good pets. Some are strong and loyal to their owners and are good at guarding things.

There are more than **300** different types of pet dog.

Irish Wolfhound

Beagle

Lhasa Apso

Grey Wolf

Fennec fox

Wolves

The grey wolf is the most closely related animal to pet dogs. Wolves live and hunt in groups called packs.

Foxes

These pointy-eared animals can be found in deserts, icy locations, mountains, and even cities. The fennec fox is the smallest fox.

Working dogs

For thousands of years, dogs have been known as man's best friend. This is because they work closely with people. Dogs work in the fields, hunt, and even sniff out people who have been buried in rubble or snow.

Early humans

The first humans were similar to apes, such as gorillas and chimpanzees. Over millions of years, they learned to walk on two legs and got smarter as their brains grew larger. They also lost most of their body hair, slowly becoming more like the humans we are today.

SEE ALSO

▶ Africa p.12
▶ Evolution p.95
▶ Fossils p.111
▶ Monkeys and apes p.170
▶ Exploration pp.180–181
▶ Stone Age p.243

Ancient humans

There were many different types, or species, of human relatives. Some of them lived at the same time and may have met each other regularly.

7 million years ago

Hominins
Early humanlike species, called hominins, developed from apes. They spent a lot of their time in trees, and began walking on two legs.

4 million years ago

First toolmakers
Homo habilis was one of the first species to use stone tools to help with work. The tools made it easier for them to get food.

Basic rock tool

3 to 2.5 million years ago

Prehumans
Australopithecus is a species of hominin that learned to walk fully upright, like humans do today.

2 million years ago

First fire-makers
Human relatives became steadily more clever and ate more meat. Homo erectus may have been using fire to cook food over a million years ago.

200,000 years ago

Hand axe

Modern humans
Modern humans appeared in Africa. The tools they made helped them adapt to other environments. They spread across the world, while other humanlike species died out.

Human evolution

The first humanlike animals were short, had small brains, and lived mostly in trees. Over many years, they began spending more of their lives on the ground.

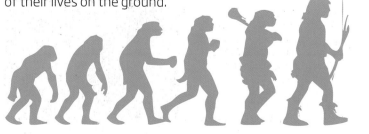

How do we know?

Ancient humans left behind bones and tools. Scientists study the bones to learn everything from how ancient humans walked to what they ate and what diseases they had. Their tools can reveal information about daily life.

Ancient skull

Earth

Earth is the planet we live on. It is the third planet away from the sun and the largest rocky planet in the solar system. Earth is about 4.5 billion years old. At the moment it is the only planet known to support life.

SEE ALSO

▶ Atmosphere p.33
▶ Earth's surface p.84
▶ Gases p.117
▶ Water pp.120–121
▶ Solar system p.233
▶ Sun p.247

Earth has seven large land masses called continents.

After seeing the first pictures from space, scientists nicknamed Earth "the blue marble."

Our home
Earth has all the right conditions for life. It is just the right distance from the sun, it has oceans of liquid water, and a blanket of gases called an atmosphere that protects it from outer space.

Earth's atmosphere is mostly made of two gases, nitrogen and oxygen.

About **70 percent** of the Earth's surface is **covered in liquid water.**

The white swirls are clouds. Thick patches of white are storms.

Habitable

Too cold

Too hot

Earth is here

Safe zone
Earth orbits the sun in what is known as the habitable zone (in green), where liquid water can exist. Closer to the sun, it is too hot, and farther away it is too cold.

Earthrise
On Earth, we see a sunrise and a moonrise as the sun and moon become visible in the sky. When astronauts orbited the moon in 1968, they saw our own planet rising in the sky.

Earth's surface

The outer layer of the Earth is called the crust. It is made up of many pieces, called tectonic plates, which fit together like a giant, ball-shaped jigsaw. Tectonic plates move very slowly, just a few centimeters each year.

SEE ALSO
▶ Earthquakes p.85
▶ Inside Earth p.135
▶ Mountains p.172
▶ Oceans and seas p.187
▶ Volcanoes p.268
▶ World p.275

Many volcanoes are found on the Ring of Fire.

Earthquakes are very common along the San Andreas Fault, a part of the Ring of Fire in California.

Pacific Ocean

Tectonic plates meet at plate boundaries.

Earth's tectonic plates
Earth's surface has seven giant tectonic plates and several smaller ones. The largest plate is below the Pacific Ocean. It covers more than one-fifth of the Earth.

KEY
Plate boundary
Ring of Fire
Volcano

Ring of Fire
Volcanic eruptions and earthquakes are common at the plate boundaries around the Pacific Ocean. This is known as the Ring of Fire.

Mountains
The Himalayas are a mountain range in Asia at the boundary between two tectonic plates. The range formed over millions of years as the plates pushed into each other, forcing the ground up. The mountains are still rising by about $1/5$ in (5 mm) every year.

Earthquakes

An earthquake is when the ground shakes. Earthquakes happen along cracks in the Earth's crust, known as faults. Small earthquakes can barely be felt by humans, but the biggest can cause enormous damage.

SEE ALSO
- Buildings p.48
- Changing world pp.50–51
- Earth's surface p.84
- Inside Earth p.135
- Rocks and minerals p.214

What causes an earthquake?

An earthquake happens when two huge areas of the ground jerk past one another, making the ground shake. The crack between them is called a fault.

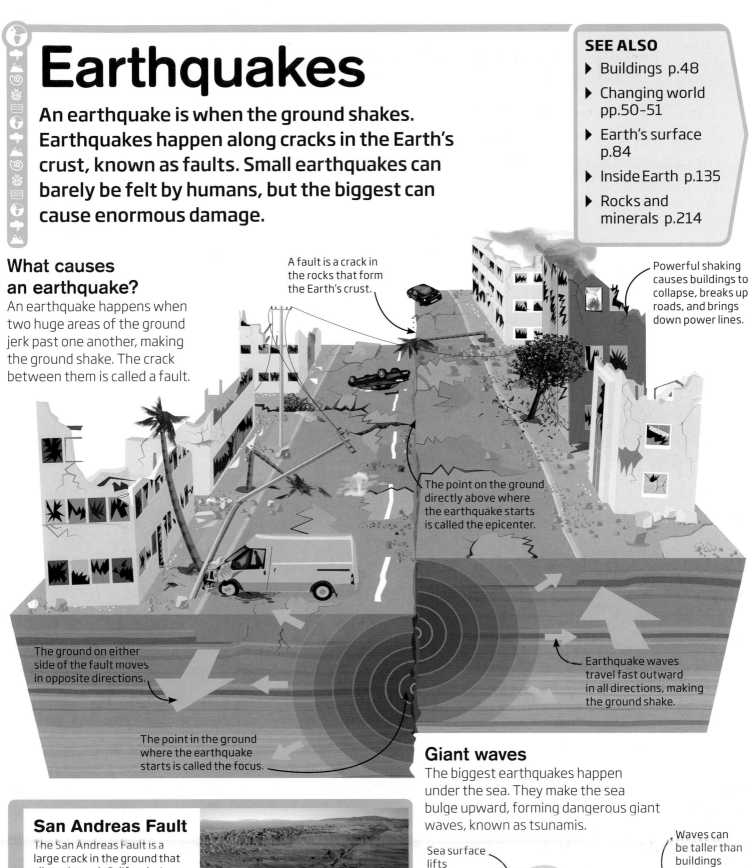

A fault is a crack in the rocks that form the Earth's crust.

Powerful shaking causes buildings to collapse, breaks up roads, and brings down power lines.

The point on the ground directly above where the earthquake starts is called the epicenter.

The ground on either side of the fault moves in opposite directions.

Earthquake waves travel fast outward in all directions, making the ground shake.

The point in the ground where the earthquake starts is called the focus.

San Andreas Fault

The San Andreas Fault is a large crack in the ground that slices through California. It marks the join between two huge pieces of the Earth's crust, called plates. Big earthquakes happen on the fault about every 10 years.

Giant waves

The biggest earthquakes happen under the sea. They make the sea bulge upward, forming dangerous giant waves, known as tsunamis.

Sea surface lifts

Waves can be taller than buildings

Earthquake pushes the seabed up

Eggs

Some young animals grow and develop inside round objects called eggs. There are different types of eggs. The size of the egg and the length of time it takes to hatch depends on the size of the animal that laid it.

SEE ALSO
- Amphibians p.15
- Birds p.39
- Fish p.101
- Life cycle p.146
- Mammals p.154
- Metamorphosis p.163

Ostrich eggs are the largest in the world.

Bird eggs

Bird eggs are hard and waterproof. They are kept warm, or incubated, by one of the parents. Most bird eggs are kept safe in a nest.

It takes 42 days for an ostrich chick to be ready to hatch.

Egg-laying mammals

Most mammals give birth to live babies. Only one group, called monotremes, lay eggs. The monotreme shown here is called an echidna.

Ostrich chick

Tortoise hatchlings are male or female depending on how warm the egg was kept.

Dogfish eggs look like leathery bags, which are sometimes called "mermaid's purses."

Leopard tortoise hatchling

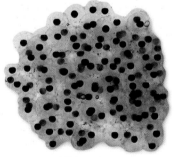

Frogspawn

Fish eggs

Most fish produce lots of eggs and don't look after them. But they do lay the eggs in places like sea grasses to keep them safe.

Reptile eggs

Reptile eggs are soft and leathery. The mother buries them in the ground and leaves them to hatch on their own.

Amphibian eggs

Amphibians such as frogs and toads lay wet eggs in water. When they are ready, the eggs hatch and tadpoles come out.

Electricity

Electricity is the flow of tiny charged particles called electrons. It is used to power lights and electrical appliances, such as kettles and televisions, in our homes, at school, and all around us.

SEE ALSO
- Atoms p.34
- Circuits p.59
- Energy pp.88-89
- Materials p.157
- Metals p.162
- Television p.251

Lightning

Lightning is a type of natural electricity called static electricity. Tiny bits of ice in the clouds rub together, charging up electricity until a big spark of lightning occurs.

Making electricity

We make electricity from different types of energy. One example is how solar panels change the sun's light energy into electricity. Also, wind turbines change the wind's movement energy into electrical energy.

Wind turbines

Using electricity

Appliances like coffee pots and televisions in our homes work when we press a switch to connect them to electricity. Electricity flows through them to make them function.

A toaster needs electricity to heat up.

The light bulb in this lamp uses electricity.

A laptop charges up using electricity.

Energy

Energy is power to make things happen. It is everywhere around us. Heat, light, and movement are types of energy. We need energy to make our bodies work and it's what we use to make electricity and power our homes. Energy can be stored and it can change from one form to another.

Fossil fuels

Fossil fuels are made from dead plants and animals squashed underground millions of years ago. Coal, oil, and gas are fossil fuels. We burn these fuels to release heat and this makes electricity in power stations.

Our bodies

Your body needs energy to move, grow, keep warm, and stay alive. The food you eat gets digested and changes inside you to give you the energy you need.

Running

Movement

Movement is a type of energy. When, for example, a roller coaster is pulled to the top of a hill, it has lots of stored energy. Then as it moves downward, the roller coaster gets faster, as stored energy changes to movement energy.

The fastest roller coaster is Formula Rossa in the United Arab Emirates. It travels at 150 mph (241 kph).

Roller coaster

Burning coals

Early steam engine

Industrial Revolution
From the late 1700s, people began to use energy in new ways, creating huge industrial growth. Movement energy from water turned wheels to drive machines to weave textiles in mills. Heat energy from steam engines drove trains and machines in factories.

Food chain
Plants take energy from the sun's light and convert it into sugar, a type of stored energy in plants. In this example, the deer eats the stored energy in the plants, which gives the deer energy. The lion eats the deer, and this food gives the lion energy.

Plants

Deer

The first **steam engine** was developed in the 1760s by Scotsman **James Watt.**

Lion

The sun
Most of the energy we use is from the sun. The sun's light energy changes to heat energy, warming planet Earth. Light helps plants grow and plants provide animals with energy.

The sun

Renewable
Renewable energy is energy made from sources that won't run out, such as sunlight, wind, and water. For example, we can use a wind turbine or a water wheel to turn movement energy into electricity.

The wind turns the blades of the turbine.

Wind turbines

Elements

An element is a material that can't be broken down into other materials. All objects are made from tiny particles called atoms, which usually join together in groups. Elements are pure materials, which means they are made from only one type of atom.

SEE ALSO
▶ Atoms p.34
▶ Electricity p.87
▶ Gases p.117
▶ Liquids p.148
▶ Metals p.162
▶ Gold pp.200–201
▶ Solids p.234

Elements everywhere

Three-quarters of the elements are part of a group called metals. They are usually solids that conduct electricity. Non-metal elements include gases, such as hydrogen and oxygen, and solids, such as carbon and sulfur.

Calcium
The metal calcium is found in rocks, living things, and milk. It helps make bones, teeth, and animal horns.

Helium
The gas helium is used in party balloons because it is lighter than air, so it floats. Helium is made inside stars.

Aluminum
The soft, light metal aluminum can be made into foil, cans, and airplane parts. It doesn't rust like some metals.

Gold
The valuable metal gold is found in its pure form in nature. It can be hammered into shapes without snapping.

The periodic table

The periodic table lists all the known elements in the universe. There are more than 100 chemical elements and we keep finding more. All the elements have a symbol and are placed in groups according to how they behave and how many particles they have inside them.

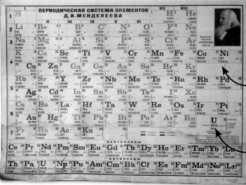

Nitrogen has the symbol Ni.

Uranium has the symbol U.

The first periodic table, written by Mendeleev

Mercury is the only metal that is liquid at room temperature.

Engineering

Engineers use math and science to solve problems. They invent and create machines, buildings, tools, and other useful inventions that make our lives easier. There are different types of engineers that specialize in different areas.

SEE ALSO
- Bridges p.46
- Buildings p.48
- Factories p.97
- Inventions pp.136–137
- Machines p.150
- Materials p.157

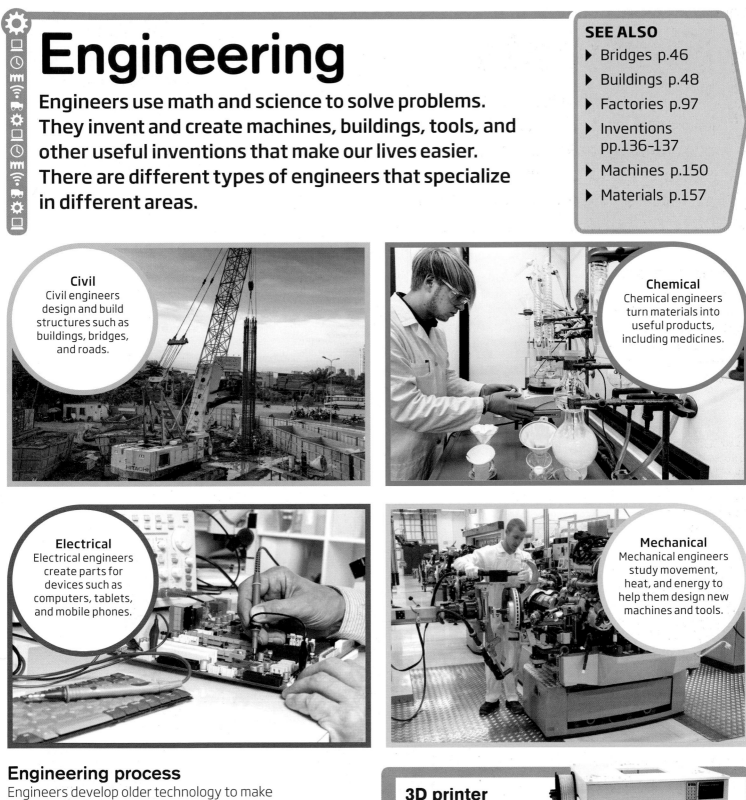

Civil
Civil engineers design and build structures such as buildings, bridges, and roads.

Chemical
Chemical engineers turn materials into useful products, including medicines.

Electrical
Electrical engineers create parts for devices such as computers, tablets, and mobile phones.

Mechanical
Mechanical engineers study movement, heat, and energy to help them design new machines and tools.

Engineering process

Engineers develop older technology to make new, better designs. An invention like the wheel has changed over time from the earliest version to a hi-tech modern one.

Stone

Wood

Rubber and metal

3D printer

Engineers can now use computer-aided design (CAD) programs to make three-dimensional (3-D) models of their designs. The 3-D printer creates the model using layers of plastic.

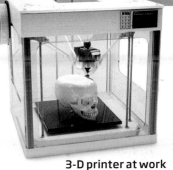

3-D printer at work

Engines

Engines power machines by turning fuel into movement. Coal, oil, or electricity is heated to create energy. The energy is then used to turn wheels or parts that move the machine forward. There are three main types of engines.

SEE ALSO
▶ Aircraft p.13
▶ Cars p.52
▶ Factories p.97
▶ Forces p.108
▶ Machines p.150
▶ Ships p.224
▶ Trains p.260

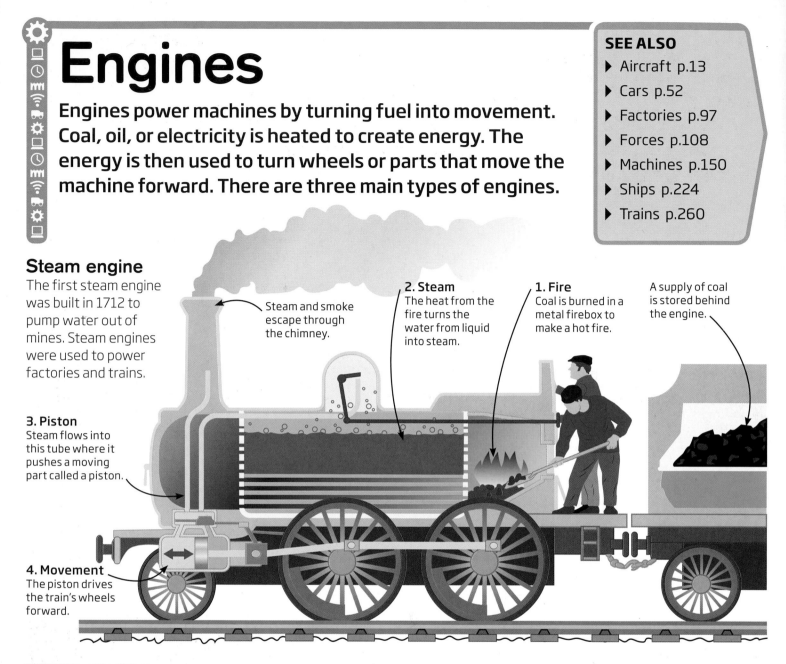

Steam engine

The first steam engine was built in 1712 to pump water out of mines. Steam engines were used to power factories and trains.

Steam and smoke escape through the chimney.

2. Steam
The heat from the fire turns the water from liquid into steam.

1. Fire
Coal is burned in a metal firebox to make a hot fire.

A supply of coal is stored behind the engine.

3. Piston
Steam flows into this tube where it pushes a moving part called a piston.

4. Movement
The piston drives the train's wheels forward.

Car engine

Car engines burn gasoline or diesel. There are four moving parts called pistons, which move up and down, making the car's wheels turn.

Jet engine

Jet engines are used for aircraft. They work by squashing, heating, and speeding up air. This hot air is blasted out backward, pushing the aircraft forward.

Erosion

Erosion is the natural movement of rocks, tiny pieces of loose rock, and soil, over long distances. Many different things can cause erosion, including wind, rivers, ice, oceans, and landslides.

On the move

Erosion moves huge amounts of rock and soil, and shapes our landscape. It is fastest in mountains, where there is lots of rain and snow, and slowest in dry places such as deserts.

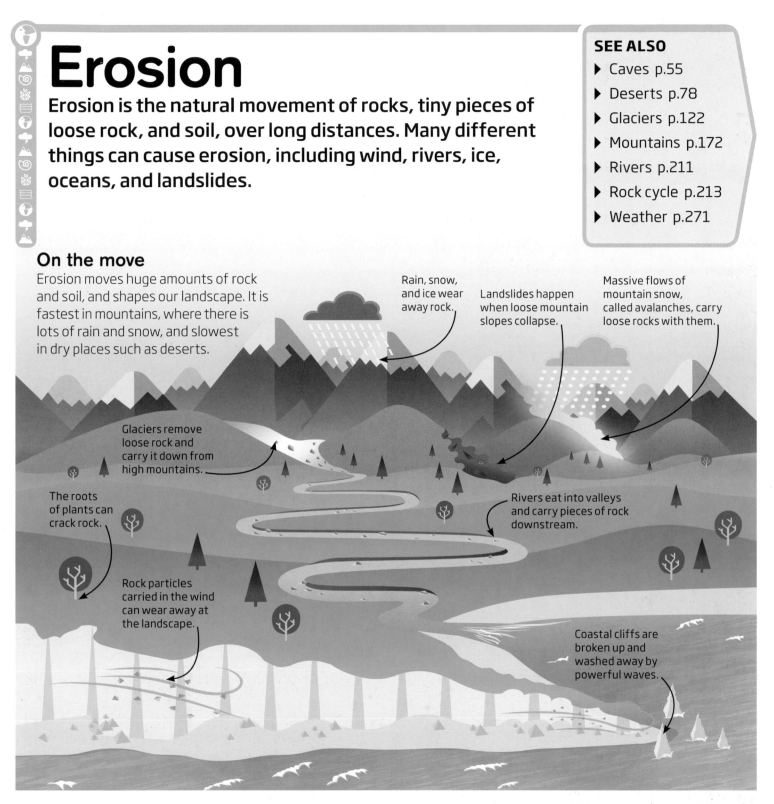

Rain, snow, and ice wear away rock.

Landslides happen when loose mountain slopes collapse.

Massive flows of mountain snow, called avalanches, carry loose rocks with them.

Glaciers remove loose rock and carry it down from high mountains.

The roots of plants can crack rock.

Rivers eat into valleys and carry pieces of rock downstream.

Rock particles carried in the wind can wear away at the landscape.

Coastal cliffs are broken up and washed away by powerful waves.

Wind sculptures

Over a very long period of time, tiny pieces of rock carried by strong winds in deserts can sandblast rocks, wearing them away into amazing shapes.

Wind-carved rock

Glacier power

Glaciers are rivers of ice that move down from high mountains very slowly. As they move, they pick up rocks that scrape away at the landscape, carving steep-sided valleys and hollows in the ground.

Europe

The continent of Europe is surrounded by ocean, except in the east, where it is joined to Asia. Much of Europe is flat, but there are several high mountain ranges, including the Alps, Pyrenees, and the Carpathians.

SEE ALSO
▶ Ancient Greece p.18
▶ Ancient Rome p.20
▶ Asia p.29
▶ World War I p.276
▶ World War II p.277

About Europe

Population: 743.1 million

Highest point: Mount Elbrus

Lowest point: Caspian Sea

Biggest desert: Oltenia Sahara

Longest river: Volga

Although it is the **second smallest** continent, Europe contains nearly **50 countries**.

This powerful meat-eater is the biggest member of the weasel family.

Wolverine

Oil Gas

Coal

Beneath the domes of this cathedral in Moscow are ten separate churches.

Eyjafjallajökull

In 2010, ash from this volcano in Iceland stopped more than 100,000 airline flights.

Ferry

Njupeskär waterfall

Brown bear

Rhythmic gymnastics

Giant's Causeway

Stonehenge

Tulips

Little Mermaid

European bison

Malbork Castle

St Basil's Cathedral

Grass snake

The building of this cathedral began in 1882. It is due to finish in 2026.

Eiffel Tower

Golden eagle

Dobšinská Ice Cave

St Sophia's Cathedral

Cossack dancing

Flamenco dancing

Sagrada Familia cathedral

Leaning Tower of Pisa

Mount Olympus

Dalmatian pelican

Mount Etna

Giant's Causeway

The Giant's Causeway is an area of hexagonal columns made of ancient volcanic rock. It is on the coast of County Antrim in Northern Ireland.

Eiffel Tower

This iron tower in Paris is 1,063 ft (324 m) high. It was completed in 1889 and is the most visited monument in the world.

The tower is made up of more than 18,000 pieces of cast iron.

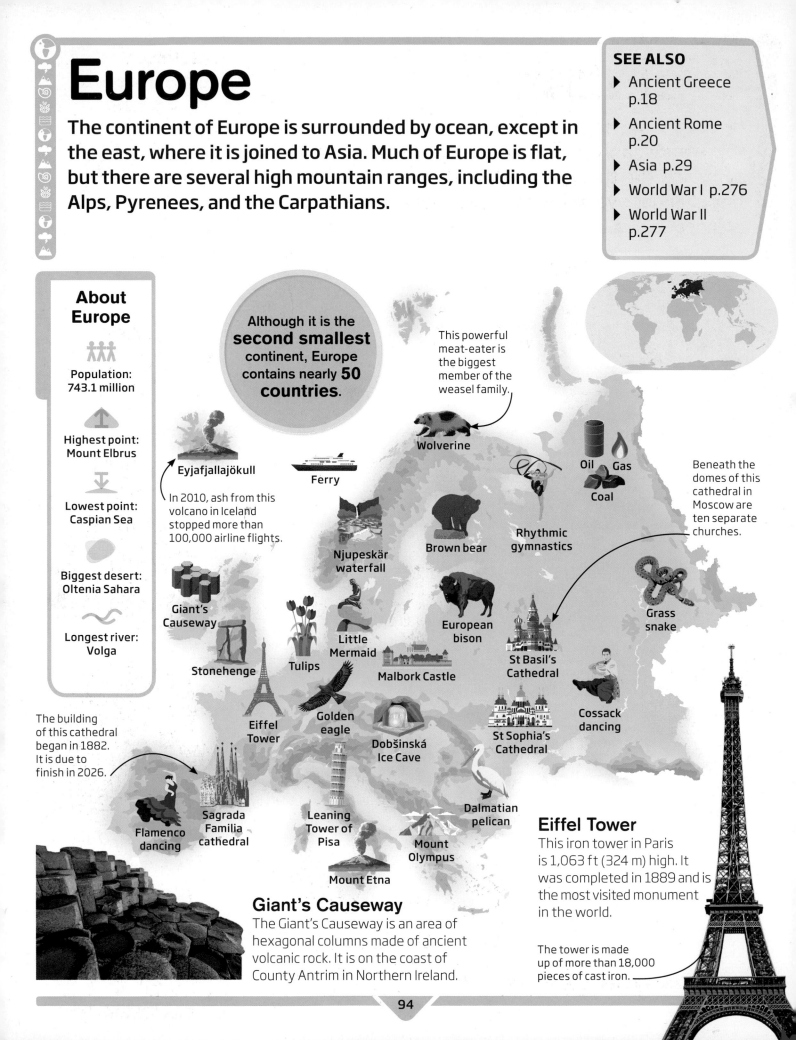

Evolution

In order to survive, an animal needs to change when the weather and food around it changes. This is called adaption. The theory of evolution is that lots of these tiny changes over millions of years create new types of living things.

SEE ALSO
▶ Dinosaurs p.80
▶ Dogs p.81
▶ Fossils p.111
▶ Genes p.119
▶ Life cycle p.146
▶ Prehistoric life p.202

Fossils

Fossils are the remains of living things that were alive millions of years ago. We study them to see how life has changed.

Ammonite fossil

Taller giraffes can reach more food.

Charles Darwin

Scientist Charles Darwin came up with the theory of evolution while traveling around the world investigating living things.

Natural selection

When an animal passes on something useful on to its children, those children are more likely to survive. This is called natural selection.

Giraffe

Selective breeding

Humans can create different shapes, colors, sizes, and personalities of baby animals by choosing their parents carefully.

Mammals first appeared and began evolving **220 million** years ago.

Labrador (Mother)   Poodle (Father)

Labradoodle (Child)

Explorers

Explorers travelled to new places to meet different people, find goods for trade, or just to see what was there! They came from all over the world and faced big challenges on their journeys. Some were successful, such as Chinese explorer Zheng He, who reached Madagascar in the 1420s. Others did not complete their missions.

SEE ALSO
▶ Europe p.94
▶ Maps p.155
▶ Exploration pp.180–181
▶ Navigation p.182
▶ Ships p.224
▶ Trade p.257

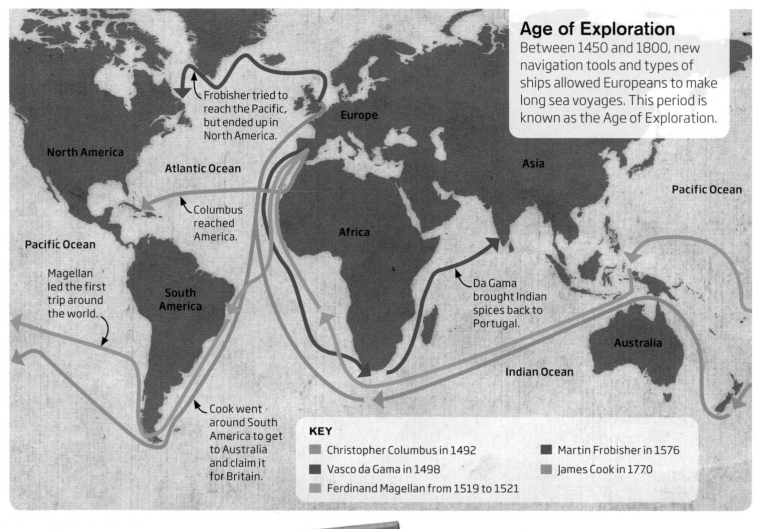

Frobisher tried to reach the Pacific, but ended up in North America.

Europe

North America

Atlantic Ocean

Asia

Pacific Ocean

Columbus reached America.

Africa

Pacific Ocean

Magellan led the first trip around the world.

South America

Da Gama brought Indian spices back to Portugal.

Australia

Indian Ocean

Cook went around South America to get to Australia and claim it for Britain.

Age of Exploration

Between 1450 and 1800, new navigation tools and types of ships allowed Europeans to make long sea voyages. This period is known as the Age of Exploration.

KEY
- Christopher Columbus in 1492
- Vasco da Gama in 1498
- Ferdinand Magellan from 1519 to 1521
- Martin Frobisher in 1576
- James Cook in 1770

Trade

Explorers discovered items they had never seen before. Merchants then traded these goods, such as food, spices, and precious metals. Pepper, for example, spread from India around the world.

Cinnamon

Black pepper

Gold

Magellan

Spanish sailor Ferdinand Magellan set out in 1519 to find a new route to Asia. He left with five ships and 270 men, but only one ship and 18 men made it back.

96

Factories

Factories are places where people and machines work to make things. When factories make many identical things at the same time, it is called mass production. Almost everything we have, use, and wear comes from a factory.

SEE ALSO
▶ Cars p.52
▶ Engineering p.91
▶ Machines p.150
▶ Robots p.212
▶ Transportation pp.258–259
▶ Work p.274

Assembly line

Things with many parts and different materials are put together at various workstations in a factory. This is called an assembly line.

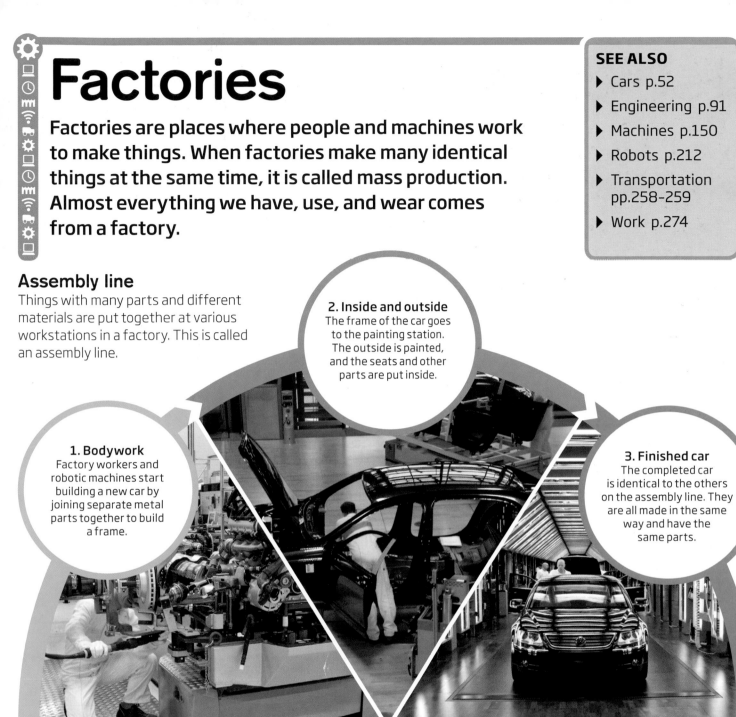

2. Inside and outside
The frame of the car goes to the painting station. The outside is painted, and the seats and other parts are put inside.

1. Bodywork
Factory workers and robotic machines start building a new car by joining separate metal parts together to build a frame.

3. Finished car
The completed car is identical to the others on the assembly line. They are all made in the same way and have the same parts.

Bottling factories

Drinks are made and bottled in factories. The same ingredients and processes are used to fill thousands of bottles every day.

Oranges enter the factory.

The oranges are squeezed.

The juice is put into bottles.

Farming

Farming is growing plants and raising animals, usually for food. Common crops include cereals, fruit, and vegetables. Farm animals include cows, sheep, pigs, chickens, and even fish. As well as their meat, cows are farmed for their milk and chickens for their eggs.

Cereal farming
Cereal crops such as wheat, corn, and barley are grown in large fields. Rice is also a cereal. It is grown in hot countries in water-covered areas called paddy fields.

Animal farming
Farmers raise pigs, cows, and chickens in large sheds or outdoors in fields. Sheep, goats, and llamas are often kept on rough or higher ground.

Fruit and vegetable farming
Crops such as pineapples and potatoes are grown outside. Others, such as strawberries and peppers, are grown all year round in glasshouses or plastic tunnels.

Fish farming
Much of the fish we eat, such as salmon and cod, is now farmed rather than caught in the wild. The fish are kept in net pens or cages in lakes, rivers, or the sea.

Feelings

Feelings are how we respond to things that happen in and to us. Feelings affect our brains, bodies, and how we behave. Being able to tell other people our feelings is important and helps us to feel connected to each other.

SEE ALSO
▶ Art p.28
▶ Brain p.45
▶ Heart p.128
▶ Language p.144
▶ Philosophy p.189
▶ Taste p.249

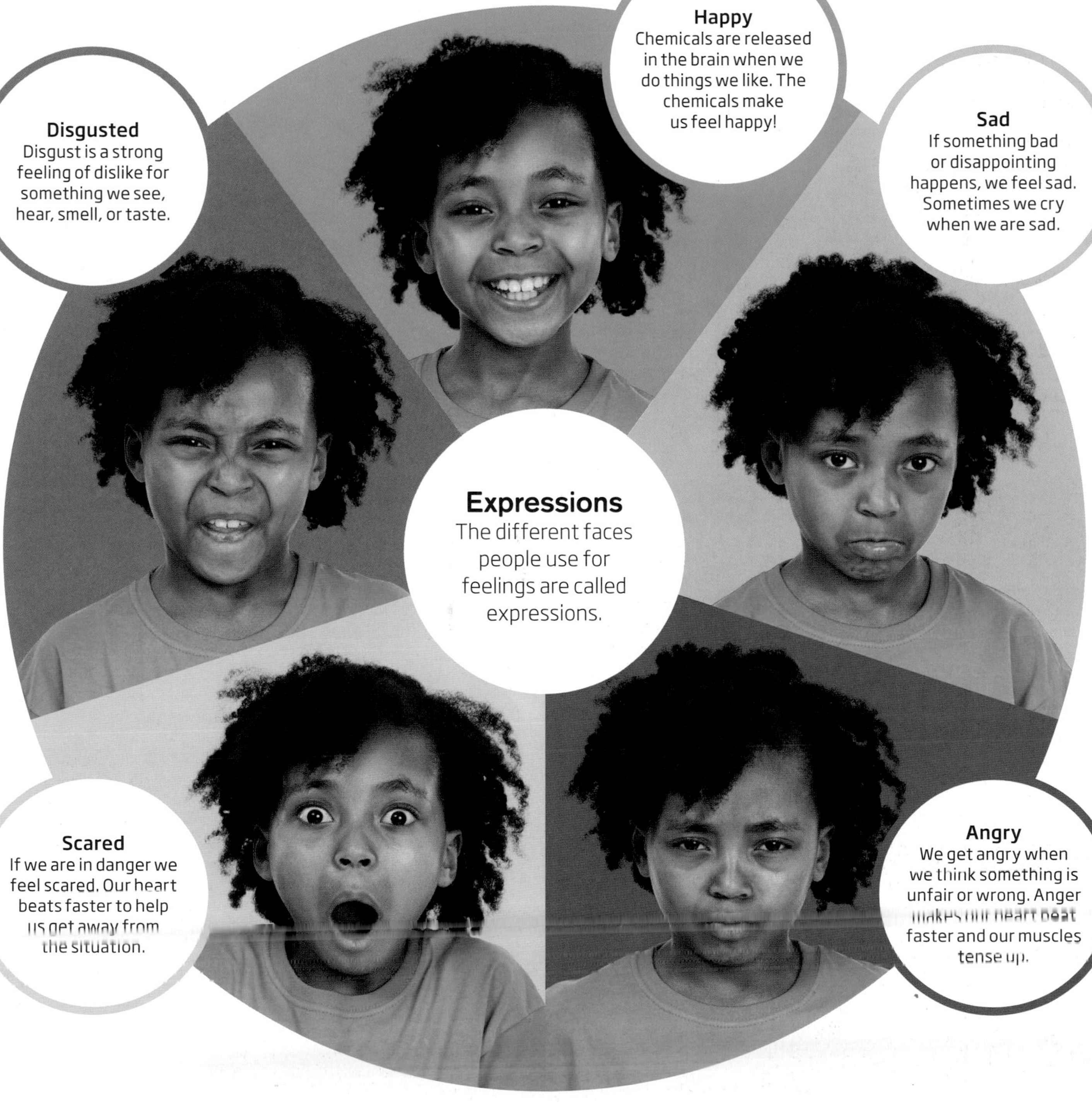

Happy
Chemicals are released in the brain when we do things we like. The chemicals make us feel happy!

Disgusted
Disgust is a strong feeling of dislike for something we see, hear, smell, or taste.

Sad
If something bad or disappointing happens, we feel sad. Sometimes we cry when we are sad.

Expressions
The different faces people use for feelings are called expressions.

Scared
If we are in danger we feel scared. Our heart beats faster to help us get away from the situation.

Angry
We get angry when we think something is unfair or wrong. Anger makes our heart beat faster and our muscles tense up.

Film

A film, or movie, is a series of still images that are quickly played one after the other, so that the pictures seem to move. Films are used to tell stories or show real events. They were first invented in the late 1800s. Live action films are recorded on cameras. Animations are usually drawn by hand or on a computer.

SEE ALSO
- Art p.28
- Storytelling pp.42–43
- Machines p.150
- Photography p.190
- Television p.251
- Theater p.253

Film types

"Genre" is a French word that means type. Films are grouped into genres when they have similar stories or styles. Common genres include action, science fiction, and documentary.

E.T. the Extra-Terrestrial (1982)

Science fiction
Sci-fi films explore themes of science and technology, such as space. "Fiction" means imaginary, and the science is often made up.

The Eagle Huntress (2016)

Documentary
Documentaries are a record of real life or actual events. They show the wonders of nature and how people live. This was one of the first film genres.

Spy Kids (2001)

Action
Action films are exciting stories about imaginary heroes or heroines. They use their strength and intelligence to stop people from doing bad things.

Around

2,000

new films are made in India every year.

Animation

Animated films bring drawings or models to life on screen. Drawings are made by hand or on a computer. Stop-motion is a type of animation that uses models. The models are photographed, moved, and photographed again.

The Wizard of Oz (1939)

Musicals

These stories are told through music, song, and dance. They became popular in the 1930s, when films were made with sound and color for the first time.

Silent films

Technology has come a long way since films were invented. The first films were in black and white, and had no sound. Background music was played live at the cinema, and actors used their faces and body gestures to tell a story.

Charlie Chaplin in
A Dog's Life (1918)

My Neighbor Totoro (1988)

Fish

Fish are animals that live in water. They are able to breathe underwater, and have fins to help them swim around. There are more than 3,000 different species of fish in the world.

SEE ALSO
▶ Life cycle p.146
▶ Pets pp.152–153
▶ Oceans and seas p.187
▶ Seashore p.220
▶ Vertebrates p.266

The body is covered in plates made of thin bone, called scales.

Gills are special organs that let fish breathe the gas oxygen underwater.

Fins steer the fish through the water.

Goldfish
Goldfish are the most popular pet fish. Newborn goldfish are shiny brown. They turn golden when they are a year old.

Lionfish
Long spines protect lionfish from other animals. They hunt at night, feeding on small fish, crabs, and shrimp.

Red lionfish

Deadly fins are used to knock out other sea animals.

Stingray
These fish are found in warm, shallow waters. Most of their time is spent buried in the sand, waiting to pounce on other sea animals.

Stinging tail has one or two poisonous spikes.

Morays have a poisonous bite.

Eel
Eels are long fish that look like snakes. They have more than 100 bones in their spine, which makes them very bendy.

Blue spots let other fish know that the stingray is deadly.

Zebra moray eel

Blue spotted stingray

Seahorse dad
Most fish don't look after their eggs. Seahorses are different–the male carries the eggs around in a pouch on its belly, until they hatch.

Flags

A flag is a piece of material showing a unique set of colors and symbols. Flags represent a country, city, religion, organization, or sport. The symbols and colors can also represent a message, such as a request for help. Flags are often flown from flagpoles outside buildings to show who the building belongs to.

SEE ALSO
▶ Africa p.12
▶ Color pp.26–27
▶ Asia p.29
▶ Governments p.123
▶ North America p.184
▶ World p.275

National flags

Each country has its own special flag, called a national flag. Most of these have colors or stripes with stars or other symbols placed on top. Each part says something about the country.

China
Red stands for communism, which is the type of government in China. The stars show communism and Chinese unity.

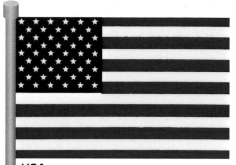

USA
The stars stand for the 50 US states. The stripes are for the original 13 states. The flag is nicknamed "the stars and stripes."

United Kingdom
The upright red cross and the diagonal red and white crosses show the English, Northern Irish, and Scottish flags of the United Kingdom.

Germany
The black, red, and gold are from the uniforms of German soldiers in the 1800s.

India
The colors stand for ideas such as peace and truth. The central wheel symbol is from the Buddhist religion.

Kenya
The shield is a sign of the Maasai people of Kenya. The color white represents peace.

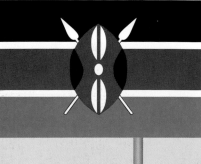

The first national flag was flown in Denmark in

1478.

Signal flags

Flags can be used to send messages. Ships use flags to ask for help if they are in trouble, or to tell other ships to keep out of the way.

"I need help"

"I need a pilot"

"Keep clear of me"

Flowers

Flowers are a part of a plant. To make new seeds, they swap tiny grains called pollen. Pollen can be spread by wind or insects. Flowers have brightly colored petals to attract insects.

SEE ALSO
- Fruit and seeds p.115
- Habitats p.126
- Insects p.134
- Plants p.194
- Shapes p.222
- Trees p.261

Flower structure

Flowers have male and female parts. To make a seed, pollen passes from the male part of one flower to the female part of another.

Stigma
This is sticky to catch any pollen that is carried to the flower.

Anthers
These are the male parts of the flower. They are covered in tiny grains of pollen.

Filament
This stalk holds up the anther.

Petals
These are brightly colored to attract insects to the flower.

Ovary
This is the female part of the flower where new seeds form.

The tallest flower is the **Titan arum.** It grows more than **10 ft (3 m) high.**

Insects

Insects help to move pollen from the anther of one flower to the stigma of another. The pollen travels on their bodies. Once transferred, the pollen fertilizes the ovary to form seeds.

Flower shapes

Different shapes of flowers attract different insects. Some insects fit down long, narrow flowers, others need big petals to land on.

Dome

Cone-shaped   Regular   Rosette   Bell-shaped

Eating

When we eat, we take in all the things we need to keep us alive and healthy. Eating food gives us the energy that allows us to think, walk, play, and work. It is also something we love to do.

Ribs with black-eyed peas and collard greens, from the US

Food around the world

People used to only eat things that were grown near them. Now, we can eat food from all over the world. Different countries have their own special recipes to make their favorite foods.

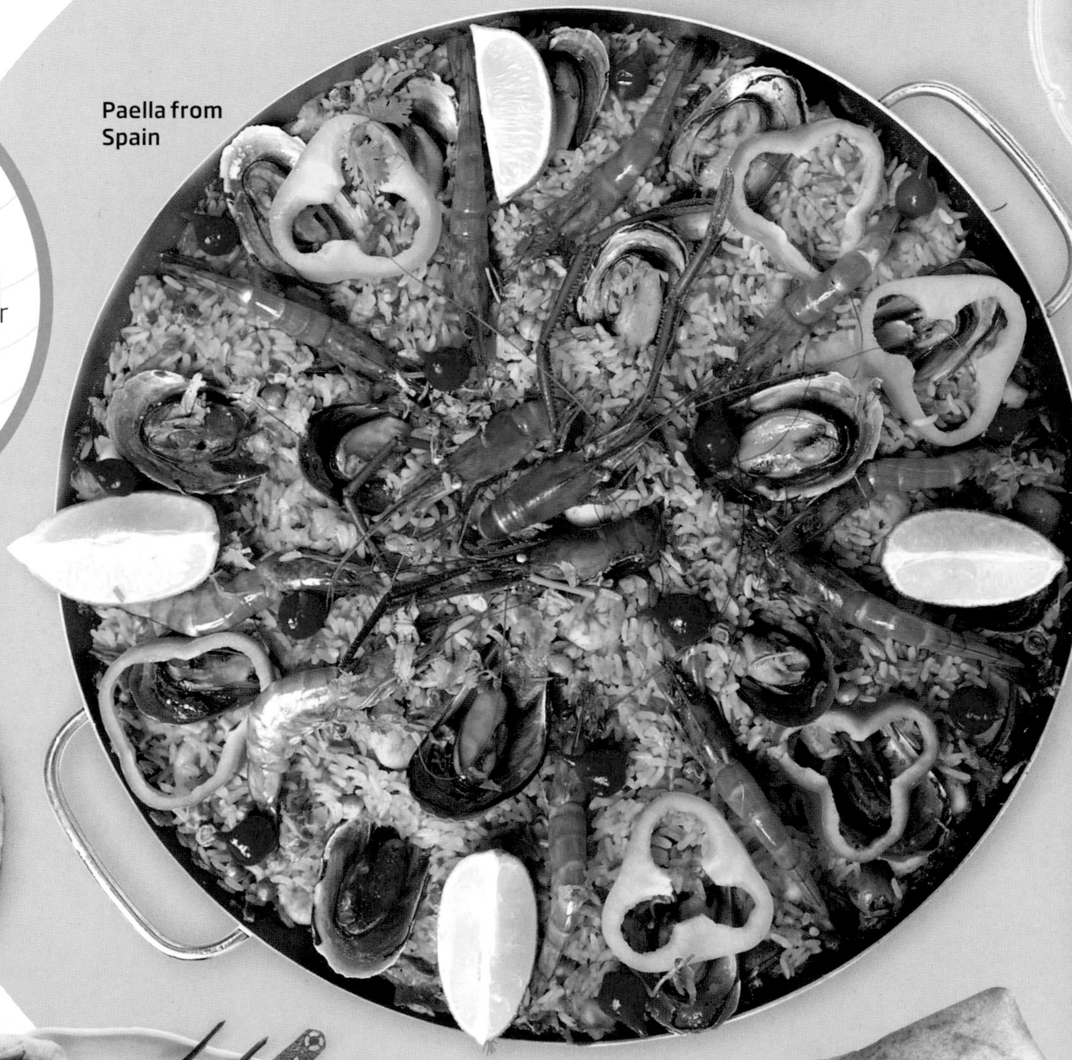

Paella from Spain

Pizza from Italy

Kebabs from Turkey

Dosa from India

Early eating

Our ancient ancestors hunted for meat and fish, and foraged for fruit, nuts, and roots. They started using fire to cook food around 400,000 years ago.

Fire

Chow mein from China

Food allergies

Some people are allergic to certain foods, which means they become ill when they eat them. These foods can include shellfish, peanuts, and milk-based foods.

Peanuts

More than
1.3
billion people
in the world work as farmers.

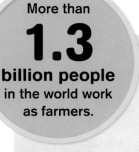

Bento box from Japan

Farming

People began farming at least 15,000 years ago. Today, almost half of the world's land is farmed for food. Farmers breed animals for their meat, milk, and eggs. They also grow plants called crops, such as wheat and oats.

Combine harvester cutting wheat

Insect protein

Insects such as mealworms and caterpillars are eaten all over the world. They don't need a lot of space to grow, so they are an environmentally friendly alternative to farmed meat.

Edible mealworms

Eating in space

Astronaut space food must be easy to eat, light in weight, quick to prepare, and not too messy. Food is often freeze-dried and put in pouches. Water is then added before eating.

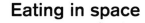

Astronaut food

Food

Humans need to eat the right mixture of different food groups to keep all the parts of the body working properly. Food gives us energy to move, grow, and repair our bodies. Types of food give our bodies the different goodness we need.

SEE ALSO
▶ Digestion p.79
▶ Energy pp.88–89
▶ Eating pp.104–105
▶ Food chains p.107
▶ Gases p.117
▶ Plants p.194

Food groups

There are five main food groups that give us the nutrients and vitamins we need to be healthy.

Carbohydrates

Bread, rice, cereal, and pasta contain carbohydrates, which give our bodies energy.

Dairy foods

Milk, yogurt, cheese, and butter contain calcium to help teeth, nails, and bones grow.

Fruit and vegetables

Fruit and vegetables have fiber, which helps break down our food. They also contain vitamins and minerals that help our bodies work properly.

Protein

Meat, fish, eggs, and beans are high in protein, which is needed to grow and repair our bodies.

Drinking

Water transports the goodness we get from food into and around our body. It then flushes waste materials out of our bodies.

Fat and sugar

Sugar and fat give our bodies energy. We can get fat from food like cheese and nuts, and sugars from fruits. Too much fat and sugar is bad for us.

Energy

When we eat, our body changes energy in food into the energy we need to move and grow. Stored energy is turned into movement energy in our bodies.

Food chains

A food chain is the passing along of energy from food.
Only plants can make their own food. All animals are part
of a food chain, either eating plants or other animals.
All animals need energy to grow, survive, and reproduce.

SEE ALSO
▶ Animal groups p.22
▶ Conservation p.72
▶ Eating pp.104–105
▶ Food p.106
▶ Habitats p.126
▶ Photosynthesis p.191

Energy on the move

Energy moves along a food chain. Each animal
in the chain gets energy from what it eats. The
arrows show how the food energy is passed along.

Producer
Plants produce their own food
by a process using light from
the sun. In a food chain, they
are called the producers.

Primary consumer
Animals that eat plants
are called primary
consumers. They are
also called herbivores.

Secondary consumer
Meat-eating animals that
eat plant-eaters are called
secondary consumers. They
are also known as carnivores.

Decomposer
These animals break down
decaying material, such as
dung, returning the goodness
to the soil for plants to use.

Food web

Animals don't just feed
on a single type of plant
or animal, so food chains
become food webs. These
can show how energy
is passed around a
whole habitat.

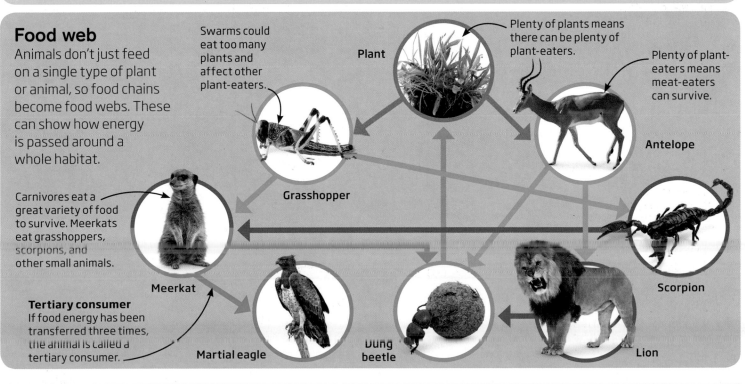

Swarms could
eat too many
plants and
affect other
plant-eaters.

Plant

Plenty of plants means
there can be plenty of
plant-eaters.

Plenty of plant-
eaters means
meat-eaters
can survive.

Antelope

Grasshopper

Carnivores eat a
great variety of food
to survive. Meerkats
eat grasshoppers,
scorpions, and
other small animals.

Meerkat

Scorpion

Tertiary consumer
If food energy has been
transferred three times,
the animal is called a
tertiary consumer.

Martial eagle

Dung
beetle

Lion

Forces

A force is a push or a pull. Forces can start things moving, speed them up, or slow them down. Some forces work through touching. Others, such as gravity, work invisibly and can affect objects a long way away.

Pushing force

A pushing force makes things start to move and can also speed them up. Your hand applies a pushing force when it moves a toy car.

A push away from the hand.

Pulling force

A pulling force also makes things start to move. It moves things forward from where the force is coming.

A pull toward the hand.

Balanced forces

Pushes and pulls can act in different directions at the same time. If they are balanced, the object moves at a steady speed, or is still. If one force is bigger, the object gets faster or slower.

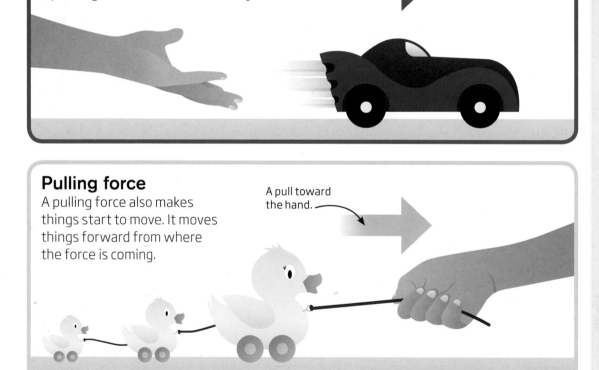

Friction pulls the car backward.

Engine power pushes the car forward.

When you sit still in a chair, the **forces** on you are perfectly **balanced**.

Gravity pulls the car down.

Gravity

Gravity pulls objects down toward the Earth. It's the force that stops us from floating off into space.

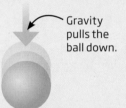

Gravity pulls the ball down.

Magnetism

Magnetism is a force that pulls objects toward a magnet, or pushes them away. Opposite magnetic forces attract each other.

The magnets pull together.

Friction

Friction is a force that slows down movement. It is created when two surfaces touch.

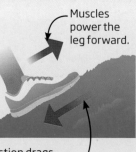

Muscles power the leg forward.

Friction drags the leg backward.

Forests

Forests are places where many trees grow. Forests grow in a wide range of places all over the world. There are different types, depending on the temperature and how much rain they get. Different trees, plants, and animals live in each type of forest.

SEE ALSO
▶ Animal homes p.23
▶ Fruit and seeds p.115
▶ North America p.184
▶ Rain forests p.204
▶ Seasons p.221
▶ Trees p.261

Deciduous forests

These forests have four seasons, with warm summers and cold winters. Many trees drop their leaves in autumn and grow them back in spring. These are called deciduous trees.

Beech trees produce spiky beechnuts in autumn.

Oak trees can live for hundreds of years.

Silver birch trees have silvery bark on their trunk.

White-backed woodpeckers peck holes in trees to find food and make nests.

Grey wolves grow thick fur in winter.

Brown bears are one of the world's largest meat-eaters.

Ferns grow in damp, shady places.

Red foxes have bushy tails to help them balance and keep warm.

Fungi live on damp, rotting wood.

Wild boars dig with their snout to find food.

Dead wood provides food and shelter for small animals.

Common shrews eat many small animals each day.

Polish forest
This large area of forest is home to many animals. Parts of the forest are protected, to keep them as they are.

Coniferous forests

These forests are found in cold, northern parts of the world. The trees have needlelike leaves. Their branches slope so that any snow slides off. These are called coniferous trees.

Black-capped chickadees nest in rotting tree stumps.

Spruce trees have sharp-tipped, prickly needles.

Jack pines have seeds in structures called pine cones.

Black bears can climb trees.

Snowshoe hares grow thick white fur in winter.

Moose grow new antlers every year.

Beavers build their homes from tree trunks.

Spruce grouses search the forest floor for needles to eat.

Lichens grow on rocks and tree trunks.

Canadian forest
These forests are covered in snow for most of the year. The plants and animals that live here must be able to survive the cold.

Fossil fuels

Fossil fuels are natural materials that formed underground millions of years ago. We dig them up or pump them out of the ground so that we can burn them to make energy to power vehicles or to make electricity. There are three types of fossil fuel: coal, crude oil, and natural gas.

SEE ALSO
▶ Carbon cycle p.49
▶ Climate change p.60
▶ Dinosaurs p.80
▶ Fossils p.111
▶ Industrial Revolution p.133
▶ Pollution p.198

How fossil fuels form

Fossil fuels are made from dead sea creatures and rotten plants. These materials are buried deep under layers of rock and soil that have built up over time. Heat and the weight of the ground above change them into fossil fuels.

Coal

Coal is dug from mines that extend deep underground, or from gigantic open pits at the surface.

1. Rotting
Dead trees rot away and are buried in mud.

2. Heat and weight
As they are buried deeper, the remains are heated and squeezed.

3. Compression
The remains are compressed (squeezed) into a layer of coal, which is called a seam.

Generating electricity

Fossil fuels are burned in power stations to make electricity. We have used fossil fuels to make electricity for many years, but burning them harms the environment.

Cooling towers at a power station.

Gas and oil

Crude oil is extracted from the earth by drilling. It is used to power vehicles and make plastics. Gas is also released through drilling. It is used for heating buildings. There are limited amounts of fossil fuels – if we keep using them, they will eventually run out.

Fossils

Fossils are the remains of plants and animals from long ago. They are usually bones or shells that have turned into stone. Some fossils are so small that we cannot see them without special equipment. Others are as tall as a building.

SEE ALSO
▸ Dinosaurs p.80
▸ Fossil fuels p.110
▸ Prehistoric life p.202
▸ Rock cycle p.213
▸ Skeleton p.228

The best fossils are found in very fine-grained rock.

This dinosaur's sharp teeth tell us that it was a meat-eater.

We only know that **dinosaurs** existed because we have found their **fossil** remains.

Dinosaur fossil
Sometimes whole animals can be found as fossils. This skeleton belonged to a small dinosaur named Coelophysis (SEE-low-FY-sis).

Complete fossil skeletons like this one are very rare.

How fossils are made
To become a fossil, an animal or plant needs to be covered up soon after it dies. Turning into a fossil takes millions of years.

147 million years ago

Death
A dinosaur dies and its body sinks into the soft mud by a river.

100 million years ago

Burial
Layers of mud, sand, and ash cover the dinosaur, and its flesh rots away.

2 million years ago

Turning to stone
The skeleton of the dinosaur slowly turns from bone to stone.

5 years ago

Discovery
Millions of years later, a scientist uncovers the fossil skeleton.

Fractions

Fractions are parts of whole numbers. They are written as one number over another number. The number on the top is usually smaller than the one on the bottom. Fractions can be used on their own or with whole numbers.

Common fractions

A whole number can be split into any number of parts to make a fraction. Here are some of the fractions we use most often.

$\frac{1}{2}$

$\frac{1}{4}$

$\frac{1}{8}$

Quarter
A quarter is 1 part out of 4 equal parts.

Eighth
One-eighth is 1 part out of 8 equal parts.

Half
Half of a number is when it is split into two equal parts.

Parts of a fraction

The top number in a fraction is called the numerator. The bottom number is called the denominator. They are divided by a line.

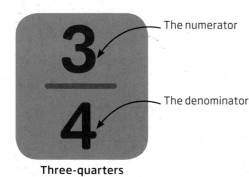

$\frac{3}{4}$ — The numerator / The denominator

Three-quarters

Decimals

Fractions can also be written as decimals. The number to the left of the decimal point is a whole number. The number to the right is the fraction.

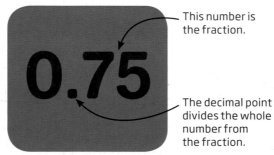

0.75 — This number is the fraction. / The decimal point divides the whole number from the fraction.

Decimal

Same but different?

Fractions can be written differently but mean the same. A half is the same amount as two quarters.

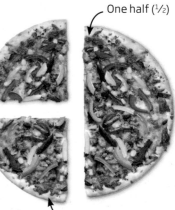

One half (½)

Two-quarters (²⁄₄)

French Revolution

For years, France was ruled by all-powerful kings, who were very rich and could do whatever they wanted. The ordinary people of France were poor. Between 1789 and 1799, the people overthrew the king and changed laws.

SEE ALSO

▶ Buildings p.48
▶ Money p.69
▶ Europe p.94
▶ Governments p.123
▶ Law p.145
▶ War pp.278-279

Marie Antoinette

The luxurious lifestyle of Marie Antoinette, the French queen, made many ordinary people angry. They thought she did not care about their problems.

The Bastille was used to keep prisoners of the king.

The Bastille

The Bastille was a royal prison in Paris. On July 14, 1789, a crowd attacked it and stole weapons that had been stored inside.

Louis was beheaded using a machine called the guillotine.

King Louis XVI was killed in 1793.

General Antoine-Joseph Santerre was a leader in the Revolution.

End of the monarchy

The king and queen tried to run away from France dressed as servants. They were caught and later executed in front of crowds of people.

Friction

Friction is a force that slows down moving things by pulling against the direction of their movement. It is created between two surfaces as they move past each other. Different surfaces produce different amounts of friction.

SEE ALSO
▶ Forces p.108
▶ Water pp.120–121
▶ Gravity p.125
▶ Materials p.157
▶ Temperature p.252

Grip or slip?
Rough surfaces grip better because they create more friction than smooth surfaces. Smooth surfaces slip past each other because they create less friction than rough surfaces.

Rubber sole
Snow boots have rough rubber soles that grip, so that the climber's feet don't slip.

Producing heat
If we rub our hands together there is friction between them. They start to get warm because friction produces heat.

Rubber grip on snow boots

Icy surface

Lots of friction
The icy surface and the sole of the boot have lots of friction between them.

Smooth bottom of the ski

Icy surface

Not much friction
The snow and the ski have little friction between them and the ski slides easily.

Skis
Smooth skis slide over an icy surface very easily. They are made of many different materials, including wood and plastic.

Fruit and seeds

Seeds store everything a new plant needs to start growing, including food. A fruit protects the seeds inside it. It also gives a plant a way to move its seeds away to somewhere they can grow.

SEE ALSO
- Animal groups p.22
- Flowers p.103
- Eating pp.104–105
- Plants p.194
- Trees p.261
- Weather p.271

Fruit

Fruit forms from the flowers of some plants. Fruit usually tastes sweet, so people and animals like to eat it.

Apple seeds sit in a core in the middle of the fruit.

Apple seeds can take up to **80 days** to begin to grow.

Apple

Peapod

Peas are the seeds inside a peapod.

How seeds grow

Many plants grow from seeds. With water, the right temperature, and soil, a seed can begin to grow into a plant.

Leaves start to make food for the plant.

Leaves unfold and shoot straightens.

Shoot bursts through the soil.

Bean seed starts to swell.

Roots grow to anchor the plant in the soil.

Shoot begins to grow upward, toward the light.

Spreading seeds

Plants spread, or disperse, their seeds in different ways.

By wind
Some plants have "winged" seeds that help their seeds fly away in the wind.

By animal
Animals eat fruit, and then poop out the seeds away from the plant.

Exploding pods
Some plants have seed pods that explode, flinging the seeds into the air.

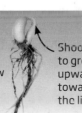

Galaxies

Galaxies are enormous groups of stars, planets, dust, and gas that are held together by the force of gravity. They come in different sizes and shapes, including spiral, elliptical, and irregular.

New stars form in the spiral arms.

Spiral galaxy

Spiral galaxies are disk-shaped with spiral arms. They are the most common type of galaxy. On average, they contain more than 100 billion stars. Our Milky Way is a spiral galaxy.

Scientist think that galaxies are mostly made of a material called **"dark matter,"** which we can't see.

All stars rotate around the center of the galaxy.

The middle of the galaxy bulges outward.

Elliptical galaxy

Elliptical galaxies are rounded in shape, and are usually made up of older stars. They are generally larger than spiral galaxies. Elliptical galaxies contain lots of stars but little gas or dust.

Irregular galaxy

Small galaxies that do not have a clear structure are known as irregular galaxies. These may be created by two galaxies colliding. They contain lots of young stars, dust, and gas.

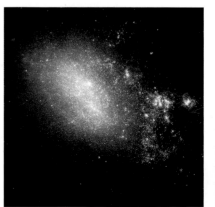

Gases

Gases are all around us–we are surrounded by a mixture of gas called air. We can keep them in sealed containers but if we open the container, the gas escapes and spreads out. Most gases are invisible.

SEE ALSO

▶ Changing states p.57
▶ Elements p.90
▶ Liquids p.148
▶ Lungs p.149
▶ Mixtures p.168
▶ Solids p.234

What gases do
Gases have things they do called properties. For example, gases can be squashed and then they push back to fill the original space. This is useful for pumping up bike tires that cushion bumps in the road as we ride.

Helium is a lighter gas than air, so helium balloons float.

Gases expand to fill their container.

Gas would escape from an unsealed container.

Blowing bubbles
Soap bubbles contain a little bit of air that pushes out toward the bubble. The soap bubble mix is stretched but pushes back, squashing the air into a sphere.

Gas particles
Gases are made from tiny particles that move away from each other in all directions at top speed. They travel long distances unless they bounce off solid barriers.

Fizzy drinks
When you see bubbles in a liquid, every one of them is full of gas. In a fizzy drink, the bubbles are the gas carbon dioxide.

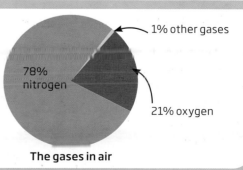

What's in air?
Air is the gas all around us. It is made of a mixture of different gases, but mostly a gas called nitrogen. We breathe in oxygen from the air for our bodies to use.

1% other gases

78% nitrogen

21% oxygen

The gases in air

Gemstones

Gemstones are minerals that can be cut and polished to make jewels. They are often set in pieces of jewelry, such as rings, brooches, and even crowns. Many gemstones, such as rubies, are brightly colored. Others, such as diamonds, are usually colorless.

SEE ALSO
▶ Elements p.90
▶ Metals p.162
▶ Money p.169
▶ Precious metals p.199
▶ Gold pp.200–201
▶ Rocks and minerals p.214

Cutting gemstones

Gemstones are found as minerals. To become sparkly jewels, they must be cut into shape. Very sharp tools are used to carefully cut the stone into exactly the right shape.

Uncut ruby

Cut ruby

Jewelry

Gems are often set in precious metals, such as gold and silver. They are used to make brooches, earrings, and other pieces of jewelry.

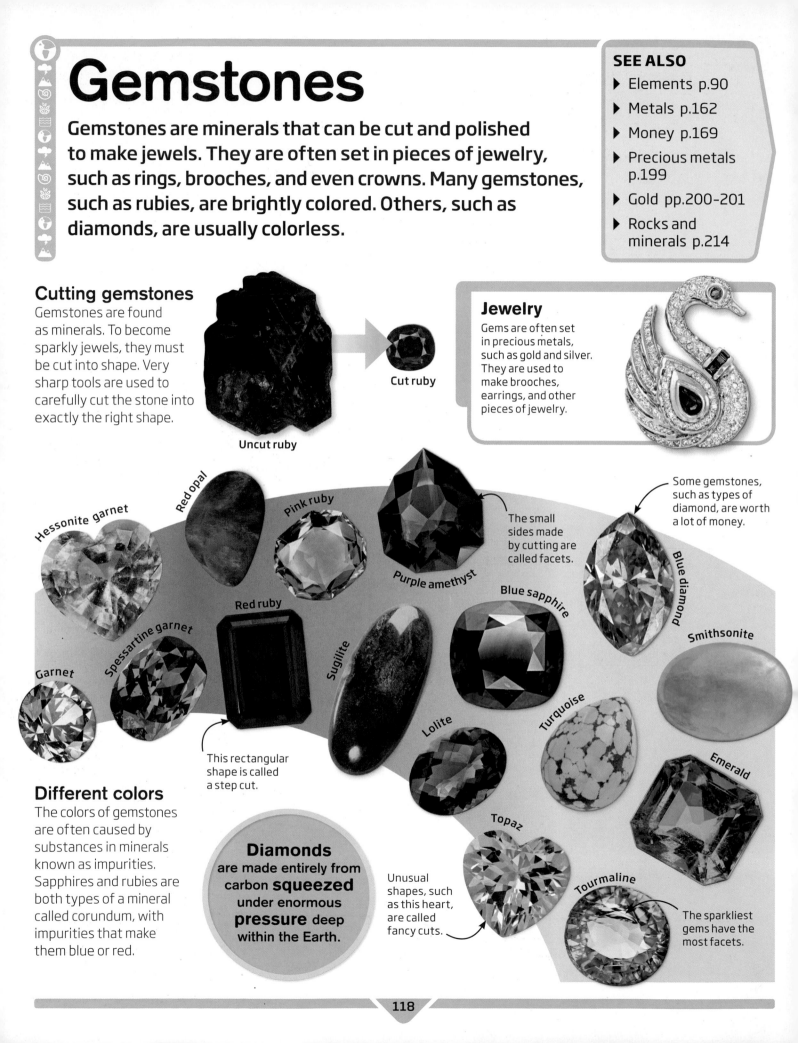

Some gemstones, such as types of diamond, are worth a lot of money.

Hessonite garnet

Red opal

Pink ruby

Purple amethyst

The small sides made by cutting are called facets.

Blue diamond

Smithsonite

Garnet

Spessartine garnet

Red ruby

Sugilite

Lolite

Blue sapphire

Turquoise

Emerald

This rectangular shape is called a step cut.

Different colors

The colors of gemstones are often caused by substances in minerals known as impurities. Sapphires and rubies are both types of a mineral called corundum, with impurities that make them blue or red.

Diamonds are made entirely from carbon **squeezed** under enormous **pressure** deep within the Earth.

Topaz

Unusual shapes, such as this heart, are called fancy cuts.

Tourmaline

The sparkliest gems have the most facets.

Genes

Genes are the instructions that make people the way they are. They include things like skin color, hair color, and height. Half our genes come from our mother and half from our father.

Inheritance

Face shape, eye color, and hair texture are passed down from either the mother's or the father's genes. Skin color works differently—it depends on the amount of a chemical called melanin in the skin.

If you unraveled all the **DNA** in a person it would reach to the sun and back **400 times**!

Mother

Father

Her hair is light brown and straight like her dad's.

Her face shape was passed on from her mother's genes.

His eyes are brown like his mom's.

His hair is black and curly like his mom's.

Her hair is curly like her mom's, and light brown like her dad's.

Child 1

Child 2

Child 3

Her skin color could be the same as either parent or anything in between.

Clones

Most animals get a mix of different genes from their parents. Clones have exactly the same genes as another animal. Dolly the sheep was the first cloned mammal. Her genes were taken from a single cell of a female sheep.

What is DNA?

Genes are made from long structures called DNA. Everyone has different DNA, except for identical twins, whose DNA is the same.

DNA looks like a twisted ladder.

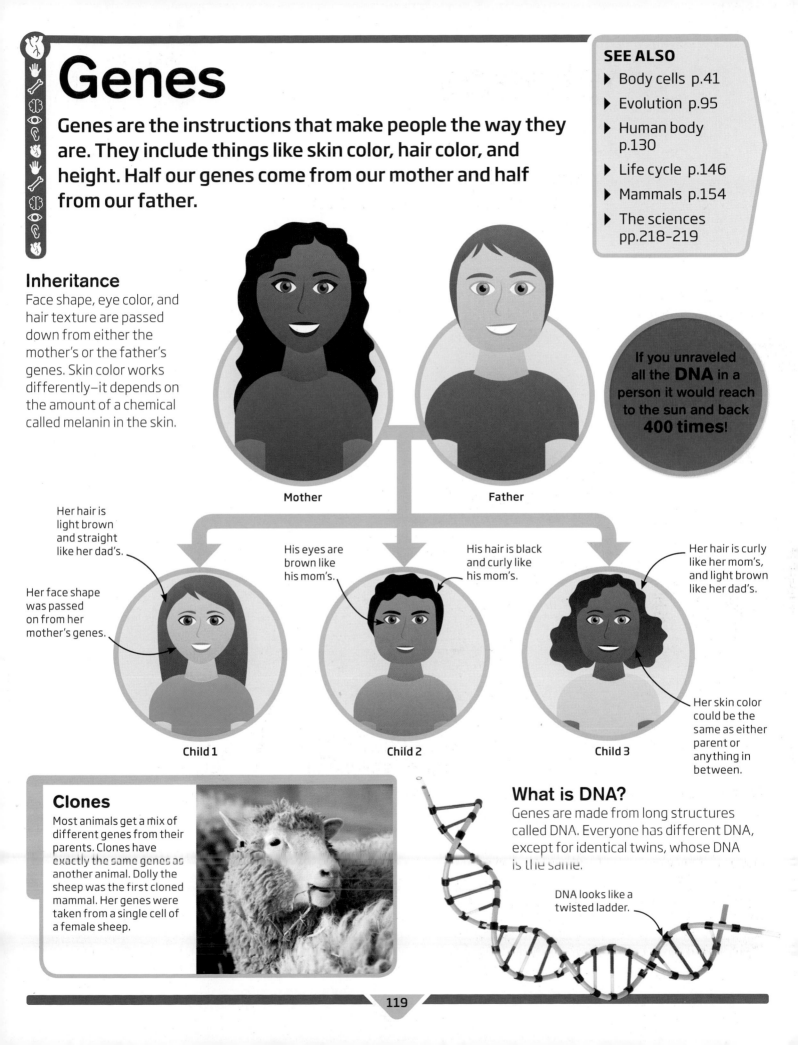

Water

Water is a clear, colorless substance that is found all around us. It forms Earth's oceans, lakes and rivers, snow and ice, and the clouds drifting overhead. All living things—including us—are mostly made of water, so without it our planet would be lifeless.

Blue planet

Nearly three-quarters of the Earth is covered by oceans and seas. Rivers and lakes stretch across the land's surface. The polar regions, near the North and South Poles, lie beneath frozen water, ice, and snow.

Planet Earth

More than 96 percent of all the water on Earth's surface is too salty to drink.

What's in water?

Water is made up of tiny particles called molecules. Each one has an oxygen (O) atom joined to two smaller hydrogen (H) atoms, so water is also known as H_2O.

H

O

H

Water molecule

Fish breathe using **special organs called gills** to extract oxygen from the water.

Water power

Rushing water is used to make power at giant hydroelectric dams around the world. As the water moves through the dam, it turns turbine machines that spin so quickly they create electricity.

About 90 percent of all frozen water on Earth is in Antarctica, around the South Pole.

Hydroelectric dam

Only 2.5 percent of the Earth's water is fresh. It is found mostly in rivers, lakes, and glaciers.

Stone for grinding wheat into flour

Grain grown in Mesopotamia

Land of the rivers
The first cities were built in Mesopotamia (now mainly Iraq) around the Tigris and Euphrates rivers. The rivers allowed goods and people to move around and provided essential water to drink, cook with, and use to water crops.

Stone sickle for cutting crops

Kayaking

Water sports
Without water there would be fewer ways for us to have fun. There would be nothing to swim in or surf on, and no kayaking or sailing. There would be no snow for skiing or sledding and we could never build a snowman.

We lose **water** from our bodies through **sweating** when we are active and play sports.

Bad for the environment
More than 200 billion plastic water bottles are used around the world each year. Making the bottles releases lots of harmful gases into the air, and only one in five bottles is recycled—the rest are thrown out as garbage.

Plastic water bottles

Glaciers

Glaciers are slow-moving rivers of ice. They form high up in mountains or regions near Earth's poles and flow downhill. The front of a glacier may melt to make a river or lake. If a glacier reaches the coast, huge blocks of it break off and float away into the ocean as icebergs.

SEE ALSO
▶ Antarctica p.24
▶ Arctic p.25
▶ Changing world pp.50–51
▶ Climate change p.60
▶ Erosion p.93
▶ Mountains p.172

How are glaciers made?
Glaciers are made from snow that builds up and turns into ice. Eventually, there is so much ice that it starts to flow downhill.

The dark streaks on the surface are rocks carried along by the glacier.

A lake of melted ice often forms at the front of a glacier.

Glaciers can wear down the sides of mountains, making them pyramid-shaped.

Signs of glaciers
Some parts of the world were once colder and covered in glaciers. As the climate warmed, the glaciers melted away. However, they left signs in the landscape that they were once there.

U-shaped valley
Glaciers carve steep-sided valleys into flatter U-shaped ones as ice and rock grind the hillside away.

Sharp ridge
An arête is a sharp ridge of rock that separates two valleys that once had glaciers in them.

Giant rocks
Glaciers can pick up giant rocks and dump them far from where they came. They are called erratics.

Governments

A government is an official group of people that runs a country. Governments keep their people safe through rules called laws. They often try to keep the peace with other countries, and can help provide services such as schools and hospitals. Most governments try to help people lead better lives.

SEE ALSO
▶ Law p.145
▶ Medicine p.160
▶ Trade p.257
▶ School pp.272–273
▶ Work p.274
▶ World p.275

How a government works

Each country has its own system of government that looks after its people. Large countries have different levels of government, while smaller countries have simpler systems.

Head of state
One person is in charge of each country, such as a president or queen. They represent it when meeting with other countries.

National government
The national government looks after the whole country. It makes laws and has people in charge of different areas, such as education.

Local governments
Local governments run smaller areas within countries. They look after local issues, such as roads and libraries.

Electorate
People in many countries choose their governments by voting in elections. They are the electorate.

Types of government

Most countries in the world are democracies. They elect (choose) who is in government. Other countries have heads of state who aren't chosen.

Democracy
In a democracy, people vote for a government and a head of state to rule them and take decisions for them.

Monarchy
A monarchy is a family system in which the job of the head of state is passed from the king or queen to their child or relative.

Dictatorship
Dictators often rule by force. They use an army to make people do what they say.

Constitutions

A constitution is a written document that sets out the aims and values of a country and how it should be ruled. The US constitution was written in 1787.

123

Grasslands

Grasslands are large areas covered in grass with just a few trees. They are dry, but get more rain than deserts do. Grasslands are known as savannas in Africa, steppes in Russia, prairies in North America, and pampas in South America.

SEE ALSO
▸ Africa p.12
▸ Animal homes p.23
▸ Birds p.39
▸ Deserts p.78
▸ Migration p.166
▸ Monkeys and apes p.170

Grassland life

Many different animals live in grasslands. Some feed on the grasses and walk long distances to find enough grass to eat. Other animals hunt and eat these plant-eaters.

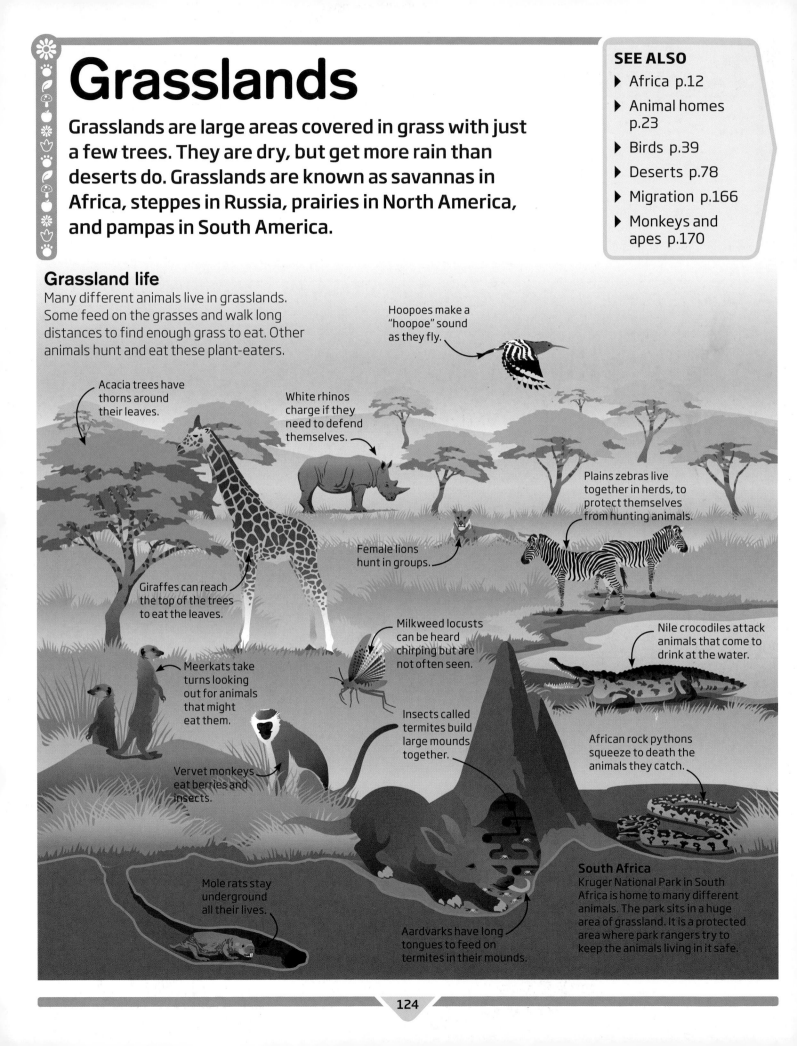

Hoopoes make a "hoopoe" sound as they fly.

Acacia trees have thorns around their leaves.

White rhinos charge if they need to defend themselves.

Plains zebras live together in herds, to protect themselves from hunting animals.

Giraffes can reach the top of the trees to eat the leaves.

Female lions hunt in groups.

Nile crocodiles attack animals that come to drink at the water.

Milkweed locusts can be heard chirping but are not often seen.

Meerkats take turns looking out for animals that might eat them.

Insects called termites build large mounds together.

African rock pythons squeeze to death the animals they catch.

Vervet monkeys eat berries and insects.

Mole rats stay underground all their lives.

Aardvarks have long tongues to feed on termites in their mounds.

South Africa

Kruger National Park in South Africa is home to many different animals. The park sits in a huge area of grassland. It is a protected area where park rangers try to keep the animals living in it safe.

Gravity

Gravity is an invisible force that pulls us back down toward Earth when we jump in the air. If we throw a ball up it comes down because of gravity. Without it, we would float off into space.

SEE ALSO
▶ Forces p.108
▶ Gases p.117
▶ Measuring p.159
▶ Moon p.171
▶ Solar system p.233
▶ Sun p.247

Falling to Earth

Earth's gravity pulls things toward it. When a skydiver jumps out of a plane, gravity starts to pull him down. Eventually he will use a parachute to slow his fall.

Air pushes up on the skydiver as he falls.

Gravity pulls the skydiver down toward Earth.

Isaac Newton

Scientist Isaac Newton realized there was a pattern behind objects falling toward Earth.

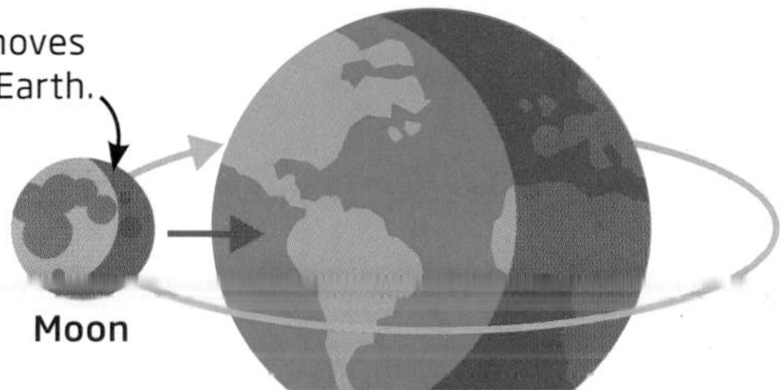

Newton came up with the theory of gravity after watching apples fall from a tree.

Earth and moon

Earth

The moon moves around the Earth.

Moon

The strong pull of Earth's gravity keeps the moon moving around it. Without gravity, the moon would disappear into space.

Habitats

A habitat is the place a plant or animal lives. Habitats around the world have different temperatures and landscapes. Animals and plants have certain features that allow them to survive in their habitats.

Tundra
This cold habitat has very few trees, plants are small, and animals often move away after the short summer.

Polar regions
Very few plants and animals can survive in the freezing temperatures of this icy habitat.

Coniferous forest
This habitat is full of coniferous trees, which keep their needlelike leaves all year round.

Tropical rain forests cover **7 percent** of Earth, but are home to **more than half** the world's plants and animals.

Desert
Rocks and sand cover this very dry habitat. Animals and plants have to be able to survive with very little water.

Rain forest
Trees grow quickly in this warm, rainy habitat. They provide food and homes for thousands of different animals.

Grassland
Grasslands have more rain than deserts, but not enough for many trees to grow. Most animals here eat grass.

Deciduous forest
This habitat has four seasons. The trees drop their leaves in autumn and grow them again in spring.

Ocean
This saltwater habitat covers 70 percent of Earth's surface. Some animals live deep down.

Hearing

Hearing happens when our ears receive a sound. Sound is a vibration that travels through the air and into our ears. The sound travels into the hidden parts of the ear and our brain identifies what we hear.

The ear
The ear is much bigger than it looks from the outside. The inner ear and outer ear are hidden inside our heads.

Inside the ear

The smallest bone in your ear is the size of a **grain of rice**.

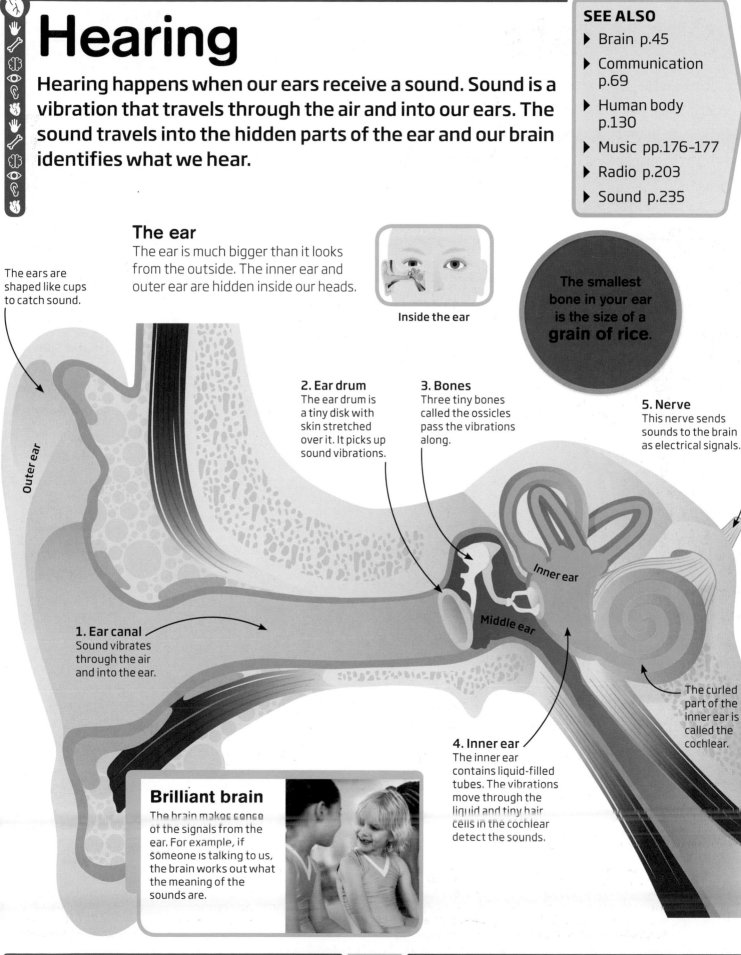

The ears are shaped like cups to catch sound.

Outer ear

2. Ear drum
The ear drum is a tiny disk with skin stretched over it. It picks up sound vibrations.

3. Bones
Three tiny bones called the ossicles pass the vibrations along.

5. Nerve
This nerve sends sounds to the brain as electrical signals.

Inner ear

1. Ear canal
Sound vibrates through the air and into the ear.

Middle ear

The curled part of the inner ear is called the cochlear.

4. Inner ear
The inner ear contains liquid-filled tubes. The vibrations move through the liquid and tiny hair cells in the cochlear detect the sounds.

Brilliant brain
The brain makes sense of the signals from the ear. For example, if someone is talking to us, the brain works out what the meaning of the sounds are.

Heart

The heart is a pump about the size of a fist. It is mainly made of muscle and it pushes blood around the body by squashing itself in and out around 80 times a minute. Blood is a liquid that carries oxygen and food around the body. If the heart stops beating, the body stops working.

SEE ALSO
▶ Body cells p.41
▶ Brain p.45
▶ Feelings p.99
▶ Human body p.130
▶ Lungs p.149
▶ Medicine p.160

Inside the heart

The heart pumps blood every second of the day. The right side of the heart sends blood to the lungs. The left side sends blood to the rest of the body.

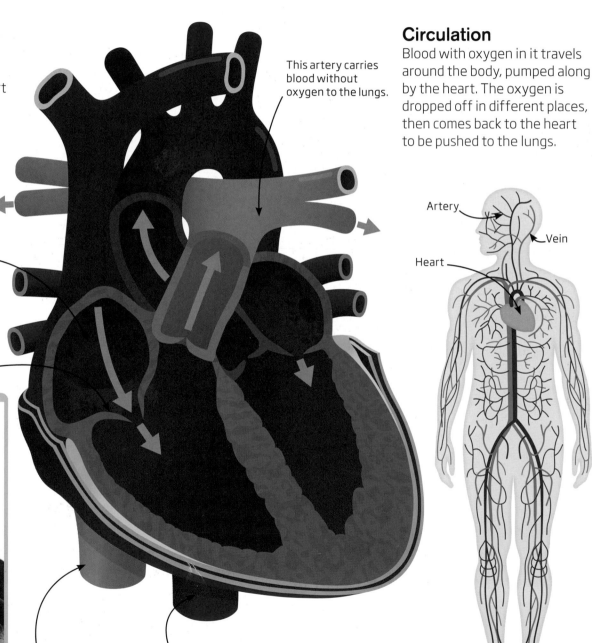

This artery carries blood without oxygen to the lungs.

Atrium
The heart has two "chambers" on each side, called atriums.

Valve
Valves are gates that only open one way, so blood can only travel in one direction.

Blood

Blood contains tiny parts called cells. Red blood cells carry oxygen and waste gas. White blood cells kill germs. Broken bits of cells stick together to make a scab when the body is cut.

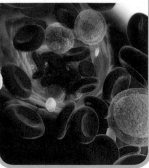

Vein
Blood arrives from the body through tubes called veins.

Artery
Blood is pushed out to the body in tubes called arteries.

Circulation

Blood with oxygen in it travels around the body, pumped along by the heart. The oxygen is dropped off in different places, then comes back to the heart to be pushed to the lungs.

Artery

Vein

Heart

Blood vessels

Hibernation

For many animals, finding enough food in winter is hard. Some animals migrate, or move, to warmer areas. Others survive by going into a deep sleep, called hibernation. They wake up again in the springtime when there is more food.

SEE ALSO
▶ Amphibians p.15
▶ Animal groups p.22
▶ Day and night p.77
▶ Mammals p.154
▶ Migration p.166
▶ Seasons p.221

Dormouse
These small mammals make cosy nests under leaves on the forest floor, or at the bottom of hedges.

The furry tail wraps around the mouse's face to keep it warm.

Bats hibernate upside down in caves or trees.

Bat
Bats enter a deep hibernation. Their heart rate drops from 400 to 25 beats per minute.

Dormice can curl up and sleep for up to seven months in a year.

Wood frog
This frog's body freezes in the winter and its heart stops beating. When the weather gets warmer, its heart starts beating again and the frog thaws out.

Wood frog

Do bears hibernate?
Bears sleep in the winter, but not very deeply, so they can be woken easily. This is called a torpor. It is like hibernation, but without such a deep sleep.

Human body

The body is made from lots of different parts called organs. Each organ has a different job to do. Organs work with muscles and other parts of the body to make important things happen, such as breathing, digestion, and movement.

SEE ALSO
▶ Biology p.38
▶ Body cells p.41
▶ Carbon cycle p.49
▶ Heart p.128
▶ Lungs p.149
▶ Monkeys and apes p.170

Body systems
Organs that are linked together are called systems. Each system has its own job, but they work together, too.

Body ingredients
The human body is made up of tiny parts called cells. The cells of the body contain lots of different ingredients. They all have different uses in the body.

Calcium helps muscles to work and the heart to keep beating.

One-fourth of our bodies is **carbon**. It is also found in diamonds!

A tiny amount of **iron** is found in the body. It makes your blood red.

Tears contain **sodium chloride**, which is the same as table salt.

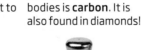

Phosphorus helps make bones strong. Matches burn using phosphorus.

Over half of the body is made of **water**. Water is found in our blood and cells.

Respiratory system
The lungs bring air into the body and send waste air out. They supply oxygen to the blood.

Nervous system
The brain thinks and controls body movement. Signals are sent to the brain through nerves.

Circulatory system
The heart pumps blood around the body in a loop to transport oxygen and food.

Digestive system
The stomach and intestines break down the food so it can be used to power the body.

Urinary system
The kidneys clean the blood and make urine from the waste. The bladder stores the urine.

Muscular system
The muscles move all the parts of the body. They make the heart pump and the lungs breathe.

Skin and hair system
The skin is a waterproof layer that protects the body from germs and sunshine. Hair keeps us warm.

Skeletal system
The skeleton is a frame of bones that protects the inner organs of the body. It also allows movement.

Imperial Japan

During the Edo period, from 1603 to 1868, Japan was ruled by a series of powerful men called shoguns. Each ruled from the city of Edo, which is now Tokyo.

SEE ALSO
▶ Art p.28
▶ Dance p.76
▶ Knights p.142
▶ Musical instruments p.175
▶ Theater p.253
▶ War pp.278-279

A horned helmet was part of a samurai's armor.

Noble samurai

Samurai were warriors who fought for a powerful lord and followed strict rules. Their way of life was called *Bushido* (bu-shi-do), "the way of the warrior."

The main weapon was a sword called a *katana*.

Art

Poets, painters, writers, and craftspeople made beautiful works of art during this time. This print from 1857 shows a traditional Japanese scene of trees and a river in the snow.

Making music

Music has always played an important part in Japanese culture. This instrument, called a *shamisen* (sha-mee-sen), is like a guitar. It provided background music for dance performances and puppet theater.

Shamisens have three strings and a square body.

Strict command

Edo society's chain of command was strict. The emperor was the leader, but the shogun was in charge of the lords, who were called daimyo. The daimyo were in charge of the samurai army.

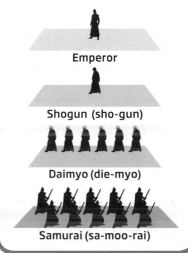

Emperor

Shogun (sho-gun)

Daimyo (die-myo)

Samurai (sa-moo-rai)

Incas

The Inca people lived in the mountains along the west coast of South America. Between 1438 and 1532 CE, their wealthy empire was the largest in the world. Society was well organized and everyone knew their place.

SEE ALSO
▶ Aztecs p.35
▶ Crafts p.75
▶ Farming p.98
▶ Maya p.158
▶ Gold pp.200–201
▶ South America p.236

Inca society
At the head of Inca society was an emperor called Sapa Inca, meaning "Great Inca." Most people were peasant farmers who worked for the emperor and in return were given food and housing.

The ancient Inca city of Machu Picchu sits in the Andes Mountains, in Peru.

The Sapa Inca was treated like a god. He was carried in a chair by servants.

Houses were made of stone and had thatched roofs.

Everybody had to bow down to the Sabu Inca.

Llamas were used for carrying goods and for their wool.

Farmers planted potatoes.

Maize, or corn, was an important food.

Sun god
This gold disk shows Inti, the Inca god of the sun. Every year the Incas held a nine-day festival of eating, drinking, and sacrifice to honor the sun god.

Inca crafts
The Incas made sacred objects from gold and silver to be used in temples. Craft workers also made fine pieces from clay, leather, and feathers.

Gold llama

Industrial Revolution

The Industrial Revolution was a time of huge growth in industry brought about by the introduction of new machinery. Factories were built to make products using large numbers of machines. The revolution began in Britain during the 1760s and later spread around the world.

SEE ALSO
▶ Buildings p.48
▶ Engines p.92
▶ Factories p.97
▶ Inventions pp.136–137
▶ Machines p.150
▶ Pollution p.198

Factory work

Factories contained rows of machines that made things in large amounts, such as textiles, iron and brass goods, pottery, and glassware. These machines were powered first by water and then by steam.

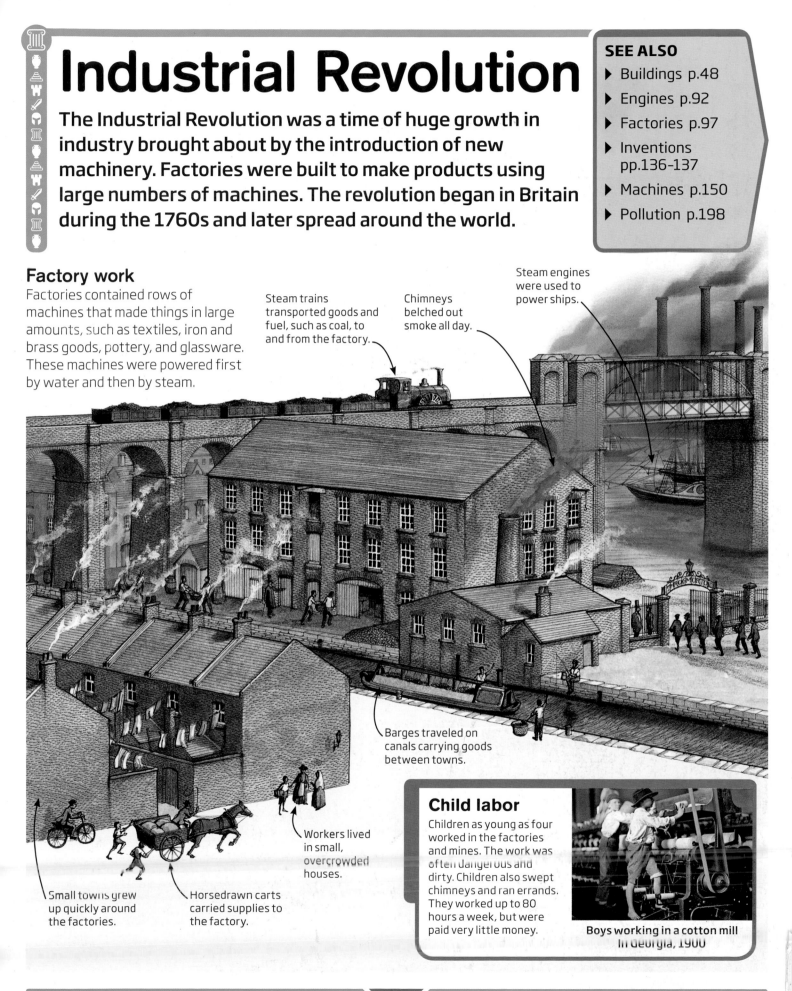

Steam trains transported goods and fuel, such as coal, to and from the factory.

Chimneys belched out smoke all day.

Steam engines were used to power ships.

Barges traveled on canals carrying goods between towns.

Workers lived in small, overcrowded houses.

Small towns grew up quickly around the factories.

Horsedrawn carts carried supplies to the factory.

Child labor

Children as young as four worked in the factories and mines. The work was often dangerous and dirty. Children also swept chimneys and ran errands. They worked up to 80 hours a week, but were paid very little money.

Boys working in a cotton mill in Georgia, 1900

Insects

Insects are the largest group of animals, and are found all over the world. They have three pairs of legs and a tough outer covering, called an exoskeleton. Many insects have wings and can fly.

SEE ALSO

▶ Animal groups p.22

▶ Eggs p.86

▶ Invertebrates p.139

▶ Metamorphosis p.163

▶ Migration p.166

Butterflies

A butterfly changes a lot in its life cycle. It starts as an egg, then hatches into a caterpillar. It wraps into a chrysalis before hatching again as a butterfly.

Feelers called antennae help the butterfly to smell nectar and stay balanced.

Swallowtail butterfly

Many insects have wings, which let them fly around.

There are more than **900,000** different types of insects in the world.

Patches of color on the butterfly's wing tell other animals that it is not good to eat.

Body parts

Insects' bodies are divided into three parts: the head, the thorax, and the abdomen. They have three pairs of legs attached to the thorax and one pair of antennae on their heads.

Thorax

Head

Abdomen

Red wood ant

Desert locust nymph

Stag beetle

Ants

Ants live together in groups called colonies, with thousands of workers and a queen. They are small but strong—ants can lift 20 times their body weight.

Grasshoppers

These insects can leap 20 times their body length. They can also fly fast, reaching speeds of up to 8 mph (13 kph).

Beetles

Beetles are found on land and in water all over the world. They have hard, shiny outer wings that close over a soft inner set of wings, to protect them.

Inside Earth

The Earth is made up of four layers. We live on its outer layer, or crust. The crust floats on a layer of extremely hot rock called the mantle. Below this, our planet's center, or core, is made of the metal iron.

The upper mantle is made of hot, partly liquid rock.

Earth's layers

Like an onion, the Earth has layers. Each layer is different. The deeper the layer, the hotter it is, with the inner core a scorching 10,800°F (6,000°C).

The outer core is made of liquid iron.

In our planet's early history, it had **no crust** and the mantle was a sea of **bubbling liquid rock.**

The inner core is a ball of solid iron.

Earth's crust is made of solid rock.

The lower mantle is made of hot, solid rock.

Magma and lava

In some places on the Earth's surface, liquid rock bubbles up to the surface, creating volcanoes. Liquid rock is called magma when it is inside the Earth and lava on the surface.

Main opening

Lava flows

Magnetic Earth

Because the Earth's outer core is liquid, it moves as the Earth spins. This creates a magnetic field around the Earth. This field keeps out harmful energy waves from space. It also lets us find directions when we use a compass.

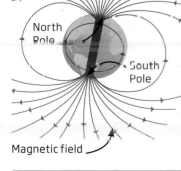

North Pole

South Pole

Magnetic field

Magma chamber

The **story** of...

Inventions

Inventions are new ideas that solve problems or prove useful to us. Thousands of years of brilliant brainpower have resulted in things and ideas that have transformed people's lives. Even in the modern world, people keep coming up with new ideas and inventions.

Hard flint was broken down to make sharp tools.

Hand axe

The hand axe was the first stone tool in prehistoric times. People dug for flint, which they shaped into handcrafted axes to cut meat, chop wood, scrape skins, and protect themselves. Hand axes were used for more than a million years.

Steam engine

The first steam engines were used to pump water out of mines. Later, engines were used to power factories and trains. George Stephenson's *Rocket* train was built in 1829.

Reaching **30 mph** (48 kph), the *Rocket* was the first vehicle to travel **faster than a horse.**

A tall chimney released steam from the engine.

A rod, or axle, links the wheels together—turning the axle uses much less energy than turning the wheel.

Wheel

The wheel was invented more than 5,000 years ago in Mesopotamia (part of modern-day Iraq). Wooden discs were attached to animal carts to carry heavy loads. Later, wheels became lighter, which made them faster and smoother.

The front wheels were pushed around by the engine.

ROCKET

Flight

In 1903, American brothers Wilbur and Orville Wright built a glider with a light engine. Although Flyer took off for only 12 seconds over 120 ft (37 m), it was the first-ever powered flight.

The Wright's *Flyer*, built in 1903.

Plastics

Plastics are cheap to make, easy to shape, and last a long time. They can be hard, soft, or bendy. The first human-made plastic was made by Belgium-born chemist Leo Baekeland in 1905. Now plastics are all around us.

Antibiotics

Infection-fighting antibiotics battle bacteria inside the body. They were discovered by accident in 1928, when Scottish scientist Alexander Fleming noticed bacteria dying around mold in his lab. The bacteria-killing chemical penicillin has since saved many lives.

Antibiotic pills

Thomas Edison (1847–1931) was an American master of invention, patenting

1,093

ideas in his lifetime, including **batteries** and **light bulbs.**

Computers

Computers are electric machines that follow instructions. Modern computers can do billions of sums every second. We use them to find, store, and share information. The idea of a computer was invented by English engineer Charles Babbage in the 1830s.

The first electronic computer, **ENIAC**, was huge, filling a room measuring 50 ft (15 m) long.

14:25
Friday, 8 May

Internet

The Internet is a network that links together computers all over the world. We use it to learn things, for entertainment, and to communicate with each other. The Internet was first thought of in 1962. Now, billions of people use it every day.

SEE ALSO
▶ Codes pp.66–67
▶ Communication p.69
▶ Computers p.71
▶ Satellites p.215
▶ Telephones p.250

How the Internet works

The Internet is made up of digital information stored on computers. The information can be uploaded or downloaded through a network.

The cloud
Information kept somewhere remote rather than on your computer is said to be "in the cloud." This information can be anything, such as facts, online games, news stories, or music.

Wi-Fi
Wireless Internet works using radio signals.

Satellite
Satellites send information between phones and the Internet.

Smartphone
Smartphones are small, handheld computers that can connect to the Internet.

Connection
Computers can connect to the Internet using cables that connect to Internet service providers.

Internet service provider
Companies called Internet service providers have massive computers. These computers provide quick access to the Internet.

Website servers

A website is a collection of linked pages. Each website has a unique Internet address called a URL. Websites are stored on computers called servers.

Web page

Computer
A laptop or desktop computer can store information and access the Internet.

Invertebrates

Invertebrates are animals that don't have backbones. They are divided into many smaller groups, such as insects and mollusks. Ninety-eight percent of all animals are invertebrates.

SEE ALSO
▶ Animal groups p.22
▶ Animal homes p.23
▶ Habitats p.126
▶ Insects p.134
▶ Vertebrates p.266

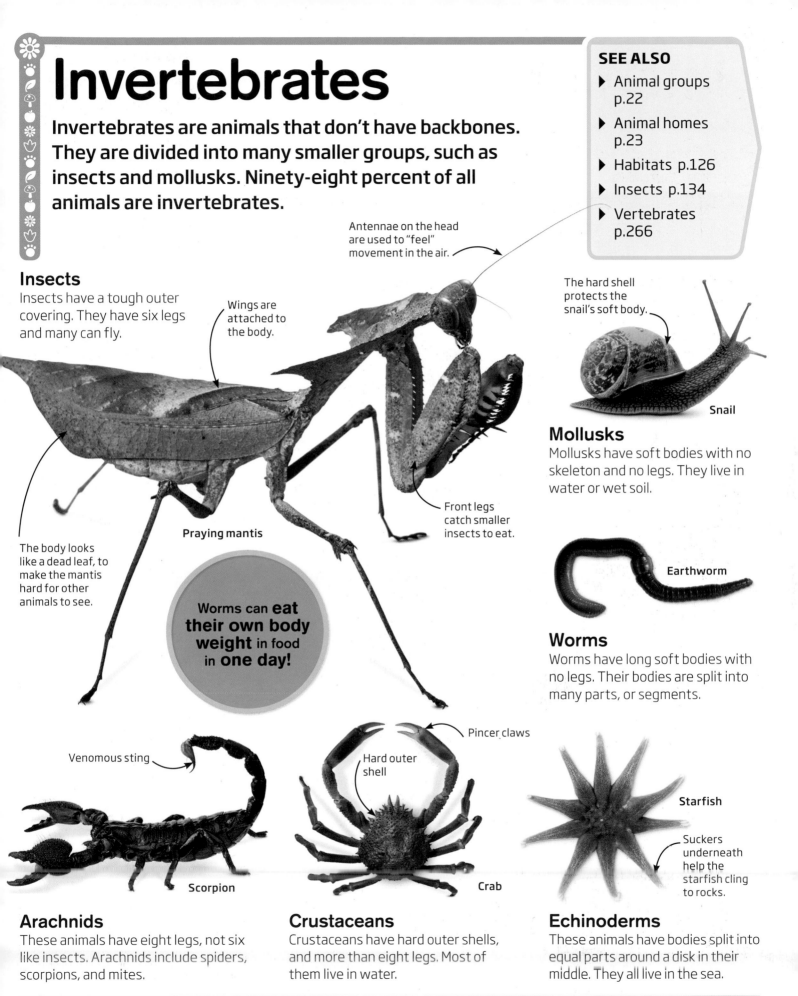

Antennae on the head are used to "feel" movement in the air.

Insects
Insects have a tough outer covering. They have six legs and many can fly.

Wings are attached to the body.

Front legs catch smaller insects to eat.

Praying mantis

The body looks like a dead leaf, to make the mantis hard for other animals to see.

Worms can **eat their own body weight** in food in **one day!**

The hard shell protects the snail's soft body.

Snail

Mollusks
Mollusks have soft bodies with no skeleton and no legs. They live in water or wet soil.

Earthworm

Worms
Worms have long soft bodies with no legs. Their bodies are split into many parts, or segments.

Venomous sting

Pincer claws

Hard outer shell

Scorpion

Crab

Starfish

Suckers underneath help the starfish cling to rocks.

Arachnids
These animals have eight legs, not six like insects. Arachnids include spiders, scorpions, and mites.

Crustaceans
Crustaceans have hard outer shells, and more than eight legs. Most of them live in water.

Echinoderms
These animals have bodies split into equal parts around a disk in their middle. They all live in the sea.

Iron Age

During the Iron Age, people began using iron tools and weapons instead of bronze ones. It started about 3,200 years ago and lasted for around 1,000 years, depending on the area. Iron tools were stronger and more durable than anything before.

SEE ALSO
▶ Bronze Age p.47
▶ Farming p.98
▶ Metals p.162
▶ Rocks and minerals p.214
▶ Trade p.257
▶ Vikings p.267

Tools

Iron tools allowed farmers and builders to work better. They were able to grow more crops, clear land for farms, and build bigger buildings.

This iron sickle would have been attached to a wooden handle and used to cut wheat.

Iron cutting edge

Weapons

Iron weapons were lighter and cheaper to make than weapons made from bronze. Well-made iron weapons were also stronger and sharper than bronze ones. Having good weapons meant societies could build powerful armies.

Hill fort

Hill forts are Iron Age villages built on the top of hills. They had earth or stone walls around them. Hill forts allowed people to see the enemy approaching and prepare themselves for attack.

Iron Age hill fort in Dorchester, UK

The walls at the base of the fort acted as a protective barrier.

Making a sword was very difficult. The best swordmakers were well paid.

Danish iron sword from the Viking period of 800–1100 CE

Making iron

Making iron items is a process that needs great skill and care. The iron must be made extremely hot before it can be shaped into a weapon or a tool. How we shape iron today is similar to how Iron Age craftsmen performed the task.

1. Dig it out
Iron is dug from the ground in lumps, called iron ore.

2. Heat it up
The iron ore is heated to high temperatures to make it melt.

3. Pour it in
The melted iron is poured into a shaped mold and left to cool.

Jupiter

Jupiter is the largest planet in the solar system, and the fifth planet from the sun. It is a "gas giant" made of hydrogen and helium. Jupiter does not have a solid surface like Earth.

SEE ALSO
▶ Astronomy p.32
▶ Atmosphere p.33
▶ Elements p.90
▶ Gases p.117
▶ Solar system p.233
▶ Solids p.234
▶ Storms p.246

King of the planets

Jupiter is so large that 1,300 Earths could fit inside it. A huge storm in its atmosphere, called the Great Red Spot, is more than twice the size of Earth. Jupiter is the third brightest object in our night sky after the moon and Venus.

Scientists have been watching the Great Red Spot storm since 1830.

Winds swirling around the **Great Red Spot** reach speeds of more than 250 mph (400 kph).

The striped bands and swirls are shaped by strong winds.

The Galilean moons

Jupiter has more than 60 moons of different sizes. Its four largest moons are called Io, Europa, Ganymede, and Callisto. They are known as "the Galilean moons" because they were discovered by the Italian scientist Galileo Galilei in the 17th century.

Io

Europa

Ganymede

Callisto

Knights

Knights were men who owned big pieces of land in Europe between the 600s and the 1600s, a time period known as the Middle Ages. They trained from age seven to be fighters and lead armies.

The helmet was shaped to help avoid direct attack.

SEE ALSO
▶ Castles p.53
▶ Clothing pp.62–63
▶ Europe p.94
▶ Flags p.102
▶ Metals p.162
▶ Sports p.239
▶ War pp.278–279

Armor

Knights wore suits of armor to protect them from enemy weapons, such as swords. The first armor was made of mail, which is rings of metal linked together. Later armor also included sheets of shaped steel.

Curved armor protected the knight's elbow.

Knights carried their shield on a strap when not using it.

Steel gloves were made of more than 40 metal pieces.

Squires

Each knight had a squire to assist him. Squires looked after their knight's armor, sharpened his weapons, and cared for his horse. Some squires later became knights.

A belt held the knight's sword and dagger.

Knights wore colorful outfits for jousting.

Mail was heavy to wear, but offered good protection.

Designs

Each knight had a special design passed down to him by his father. Knights put their design on their shield so others would recognize them in battle. Men called heralds recorded which knight had which design.

Jousting

At jousts, crowds watched as knights on horseback raced at each other holding blunt, wooden sticks called lances. They scored points by hitting the other knight or knocking him off his horse.

Lakes

A lake is a large body of water surrounded by land. Most lakes contain fresh water, but some are salty. Lakes are usually found in high areas or near large rivers. The water in lakes comes from streams or rivers around them.

SEE ALSO

▸ Climate change p.60

▸ Factories p.97

▸ Farming p.98

▸ Water pp.120–121

▸ Rivers p.211

▸ Water cycle p.270

How we use lakes

Lakes provide water for factories, farming, energy, sports, and homes. Nearly all lakes are natural but some, known as reservoirs, are made by people.

Lakes form when water fills hollows in the landscape.

Lakes provide water for us to drink, wash up, and bathe and shower.

Many lakes have an outlet, such as a river, from which water leaves.

Lake water is used for farming, making goods, and producing electricity.

Oxbow lakes

Rivers sometimes change their course. When they do, bends in them may become cut off to form U-shaped bodies of water called oxbow lakes.

A deep bend, or meander, forms in the course of the river.

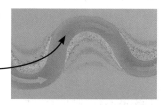

The river makes a shortcut and changes its course.

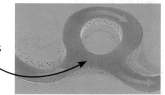

An oxbow lake forms as the river's new course separates from it.

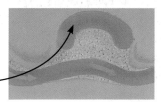

Wet or dry?

Lakes can dry out if there is a long period without rain, called a drought, or if the climate changes. They may reappear when the rain returns or stay dry forever.

Language

Language is how people communicate. Across the world, people speak many different languages. There are more than 7,100 in total, some spoken by millions of people and others by just 100. These languages often sound very different from one another, and can look different when written down.

SEE ALSO
▶ Ancient Rome p.20
▶ Storytelling pp.42–43
▶ Books p.44
▶ World p.275
▶ Writing p.280

The most-spoken languages

There are almost 7.5 billion people in the world today. About one-third of them speak one of five languages, which are used by countries all over the world.

您好
nee-how

مرحبا
marr-hah-bah

नमस्ते
nuh-muh-stay

Hello

Hola
o-la

Mandarin
This is the most spoken language in the world. Forms of Mandarin Chinese are used all over China.

Arabic
This is spoken across North Africa, the Middle East, and in many other countries.

Hindi
This is one of the official languages of India. It is also an official language in Fiji.

English
English is now spoken in every continent and in many countries, including the US.

Spanish
This is spoken in Spain and parts of South and Central America, eastern Asia, and Africa.

| 295 million | 310 million | 360 million | 405 million | 955 million |

Sign languages

People sometimes use hand shapes, body movements, and facial expressions to talk, rather than spoken language. This is called a sign language. It is useful if someone cannot hear or speak.

"No" in American sign language

"Yes" in American sign language

Dead languages

Some languages die out when their speakers start using another language. Latin was once spoken in the Roman Empire, which included much of Europe. It's now a dead language, but can still be read and written.

Latin words from the Roman Empire.

Law

Laws are official rules for people to follow. The government writes laws for the whole country. Some laws stop people from doing bad things (crimes), such as stealing. These are called criminal laws. Other laws try to improve life, such as making sure people are paid a fair amount of money for doing work.

SEE ALSO
▶ Changing world pp.50–51
▶ Codes pp.66–67
▶ Governments p.123
▶ Trade p.257
▶ Work p.274
▶ World p.275

Law court

If someone doesn't follow the law, they can be punished. A criminal law court is where it is decided if someone has committed a crime, and if they should be punished. This process is called a trial.

Defendant
The defendant is the person who is said to have committed the crime.

Judge
The judge controls the court, and may give the defendant a punishment, such as imprisonment, if they did the crime.

Witness
A witness is someone who knows something about the crime. They tell the court what they know.

Defense
Defense lawyers try to stop the defendant from being punished by arguing for them.

Prosecution
Prosecuting lawyers try to make the judge and jury believe that the defendant did the crime.

Jury
A group of usually 12 ordinary people hear about the crime and decide if the defendant did it.

In the UK, it is **against the law** to deliberately disturb someone by knocking on their front door.

Public
Ordinary people are allowed into courts to see what decisions are made.

Police

The police make sure people follow laws. They capture people who might have broken laws. This is called putting someone under arrest.

Police cars travel at high speeds to catch criminals.

Police car

First laws

One of the earliest sets of laws was drawn up by King Hammurabi of Babylon, who ruled from 1792 to 1749 BCE. There are 282 laws about the family, trade, and wages.

Hammurabi's laws

Life cycle

Like all animals, humans are born, grow up, and can have children of their own. This is called a life cycle. There are many different stages that a human goes through on their journey from birth to adulthood.

Baby
Babies are very small and can't feed themselves or talk. They need parents or carers to take care of them.

Toddler
Toddlers learn how to walk, talk, and feed themselves. They grow teeth called milk teeth, which fall out and are replaced with adult teeth.

Growing up
Everyone starts life as just two cells. We grow into children and eventually adults.

Child
Children grow and learn quickly. They are smaller than adults and still have a lot of skills to learn.

Sperm and egg
A sperm cell joins an egg cell inside the mother's womb. After nine months, the cells have grown into a baby.

The oldest person recorded died at 122 years and 164 days old.

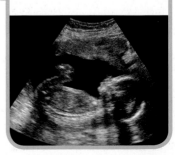

Unborn baby
Babies grow inside the mother's womb. Doctors look at the growing baby using a process called an ultrasound. At 12 weeks a baby is about the size of a lime.

Adult
Adults can make their own children. Males produce sperm cells and females produce egg cells.

Teenager
Chemical signals called hormones tell the body to start changing from a child into an adult.

Light

Light is a type of energy that bounces off objects and into our eyes—we need it to see things. Light can change into other types of energy such as heat or electricity. Dark is the absence of light.

SEE ALSO
▶ Color pp.26–27
▶ Energy pp.88–89
▶ Invertebrates p.139
▶ Materials p.157
▶ Sight p.226
▶ Sun p.247

White light

White light is actually made from all the colors of the rainbow. We can split white light into colors by shining it through a prism.

Light travels in straight lines.

The light bends as it hits the prism. This is called refracting.

White light is split into seven colors.

Light sources

The main source of light on Earth is the sun. Artificial light sources include light bulbs, candles, and oil lamps. Some animals, such as jellyfish and fireflies, produce their own light.

The sun is a natural light source.

A candle is an artificial light source.

Shadows

A shadow is a dark area where light is blocked by an object. It takes the shape of the object blocking the light.

Reflection

More light bounces off shiny surfaces like mirrors or still water. This is called a reflection.

Some jellyfish can glow in the dark.

Liquids

Liquids are runny materials. They can be poured into things, and move to fit the shape of their container. Liquids make a pool, not a pile. We drink liquids including water. When a liquid cools, it can become a solid. Heating a liquid can create a gas.

SEE ALSO
▶ Atoms p.34
▶ Changing states p.57
▶ Gases p.117
▶ Rivers p.211
▶ Solids p.234
▶ Water cycle p.270

What liquids do

The things a liquid can do are called its properties. For example, liquids can be heated to cook things. Liquids are good at mixing because of the way they flow and move. Some liquids flow more easily than others, but they all change shape to fit their containers.

Around **75 percent** of your brain is made of **water.**

Liquids can be poured.

Liquids move to fit the shape of their container.

Dissolving

Some materials dissolve (disappear into) liquids. If we add salt to water, it becomes salty water. We can't see the grains of salt because they have dissolved into the water to make salt water.

Water   Salt   Salt water

Liquid particles

Liquids are made from tiny particles that move around quickly and stick together in groups. When they cool, they slow down to eventually become solid.

Water

Two-thirds of the Earth's surface is covered in water. Water is essential because living things need water to survive. Animals drink water and plants take water in from the ground or air. Most living things are made up of at least half water.

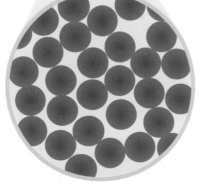

Lungs

We breathe air in and out of our lungs. The lungs take oxygen from the air and transfer it to the blood. Every part of the body needs oxygen, so the lungs collect it and the blood carries it around the body.

SEE ALSO

▶ Brain p.45
▶ Gases p.117
▶ Heart p.128
▶ Human body p.130
▶ Skeleton p.228
▶ Sound p.235

Lungs

The lungs are two spongy bags filled with tubes and air sacs. The air sacs are where gases change places. Oxygen is breathed in and carbon dioxide is breathed out.

Bronchi
These two air tubes connect the trachea to the lungs.

Bronchioles
The air goes into these tiny tubes. Each one ends in air sacs called alveoli.

Diaphragm
This muscle changes the shape of the lungs so we can breathe in and out.

Nose
Air enters and leaves our bodies through our nose and mouth.

Trachea
This tube carries air into our lungs. It is also known as the windpipe.

Oxygen is taken into the blood and carbon dioxide is sent out of the blood in the air sacs.

Alveoli, or air sacs

Breathing

Muscles work together to let us breathe in and out. We have a diaphragm muscle below the lungs and more muscles around the ribcage. They change the size and shape of the lungs.

Air enters the lungs as we breathe in.

The rib muscles pull up to make the ribcage bigger.

The diaphragm pulls down to pull air into the lungs. The lungs get bigger.

Air leaves the lungs as we breathe out.

The rib muscles relax so the ribcage gets smaller.

The diaphragm relaxes and the lungs get smaller, pushing air out.

Voice box

The voice box is in the throat. It stops food from getting into the lungs and makes us cough if any food gets in. The voice box also lets us speak and sing.

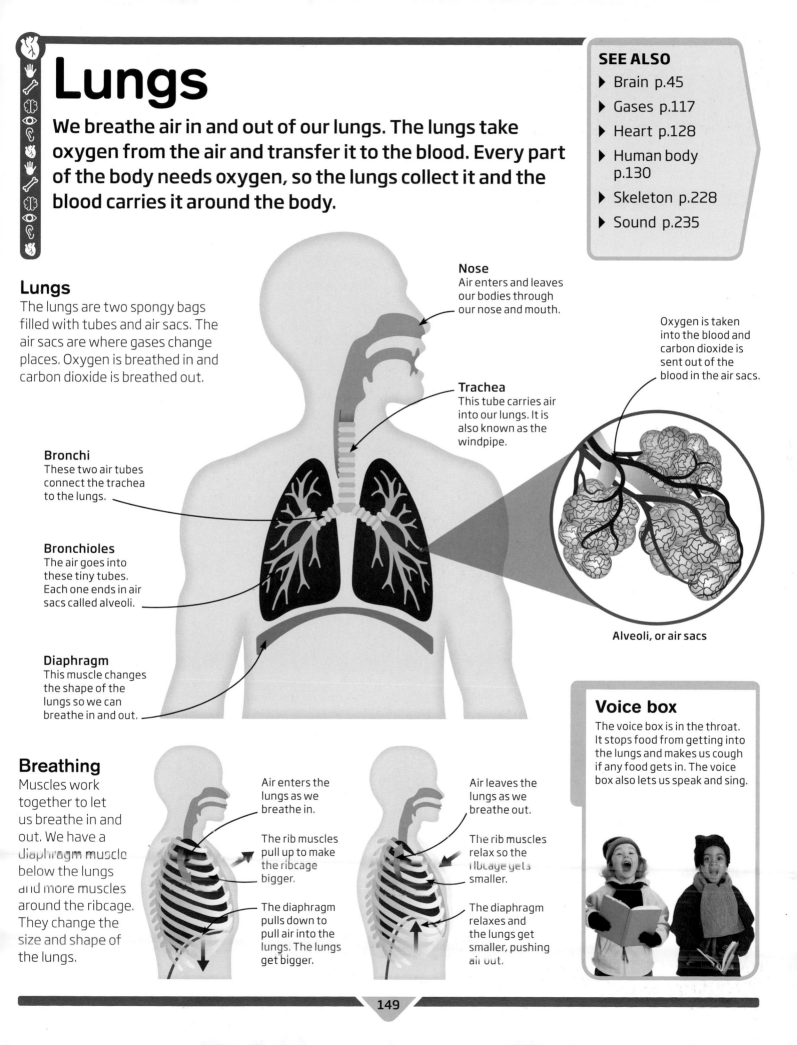

Machines

Machines help us do things. They usually perform tasks that are too big, small, boring, long, or dangerous for people to do. Most modern machines are powered by electricity or gas.

Simple machines

Simple machines reduce the effort needed to do things. A person must operate the machine, but only a small amount of effort is required to move heavy objects.

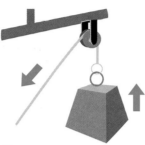

Pulley
A pulley uses a rope or chain looped over a wheel to lift heavy loads.

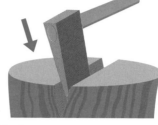

Wedge
Made of wood or metal, this triangular tool can be used to push things apart.

Screws
These sharp metal pins are used to attach things. As the screw is turned, it moves down and around.

The operator sits in the driver's cabin.

Big machines

Backhoes are made up of several simple machines. They are powered by engines.

Lever
Levers move like arms. This one raises a metal scoop to collect building materials.

Wheel
Wheels make it easier to move heavy things around.

Why we use machines

Machines are usually more efficient and reliable than human workers. This is because they can do things without ever becoming bored, tired, slow, or distracted.

Neat work
A sewing machine can sew more neatly and more quickly than most people can by hand.

Repetitive work
Automatic cash machines don't sleep, so they can give out money 24 hours a day.

Dangerous work
Robots are used to study active volcanoes, so people do not have to put themselves at risk.

Magnets

Magnets are objects that other magnets and some metals stick to. They have two sides, or ends, called poles. The area all around the magnet where the magnet acts is called the magnetic field.

SEE ALSO
▶ Compass p.70
▶ Earth p.83
▶ Electricity p.87
▶ Inside Earth p.135
▶ Forces p.108
▶ Materials p.157

Magnetic materials

Materials that magnets stick to are called magnetic materials. Any metal that contains iron is magnetic, but most metals are not magnetic.

This paperclip is being attracted to the magnet.

The largest **magnet** on Earth is **Earth** itself. The whole planet is a magnet with **two poles**.

The paperclips contain iron, so they stick to the magnet.

Magnetic force

Two identical poles repel each other, pushing each other away. Two opposite poles attract each other and stick.

Two south poles push each other apart.

N   S   S   N

S   N   S   N

A north and a south pole attract each other.

Magnetic field

The magnet acts on things that are nearby. The region where the magnet attracts or repels magnetic materials is called the magnetic field.

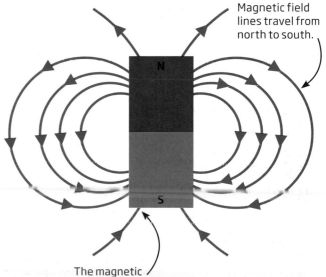

Magnetic field lines travel from north to south.

The magnetic field is strongest at the poles.

The **story** of...

Pets

Pets have become an important part of humans' lives. Many animals are kept as companions, for work, or to help people go about their daily lives. It is estimated that 44 percent of homes in the world have a pet.

Canaan dog

Pets big and small

Pets aren't just dogs and cats—we keep all sorts of animals as pets. They vary from big dogs and horses to small snakes and hamsters. Each species needs a special diet and room to exercise.

First pets

Dogs were the first animals to be kept as pets. They were used for hunting—helping early humans to catch food. Ancient art from 12,000 years ago shows humans and dogs together.

Dog

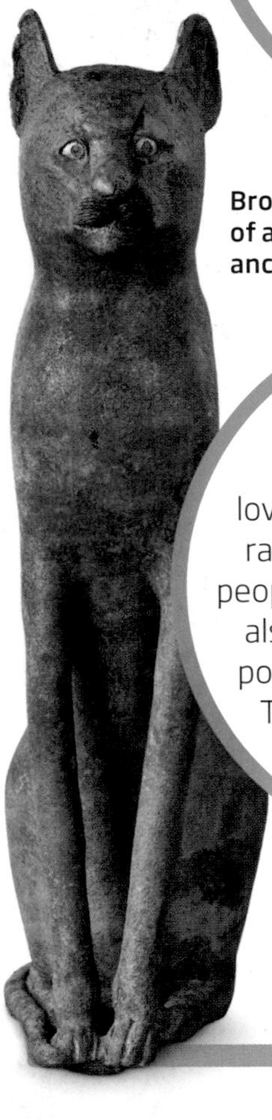

Bronze statue of a cat from ancient Egypt

Bearded dragon

Goldfish

Holy cats

The ancient Egyptians loved cats. They caught mice, rats, and snakes, which kept people's homes clean. Cats were also believed to have special powers for guarding children. The punishment for killing a cat was death.

Hamster

Gerbil

Snake

Helpful pets

Dogs are good at keeping people company. They are also easy to train, and can be used to help people with disabilities. A dog can be a person's eyes or ears, and help them get around.

Guide dogs are specially trained to help people who need help seeing.

Pets in space

For years, animals have helped scientists answer questions about how humans would survive in space. Dogs Belka and Strelka (above) were sent into space on the *Sputnik 5* in 1960. They returned safely to Earth using a parachute.

Budgie

Cat

Rabbit

Guinea pig

Not pets

It is illegal to keep some animals. Wild animals, such as monkeys, can even be dangerous. Before getting a pet, make sure you know that the animal has come from a good home and has not been taken from the wild.

Tarantula

Mammals

Mammals are animals that have body hair and feed their babies on milk made by the females. They are warm-blooded, which means their bodies stay the same temperature. There are many different groups of mammals.

SEE ALSO
▶ Animal families p.21
▶ Animal groups p.22
▶ Food chains p.107
▶ Habitats p.126
▶ Vertebrates p.266

Mammal babies

Mammals give birth to live babies. Parents feed and care for their young until they can look after themselves.

A mother elephant is pregnant for nearly **two years** before its baby is ready to be born.

Gemsbok's horns grow longer each year.

Each hoof has a hard covering.

Gemsbok

Cheetahs have sharp hearing to help them catch animals to eat.

Plant-eaters

Animals that eat plants are called herbivores. They have special teeth for cutting and chewing leaves.

Cheetah

Fur or hair on the body keeps mammals warm.

Meat-eaters

Meat-eating animals are called carnivores. They hunt other animals for food.

Asian elephants

Pouched mammals

Some animals, called marsupials, look after their babies in a special pouch. The baby stays in the pouch, drinking milk until it is big enough to leave.

The pouch is a warm place for the baby.

Red kangaroo

Dolphins

Not all mammals live on land. Dolphins are mammals that live in water. They come up to the surface to breathe through a blowhole at the top of their head.

Maps

A map is a detailed picture of what the ground looks like from above, as if you were flying over it. Maps tell us how big an area is and what can be found there. Maps can be of anything, from the whole world to the insides of buildings.

SEE ALSO

▶ Compass p.70
▶ Explorers p.96
▶ Measuring p.159
▶ Exploration pp.180–181
▶ Navigation p.182
▶ Transportation pp.258–259

Using a map

We can use a map to work out the height of the land, to follow roads and railroads, or to find our way to a hospital or school.

The map is divided into a grid with squares for different areas.

The scale bar shows the real-life distance between points on the map.

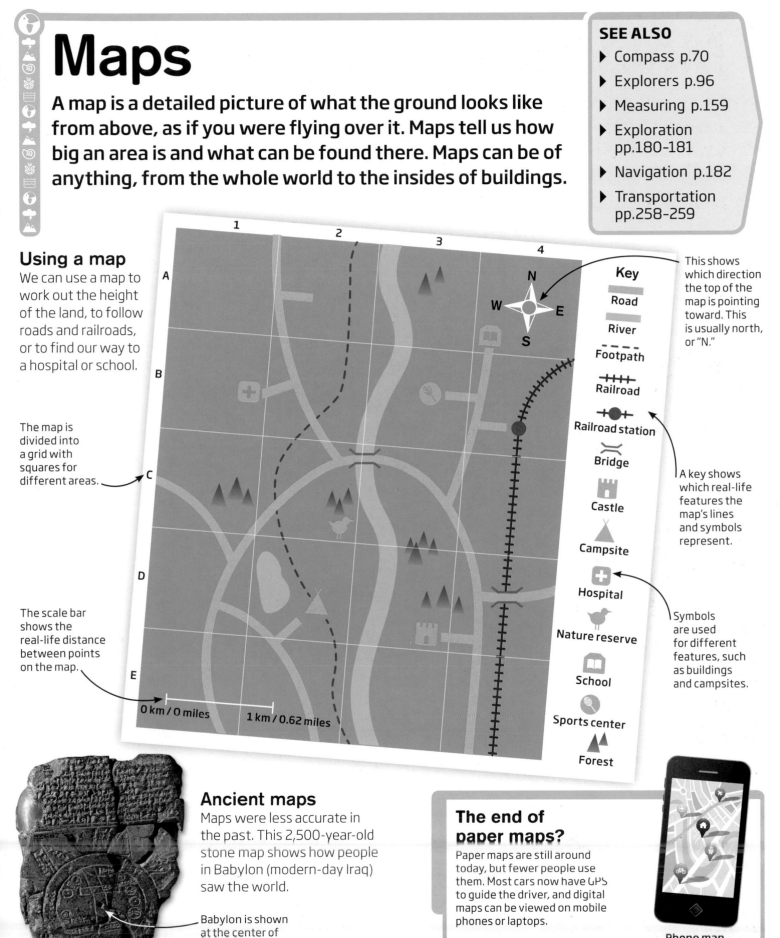

This shows which direction the top of the map is pointing toward. This is usually north, or "N."

Key

Road
River
Footpath
Railroad
Railroad station
Bridge
Castle
Campsite
Hospital
Nature reserve
School
Sports center
Forest

A key shows which real-life features the map's lines and symbols represent.

Symbols are used for different features, such as buildings and campsites.

0 km / 0 miles   1 km / 0.62 miles

Ancient maps

Maps were less accurate in the past. This 2,500-year-old stone map shows how people in Babylon (modern-day Iraq) saw the world.

Babylon is shown at the center of the world.

The end of paper maps?

Paper maps are still around today, but fewer people use them. Most cars now have GPS to guide the driver, and digital maps can be viewed on mobile phones or laptops.

Phone map

Mars

Named after the Roman god of war, this rocky planet has huge volcanoes, ice caps, and deep canyons. It was once a wet, warm world where water flowed. Now, Mars is a cold, dry world covered in craters.

SEE ALSO
▸ Ancient Rome p.20
▸ Asteroids p.30
▸ Elements p.90
▸ Rocks and minerals p.214
▸ Space travel p.237
▸ Volcanoes p.268

Mars' surface features a giant volcano called Olympus Mons.

Thousands of craters formed when asteroids hit Mars 3.5 billion years ago.

Red planet

Mars is called the red planet because its surface is covered in a layer of reddish dust. When the wind blows, this dust enters the atmosphere and turns the sky red.

Mars is about half the size of Earth.

Cameras photograph and video details on the surface.

Spirit rover

Instruments take rock samples.

Mission to Mars

Since 1976, spacecraft have visited Mars to study its surface. Two twin rovers called *Spirit* and *Opportunity* arrived on Mars in 2004, and *Opportunity* is still exploring.

Moons of Mars

Mars has two tiny moons called Deimos and Phobos. These rocks may have started as asteroids. Phobos is the largest, measuring 16 miles (27 km) in length.

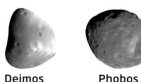

Deimos   Phobos

Materials

Materials are what all things in the world are made of. We describe them using their properties, which are how they behave and what they do. They can be hard, bendy, waterproof, or magnetic. Materials will either float or sink, and electricity can pass through some of them.

Solubility

Solubility is how easily something dissolves (mixes into) liquid. If you put salt in water, the salt dissolves into it, so salt is soluble. Soluble materials can be solids, liquids, or gases.

Sand is insoluble—it does not dissolve in water.

This purple powder dissolves into the water.

Conducting heat

Metals are good at conducting heat, which means when something hot touches them, the heat transfers into them. Wood, plastic, and rubber are poor conductors of heat. Both properties are useful in saucepans.

The rubber handle stays cool, so we can pick up the pan.

The flame causes the metal pan to heat up.

Conducting electricity

Copper conducts electricity, which means it allows electricity to flow through it. Plastic is an electrical insulator, which doesn't conduct electricity. Both are useful in wire cables.

Copper wire lets electricity travel through it.

Plastic stops electricity from leaking out of the cable.

Flammability

Flammability is how easily something catches fire and burns. Dry wood is highly flammable, which means it catches fire and burns easily, giving off heat.

Dry wood catches fire and burns easily.

Non-flammable stones stop the fire from spreading.

Maya

The Maya people lived in Central America from 1000 BCE to 1600 CE. They built great cities from stone and farmed maize, beans, and squash. The Maya had many gods, who they built temples for. They were skilled mathematicians and developed a calendar.

SEE ALSO
▶ Art p.28
▶ Aztecs p.35
▶ Farming p.98
▶ Incas p.132
▶ Games pp.240–241
▶ Religion p.208

Mayan gods

The Maya worshipped many different gods. They believed the gods controlled the world around them, including animals and the weather.

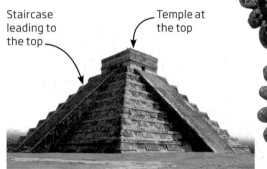

Staircase leading to the top

Temple at the top

Mayan pyramid at Chichén Itzá, Mexico

Temples

Many Mayan temples were built on top of stone pyramids. Priests at the temples sacrificed animals, sang, and danced to honor the gods.

Mayan sport

The Mayans played a sacred ball game. Players hit a large rubber ball to different parts of a court to win points. They could only use their forearms and hips.

Mayan gods were often shown wearing large hats decorated with holy symbols.

Chaac was shown with the nose and fangs of a snake.

Balls of incense were burned to honor the gods.

Chaac was the brother of the **sun**. When he cried, his **tears fell as rain**.

Chaac, the Mayan rain god

Measuring

We measure things to find a number that shows the size or amount of something. Being able to measure things lets us record and compare them. We use many different types of measurements, as well as various tools for measuring.

SEE ALSO
▶ Ancient Egypt p.17
▶ Astronomy p.32
▶ Clocks p.61
▶ Earth p.83
▶ Numbers p.185
▶ Volume p.269

Measuring tools

Different tools let us measure time, size, distance, speed, weight, and volume. Volume is the amount of three-dimensional space something takes up.

Digital scales for measuring weight

Cup for measuring liquid

Clock for measuring time

Different-sized cups for measuring cooking ingredients

Thermometer for measuring temperature

Ruler for measuring length

Spoons for measuring small amounts of ingredients

Weighing through history

People have always wanted to be able to compare amounts of things. The ancient Egyptians invented their own, very accurate system of weights and simple scales to measure the goods they bought and sold.

Big and small

All objects can be measured one way or another. A box of eggs fits easily on weighing scales, but the Earth is so big it can only be weighed using complicated scientific calculations.

A box of six eggs weighs about 10 oz (300 g).

Earth weighs 13.2 billion trillion lbs (5.9 trillion trillion kg).

159

Medicine

Medicine is used to treat and prevent sickness. Medicine can be made from plants or from chemicals in a science lab. Doctors are trained to discover different problems and find the right treatment or medicine to make people better.

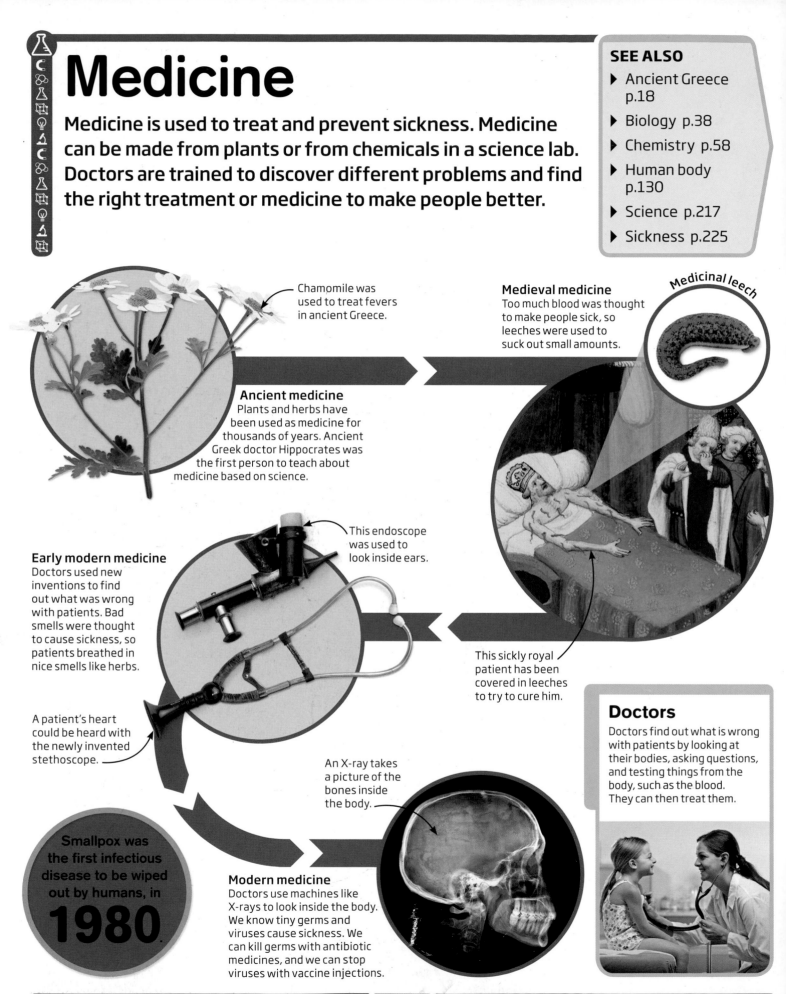

Chamomile was used to treat fevers in ancient Greece.

Medieval medicine
Too much blood was thought to make people sick, so leeches were used to suck out small amounts.

Medicinal leech

Ancient medicine
Plants and herbs have been used as medicine for thousands of years. Ancient Greek doctor Hippocrates was the first person to teach about medicine based on science.

This endoscope was used to look inside ears.

Early modern medicine
Doctors used new inventions to find out what was wrong with patients. Bad smells were thought to cause sickness, so patients breathed in nice smells like herbs.

This sickly royal patient has been covered in leeches to try to cure him.

A patient's heart could be heard with the newly invented stethoscope.

An X-ray takes a picture of the bones inside the body.

Doctors
Doctors find out what is wrong with patients by looking at their bodies, asking questions, and testing things from the body, such as the blood. They can then treat them.

Smallpox was the first infectious disease to be wiped out by humans, in **1980**.

Modern medicine
Doctors use machines like X-rays to look inside the body. We know tiny germs and viruses cause sickness. We can kill germs with antibiotic medicines, and we can stop viruses with vaccine injections.

Mercury

Mercury is the smallest planet in the solar system. Despite this, it can often be seen from Earth at sunrise and sunset. The average temperature is a scorching 332°F (167°C) because this planet is closest to the sun.

SEE ALSO

▶ Ancient Rome p.20

▶ Asteroids p.30

▶ Water pp.120–121

▶ Moon p.171

▶ Solar system p.233

▶ Sun p.247

Fast mover

This planet takes its name from the speedy Roman messenger god. Mercury moves faster across Earth's sky and faster around the sun than the other planets.

Mercury is a dry, rocky planet with no liquid water.

Craters were made when asteroids hit Mercury billions of years ago.

Large solar panels kept MESSENGER working by turning the sun's rays into electricity.

Temperatures on Mercury can soar to **800°F (430°C)** in the day and drop to **−290°F (−180°C)** at night.

Exploring Mercury

Between 2011 and 2015, the robotic space probe MESSENGER explored the surface of Mercury. The information collected allowed scientists to make complete maps of Mercury for the first time.

Mercury

arth's moon

Tiny planet

Mercury is a very small planet. It is only slightly bigger than Earth's moon. The planets Jupiter and Saturn both have moons that are bigger than Mercury.

Metals

We find metals in rocks. Metals can be strong or bendy, and they let electricity pass through them. These features are useful for making many things, from wires to buildings. Metals can be used on their own or mixed together.

SEE ALSO

▶ Bicycles p.36
▶ Elements p.90
▶ Iron Age p.140
▶ Liquids p.148
▶ Magnets p.151
▶ Meteorites p.164

Bicycle basics

A bicycle is made from a combination of strong and bendy metals. The type of metal used for each part depends on what it needs to do.

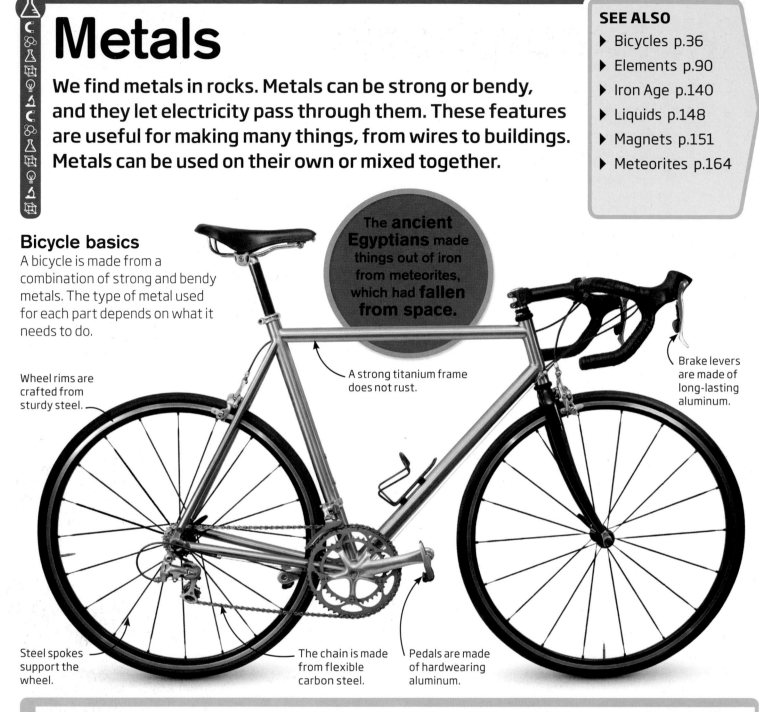

The **ancient Egyptians** made things out of iron from meteorites, which had **fallen from space.**

Wheel rims are crafted from sturdy steel.

A strong titanium frame does not rust.

Brake levers are made of long-lasting aluminum.

Steel spokes support the wheel.

The chain is made from flexible carbon steel.

Pedals are made of hardwearing aluminum.

Metal from mines

People dig tunnels underground to find metal in places called mines. Usually, the metal found in mines is not pure, which means it has rock and gas mixed in it. These materials need to be separated from the metal before we can use it.

1. Ore
An ore is a rock that contains metal. The ore is discovered and dug out of the mine.

2. Melting
The ore is heated to melt and remove the metal. Chemicals are added to help remove gases.

3. Cooling
The metal cools into a solid. It can be heated up and hammered into useful shapes.

Metamorphosis

Some animals go through amazing changes between birth and adulthood. Their appearance changes so much that their fully grown shape is completely different to the newborn one. This process is called metamorphosis.

SEE ALSO
▶ Amphibians p.15
▶ Animal groups p.22
▶ Eggs p.86
▶ Insects p.134
▶ Life cycle p.146

Birth of a butterfly

Becoming a beautiful butterfly is a long process involving many stages and different forms. The process takes between a month and a year.

2. Caterpillar
A hungry caterpillar emerges from the egg. It eats leaves and begins to grow. Although it starts life small, the caterpillar develops quickly.

Metamorphosis is a Greek word meaning **"change in shape."**

1. Eggs
Butterflies start out as tiny eggs, laid on plants. The size, shape, and color of the egg depends on the type of butterfly.

3. Chrysalis
The caterpillar wraps itself in a protective layer called a chrysalis. Inside, the caterpillar completely changes its body shape.

The chrysalis is attached to a branch or leaf.

4. Butterfly
Once the changes are complete, a butterfly emerges from the chrysalis. In a few hours, the butterfly can fly, and the life cycle begins again.

Frogspawn

Tadpole

Adult frog

Froglet

Becoming a frog

The life cycle of a frog has many stages. A female lays many eggs, called frogspawn, usually in water. These hatch into tiny tadpoles with gills for breathing. Tadpoles grow bigger and develop legs. Over a few more weeks, a froglet loses its tail, grows a frog's tongue, and becomes an adult.

The chrysalis is left empty.

The wings need to dry out before the butterfly can fly.

Meteorites

Meteorites are pieces of space rock (asteroids and comets) that reach the surface of the Earth. They come in many different sizes, from tiny pebbles to rocks the size of a house. Only big meteorites can create craters when they hit the ground.

SEE ALSO
▶ Asteroids p.30
▶ Atmosphere p.33
▶ Comets p.68
▶ Metals p.162
▶ Rocks and minerals p.214
▶ Solar system p.233

Space rocks

Meteorites are made of materials that are also found on Earth. There are three main types.

Stony-iron
Stony-iron meteorites are a mixture of metal and rock. They are very rare.

Stony
Most meteorites that are found are stony. They come from the crusts of asteroids.

Iron
Iron meteorites are made of iron and nickel metals. They come from the cores of asteroids.

Asteroid

Meteoroids are small pieces of asteroids and comets.

Meteoroid

Space

The atmosphere is a layer of gases around the Earth.

Atmosphere

Meteor

Meteorite

Earth

Changing names

The name of a space rock changes as it approaches Earth. In space, it is a meteoroid; in the atmosphere, it is a meteor; and on the ground, it is a meteorite.

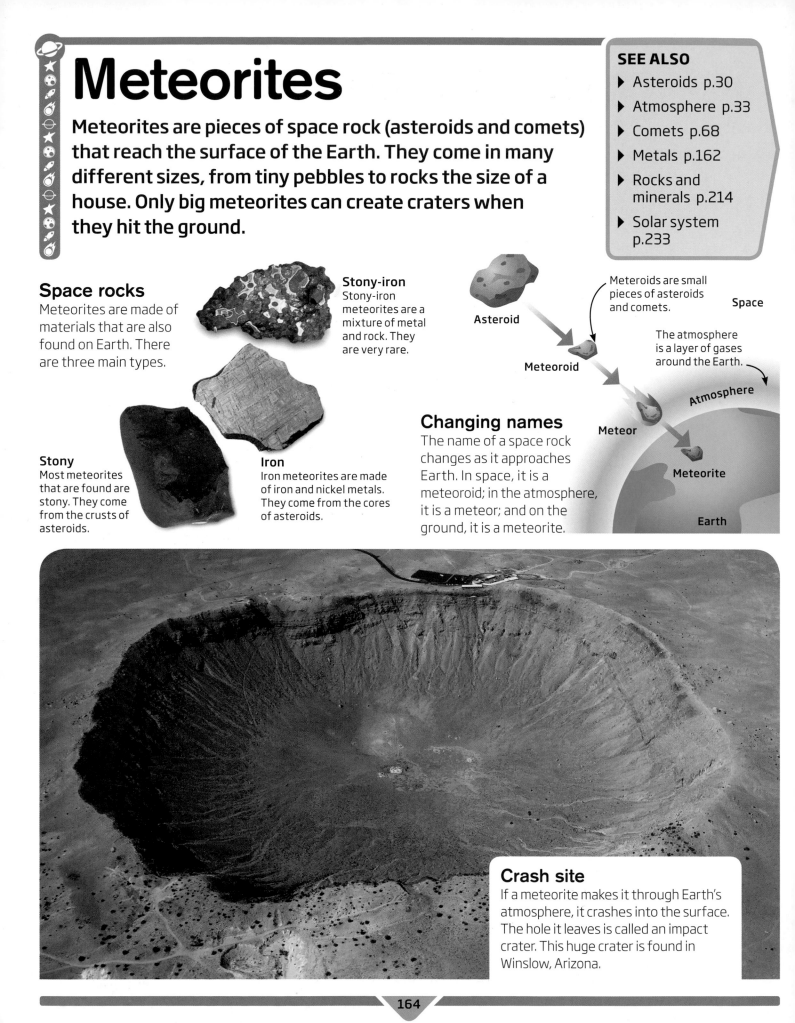

Crash site

If a meteorite makes it through Earth's atmosphere, it crashes into the surface. The hole it leaves is called an impact crater. This huge crater is found in Winslow, Arizona.

Microscopic life

Microorganisms are very tiny living things. They are all around us–in the air, in our bodies, and in water. Most microorganisms are so small that they can only be seen through a magnifying machine called a microscope.

SEE ALSO
▶ Body cells p.41
▶ Food chains p.107
▶ Inventions pp.136-137
▶ Invertebrates p.139
▶ Sickness p.225

Types of microscopic life

There are many kinds of microscopic life. Some are harmful and spread illness. Others are helpful, such as the bacteria in our stomach, which break down our food.

Plankton
Plankton are microscopic plants and animals that live in water.

Virus
Viruses attack the cells of plants and animals, causing sickness.

Bacteria
Some bacteria help our bodies use food. Others cause illness, such as cholera and tetanus.

Humans have **trillions of bacteria** in their bodies to help them survive.

Dust mites look like tiny bugs.

Scientists put samples on glass slides to examine them in closer detail under a microscope.

Dust mites

These microscopic bugs live all around us. They live in people's homes and eat flakes of dead skin that drop off us.

Microscope

Microscopes use lenses to enlarge, or magnify, things. This lets us look at things much smaller than what we can see with just our eyes.

Migration

Some animals make long journeys each year. These journeys are called migrations. Animals migrate to find water, to spend winter in warmer places, or to find the best place to mate and have their babies.

SEE ALSO
▶ Birds p.39
▶ Insects p.134
▶ Mammals p.154
▶ Metamorphosis p.163
▶ North America p.184
▶ Seasons p.221

North America

Monarch butterfly

Monarch butterflies fly thousands of miles to get from North America to Mexico. Butterflies that arrive in Mexico hatch from eggs laid by butterflies in North America. These live until the spring, when they can lay eggs on their own.

Key

➤ Autumn
➤ Spring
➤ Summer

Autumn
As the temperature drops and there is less food for the butterflies, the young ones begin their long migration south to warmer areas.

Summer
Once the caterpillars have turned into butterflies, they are ready to fly farther north in large groups, to mate and lay eggs.

Spring
The butterflies travel north to lay their eggs in the warm spring air, and then die. There will be plenty of leaves for the caterpillars to eat when they hatch.

Mexico

Winter
Huge numbers of butterflies come together in the forests in the winter to rest.

Thousands of butterflies migrate together.

Arctic tern

These small birds have the longest migration of all animals. They fly back and forth between the North and South Pole areas. They fly for eight months of every year.

Caribou

These hoofed animals from the Arctic travel in enormous herds. They walk up to 30 miles (50 km) a day for three months to spend their summer in open areas and winter in forests.

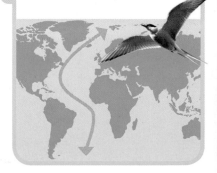

Milky Way

The Milky Way is a galaxy, or group of stars. It contains more than 200 million stars, including our sun. Astronomers think that the Milky Way is shaped like a spiral, with two main arms.

SEE ALSO
▶ Astronomy p.32
▶ Constellations p.73
▶ Earth p.83
▶ Galaxies p.116
▶ Solar system p.233
▶ Stars p.242
▶ Universe p.263

Home galaxy

Our solar system is located about halfway between the center and the edge of the Milky Way. It turns around its center once every 240 million years.

Scutum-Centaurus Arm

The Milky Way will crash into another galaxy, the Andromeda galaxy, in about **4 billion years.**

The center is shaped like a long bar.

The spiral arms are made of stars, gas, and dust.

Everything in the galaxy rotates around its center.

Our solar system is located here, in a small arm called the Orion Spur.

Perseus Arm

Edwin Hubble

Edwin Hubble was a famous American astronomer of the 20th century. He was the first person to realize that there are other galaxies beyond the Milky Way. He also measured the distances between galaxies.

View from Earth

From Earth, we can see the Milky Way as a faint white band across the night sky. The light we see is created by billions of shining stars.

The Milky Way from Earth

Mixtures

A mixture is made when we mix different materials together and they can be easily separated back out into their original parts. Mixtures can be made from solids, liquids, and gases. There are three main ways of separating mixtures.

Sifting

We can use a sifter to separate large solids from small ones, or solids from liquids. A sifter is made from crisscrossed wire with small holes that let some solids through.

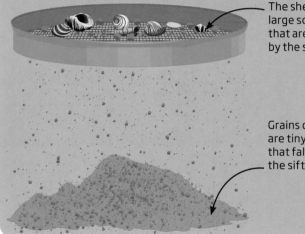

The shells are large solids that are caught by the sifter.

Grains of sand are tiny solids that fall through the sifter.

Filtering

Filters are made from materials with tiny holes in them. The holes catch solids that are too big to fit through, but let liquids pass.

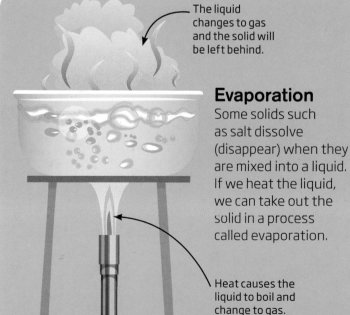

A mixture of sand and water is poured into the filter.

The filter catches the sand but not the water.

The water that lands in the beaker has no sand in it.

Evaporation

The liquid changes to gas and the solid will be left behind.

Some solids such as salt dissolve (disappear) when they are mixed into a liquid. If we heat the liquid, we can take out the solid in a process called evaporation.

Heat causes the liquid to boil and change to gas.

Compounds

Some materials that are joined together can't be easily separated by sifting, filtering, or evaporation. These materials are not mixtures, they are compounds. Iron and sulfur make the compound iron sulfide.

Iron sulfide

Money

We exchange money for things we want to buy, such as food, clothes, and electricity. Money has a number value, and it is made up of coins and bills. Some objects are expensive and worth more money than others.

SEE ALSO
▶ Measuring p.159
▶ Metals p.162
▶ Numbers p.185
▶ Plastic p.195
▶ Precious metals p.199
▶ Work p.274

Currency

The different units of money used around the world are known as currency. In the US, for example, the currency is the dollar, and in Japan the currency is the yen.

Early currency

Before coins were invented, people exchanged other things as money, including cattle, salt, grain, and even shells.

A type of shell that was once widely traded.

Cowry shell

Digital money

Banks store money for people in bank accounts. People can pay into or take money out of their bank account. They can use a card or phone to spend the money from the bank in a shop.

Ancient coins

The first coins were used nearly 3,000 years ago. They were made from gold and silver. Different coins were made across the ancient world.

Chinese Han Dynasty coin

Ancient Greek coin

Roman Emperor Antonius Pius.

Ancient Egyptian coin

Ancient Roman coin

Value

An object that takes a lot of time to make or uses expensive materials is said to have a high value. It will cost more money than something that is quick and easy to make and uses cheaper materials.

High-value sports car   Low-value toy car

Modern money

Coins today are made from a mix of metals called alloys. We also use bills made from cotton-paper or plastic.

British pence

Indian rupee

American cent

Danish krone

European euros

Japanese yen

Mexican peso

South African rand

A springbok–the national animal of South Africa.

Earning money

People exchange their time for money, too. This vet gets paid for the time she spends making animals better. She goes to work and earns money.

Vet at work

Monkeys and apes

Apes, monkeys, and lemurs belong to a group of animals called primates, which also includes humans. Most primates are smart and like to play. Primates are the only animals with hands that can grab things.

SEE ALSO
▶ Africa p.12
▶ Early humans p.82
▶ Habitats p.126
▶ Rain forest p.204
▶ South America p.236
▶ Vertebrates p.266

Apes
Apes do not have tails and can stand more upright than monkeys. They use their huge, strong arms to climb trees and hang from branches.

Old World monkeys
From Africa and Asia, these monkeys live in many different places, such as swamps and mountain forests.

Rhesus macaque

Squirrel monkey

New World monkeys
From South America, these monkeys spend most of their time in the trees. They use their tails to swing from branch to branch.

Chimpanzee

Chimpanzees live in groups of up to

120

animals.

Lemurs
Lemurs are only found on the African island of Madagascar. Most of them live in trees, and are good climbers.

Ring-tailed lemurs

Tool use
Chimpanzees are some of the smartest animals in the world. They use tools to open hard nuts or find insects to eat. Young chimpanzees learn how to use tools from the older members of their group.

Moon

The moon is a round, rocky, airless "body" that circles the Earth. It is the most familiar object in the sky after the sun. People have visited the moon, but not since 1972.

SEE ALSO
- Asteroids p.30
- Atmosphere p.33
- Comets p.68
- Earth p.83
- Solar system p.233
- Tides p.254

Rocky body
The moon is large and rocky with a dusty, airless surface. It is about one-quarter the width of the Earth.

Man on the moon
The moon is the only object in the solar system that has been visited by humans. American Apollo space missions landed 12 people on the moon between 1969 and 1972.

The dark areas are where there used to be seas of liquid rock.

The moon's surface is covered with pits left by space rocks that crashed into it.

Moon creation
Scientists think the moon was created when a small planet, Theia, crashed into the Earth 4.5 billion years ago. As a result, rocks on the moon are similar to rocks on Earth.

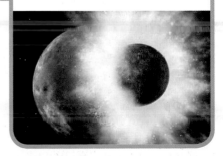

Moon's orbit
The moon travels around the Earth. This is called an orbit. The moon takes 27.3 days to make its orbit around our planet.

The shape of the moon's orbit is a slightly squashed circle.

Earth

We always see the same side of the moon facing Earth.

Moon

Mountains

Mountains are tall, rocky features on the Earth's surface. They usually have very steep sides and tower over the surrounding landscape. The tops of mountains are called summits, and they are often covered in snow, even in summer.

SEE ALSO
▸ Earth's surface p.84
▸ Evolution p.95
▸ Glaciers p.122
▸ Rock cycle p.213
▸ Rocks and minerals p.214
▸ Volcanoes p.268

Mountains around the world

Every continent has mountains. Most mountains are in rows, or ranges, that can be thousands of miles long.

The Andes mountain range runs the length of South America.

The summit

Mountain life

Mountain animals must be able to survive on steep rocks without much oxygen to breathe. Mountain goats are good at climbing and eat small plants.

How are mountains made?

Most mountains are formed over millions of years, as huge pieces of the Earth's crust push into each other. Where they meet, the ground is forced up, making mountain ranges.

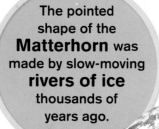
The pointed shape of the **Matterhorn** was made by slow-moving **rivers of ice** thousands of years ago.

This mountain is called the Matterhorn. It is part of a range in Europe called the Alps.

The treeline is the highest point on the mountainside where trees can still grow.

Muscles

Muscles are stretchy cords that pull parts of the body to make them move. They work in teams. Some muscles work without us thinking, others move when we choose to move them. Every time we blink, smile, or move, it is with the help of muscles.

SEE ALSO
▶ Body cells p.41
▶ Feelings p.99
▶ Human body p.130
▶ Skeleton p.228
▶ Sports p.239
▶ Games pp.240-241

Muscular system

Most of our muscles are wrapped around the bones of our skeletons, forming the muscular system. They move our bodies by pulling on the bones.

Muscles are attached to bones by tendons.

The biggest muscle in our body is in our bottom. It is called the gluteus maximus.

Bicep muscle

Tricep muscle

Working in pairs

Muscles only pull—they can't push. To lift your arm up, biceps pull and triceps relax. When triceps pull and biceps relax, the arm moves back down again.

Stomach muscles are called abs.

Upper thigh muscles are called quads.

Face muscles

The muscles in our face move the eyes and mouth and help us to express our feelings to others. For example, we show we are happy by smiling.

You use **300** different muscles just to stand up.

Exercise

The more we move our muscles, the stronger they get. After exercise, the body repairs any damage to muscle cells by making new muscle fibers. This is why muscles become bigger and stronger the more you use them.

Mushrooms

A mushroom is the fruit of a fungus. Fungi are neither animals nor plants. They feed on living and dead animals and plants. Many fungi are very poisonous–you should not touch or pick them.

SEE ALSO

▶ Animal groups p.22

▶ Color pp.26–27

▶ Fruit and seeds p.115

▶ Life cycle p.146

▶ Plants p.194

Fly agaric

Cap
This is the head of the mushroom. It protects the gills.

All parts of the fly agaric mushroom are **poisonous**. It was used to kill flies in medieval times.

Gills
These delicate structures hold the mushroom's spores.

Parts of a mushroom
Mushrooms scatter tiny, seed-like spores, so that fungi can spread. Many are brightly colored.

Ring
This protects the gills. It breaks away as the cap grows.

Stem
This supports the cap and supplies the mushroom with the water and food it needs to stay alive.

Roots
These underground tubes collect water and food.

Fungi
There are many different types of fungus. Most of them grow in damp places, such as grassy fields and shady woodlands.

Devil's fingers

Green elfcup

Yellow jelly antler

Spores
Spores are tiny cells from which new fungi grow. They are released into the wind when a fungus bursts open. The spores are carried away in the wind. When they fall, they can grow into new fungi.

Puffball

Musical instruments

An object used to make musical sounds is called a musical instrument. Musical instruments make sounds in different ways—some have strings that vibrate, others a hole to blow into or a surface to beat. We put musical instruments into four groups based on how they make sound.

SEE ALSO
▸ Dance p.76
▸ Hearing p.127
▸ Music pp.176–177
▸ Orchestra p.188
▸ Radio p.203
▸ Sound p.235

Strings

The sound of stringed instruments comes from their vibrating strings. Players pluck the strings with their fingers or move a bow across them.

Drawing a horsehair bow over the violin's strings makes them vibrate.

Wind

Wind instruments such as the trumpet or flute are made of tubes of wood or metal, which might be straight or looped. Musicians play wind instruments by blowing into them.

Pressing valves on a trumpet changes the tube's length to make a higher or lower sound.

Keyboard

Musicians play instruments such as pianos and synthesizers by pressing keys on a keyboard. Piano keys cause a tiny hammer to hit a string, which produces a particular sound called a note.

A modern grand piano has 88 keys.

Percussion

Percussion instruments such as drums make a sound when they are hit. Some, such as bells and xylophones, can make different notes (sounds). Others, such as rattles, produce a noise when shaken.

Traditional drum heads are made from animal skin.

The **story** of...

Music

Since the earliest times, people have felt the need to make music. We can express our feelings by singing or playing instruments. Musicians organize sound into tunes and regular patterns known as rhythms. A steady rhythm can inspire people to dance.

Musicians rehearsing in Brazil

Playing together
Many people enjoy getting together to make music. Players and singers perform in concerts or just for fun.

The American Symphony Orchestra performs in New York

Classical music
Most music performed in concert halls is known as classical music. It is played by orchestras or groups of musicians called ensembles, and sung by choirs. Classical music began hundreds of years ago, but is still written, played, and enjoyed today.

Pop and rock
Most of the music we hear on the radio is rock or pop music. Before pop music, most music was classical or traditional. Pop music introduced electronic instruments, a strong beat, and words that are easy to sing along to. It quickly became popular all over the world.

This part changes the vibrations of the strings into an electric signal.

Singing
Singing is an important part of music-making all over the world. Singing helps us to express our feelings. A singer can sing alone, or with others as part of a choir.

Kalengo drum from Nigeria

Around the world
There are different types of music and musical instruments all over the world. Singing styles are varied too. African music is often very rhythmic and exciting, while Asian music emphasizes the tune.

First instruments
The first instruments were probably rattles and drums made of wood or bone. Instruments that make a sound when you blow them appeared more than 40,000 years ago.

Bone flute from around 800 BCE

Pan flute from South America

Guiro from Central America

The longer the pipe, the lower the sound it makes.

Notes can be made by pressing the string on the fingerboard and plucking the strings further down.

The sound the guitar makes is created by turning these knobs, which tighten or loosen the strings.

1932
The year the first electric guitar was sold.

Gibson electric guitar

Modern sounds
The first musical instruments made sounds when people touched or blew them. Now we also have instruments powered by electricity. Modern synthesizers can copy other instruments and make completely new sounds too.

Notation
Musicians write music down using a system of symbols called musical notation. The dots on and between the lines tell the performer which notes to play or sing.

This is the music for "Twinkle Twinkle Little Star."

Synthesizer

Myths and legends

Myths and legends are stories. In the past, people invented myths to answer big questions, such as where our world came from. Unlike myths, legends are often based on real events, but the details have changed a lot over time, so there is not much truth left!

SEE ALSO

▶ Ancient Egypt p.17
▶ Ancient Greece p.18
▶ Storytelling pp.42–43
▶ Books p.44
▶ Writing p.280

Mythical creatures

Myths often include strange creatures, which sometimes have a mix of features from different animals. Mythical creatures can be terrifying monsters, or friendly beasts like the Chinese dragon.

Minotaur
The minotaur is a scary monster with a human body and the head of a bull. He appears in an ancient Greek myth.

Chinese dragon
The Chinese dragon has four legs and a long, snakelike body. In China, dragons are a symbol of good luck.

Griffin
The griffin is part lion and part eagle. In Greek myths, griffins stand guard over treasures.

Legendary heroes

Many myths and legends tell the stories of brave people called heroes. Hua Mulan is the hero of a Chinese legend. She pretends to be a man and takes her elderly father's place as a soldier.

This is a modern statue of Hua Mulan. Her story has been told in many books and films.

"Myth" comes from the **Greek** word **"mythos,"** which simply means **"story."**

Creation myth
Many myths are about how the world was created. An Egyptian myth says that the first people in the world were shaped out of clay on a potter's wheel, by a ram-headed god called Khnum.

Native Americans

People first moved from Asia into the Americas more than 25,000 years ago. When Europeans first arrived in the Americas in the late 1400s, there are thought to have been 50 million people already living there in tribes. These people are known as Native Americans.

SEE ALSO
▶ Arctic p.25
▶ Art p.28
▶ Dance p.76
▶ North America p.184
▶ Religion p.208
▶ Homes pp.244-245

The center of this mask shows the sun god.

Cultural areas

There were once hundreds of Native American tribes, each with its own traditions. This map shows the ten Native American cultural areas. The tribes of each area often shared similar customs or ways of life.

KEY

Plateau	Southeast
Northwest	Southwest
Arctic	Plains
Subarctic	Great Basin
Northeast	California

Art and beliefs

Native Americans had many gods and beliefs. Some rituals involved dance, and people often expressed their beliefs through art. For example, the Bella Coola tribe used this carved mask for dance ceremonies.

By the early **16th century**, the Native American population had fallen to **only 400,000** due to disease brought by the Europeans.

Finding food

Some tribes grew crops such as potatoes, corn, or tomatoes. Other tribes relied on hunting wild animals, such as buffalo, or gathering plants.

Homes

Native Americans lived in different kinds of homes. Northeast farmers had longhouses, which were homes built for several families. Plains hunters used tents called tepees.

The **story** of...

Exploration

Humans have explored the land, sea, and sky, and we are starting to explore space. Since our first travels on land, we have made new technology to let us sail and fly. Distant countries can work together because of world exploration. We might even live in space one day!

Leaving Africa

Humans first lived in Africa. They started to leave this continent in large groups between 80,000 and 70,000 years ago. They went by foot to the nearby continent of Asia, and later traveled by boat to Australia.

EUROPE
ASIA
NORTH AMERICA
AFRICA
SOUTH AMERICA
AUSTRALIA

The first people lived in Africa. They slowly spread around the world.

Trade

In the past, people traveled many miles by land and sea to buy things from other countries. Merchants found new routes between distant lands, and bought or traded items such as spices. These goods were then brought home to sell.

Ginger

Cinnamon

Cloves

Vasco da Gama found the **first sea route** from Europe to India in the 15th century.

Reaching the poles

The freezing North and South poles were unexplored until the early 1900s. The first explorers traveled in sleds pulled by dogs and wore fur for warmth.

American explorer Robert Peary, in 1909

This ship carried Christopher Columbus to an island off the coast of America in 1492.

The *Santa Maria*

A deep-sea hatchet fish

Under the sea
Oceans are many miles deep in places. These black depths are largely unexplored. The few crafts that have reached the bottom of ocean trenches have found mysterious new creatures.

Age of exploration
In the 1400s, Europeans traveled by ship to distant places they had never been to before, including America. These long trips were called expeditions.

Around the world
As technology advances, new opportunities for exploration open up. The first flight around the world was made in 1924 by a plane that ran on fuel. In 2016, *Solar Impulse 2* made the first around-the-world flight using sunlight converted into power.

Solar cells on the wings of *Solar Impulse 2* use sunlight to power the plane.

Wind blew into the sails to power the ship.

In 1961, Yuri Gagarin became the first man in space.

Space exploration
A Russian spacecraft called *Sputnik 1* first flew around the Earth in 1957. Humans soon made it into space, too, and landed on the moon in 1969. Since then, we've used robots to visit every planet in the solar system, as well as comets.

Navigation

Navigation is finding where you are and where you are going. We can use the sun, stars, a compass, and paper maps to navigate. Today, most modern transportation receives signals from satellites in space to show where it is on Earth. This is called GPS.

SEE ALSO
▶ Compass p.70
▶ Constellations p.73
▶ Light p.147
▶ Maps p.155
▶ Radio p.203
▶ Satellites p.215

How does GPS work?

The Global Positioning System (GPS) uses signals from a group of satellites in space to work out exact locations on Earth.

3. Signal speed
The satellite signals are sent as radio waves. The phone can tell how far the signal has traveled by how long the signal has taken to reach it.

4. Mobile phone
The mobile phone works out where it is on Earth by looking at how far it is from each of the four satellites.

1. Orbiting satellites
Satellites go in a steady circle around the Earth. There are always at least four GPS satellites in range of your phone.

2. Location and time
The satellite sends out a signal that includes where it is and the exact time.

Latitude and longitude

Maps of Earth have grid lines of latitude and longitude to show where places are. Every place has a unique latitude and longitude number in degrees.

Latitude lines run across.

90°
60°
30°
0°
30°

Longitude lines run up and down.

90° 60° 30° 0°

Map and compass

Without GPS, we can still navigate using a paper map and a compass. The compass shows the direction North, which helps us work out which direction we need to go.

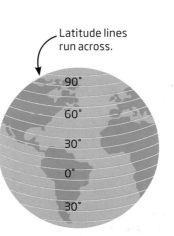

Neptune

Neptune lies in the freezing cold, dark outer parts of the solar system. It is the eighth planet and the farthest planet from the sun. Neptune is often called the "twin planet" of Uranus because it is made up of similar ices and gases. It is four times larger than Earth.

SEE ALSO
▸ Atmosphere p.33
▸ Gases p.117
▸ Liquids p.148
▸ Pluto p.196
▸ Solar system p.233
▸ Uranus p.264

Wispy clouds made of frozen methane gas are found high in Neptune's atmosphere.

The windy planet

Neptune is known as "the windy planet" because it has powerful winds in the outer layers of its atmosphere. Winds can reach speeds of more than 1,500 mph (2,400 kph), about twice the speed of sound.

Neptune gets its blue color from methane gas in the upper atmosphere.

Scientists think that Neptune's largest moon **Triton** is an icy **minor planet** that got caught by Neptune's gravity.

Hydrogen and helium gases make up most of Neptune's atmosphere.

The sun

God of the sea

Neptune was named after the Roman god of the sea, who is usually pictured carrying a three-pronged spear called a trident. The planets Mercury, Venus, Mars, Jupiter, and Saturn are also named after Roman gods.

Beyond Neptune

There are thought to be several thousand icy "minor planets" that orbit the sun beyond Neptune. The first, and largest, minor planet that was discovered is Pluto.

North America

North America stretches from the icy Arctic in the north to tropical Central America in the south. Huge areas of grassland, called prairies, cover much of North America. There are also mountains, forests, deserts, and some of the world's biggest lakes.

SEE ALSO
▶ American West p.14
▶ Arctic p.25
▶ Aztecs p.35
▶ Native Americans p.179
▶ South America p.236

Alaskan salmon

Grizzly bear

Inuit drummers

Polar bear

About North America

Population: 579 million

Highest point: Denali

Lowest point: Badwater Basin

Biggest desert: Great Basin Desert

Longest river: Missouri

Totem pole

Yellowstone is on top of a huge volcano known as a supervolcano.

Rocky Mountains

Wheat

Beaver

Canadian Mountie

Moose

The moose is the largest member of the deer family.

Yellowstone National Park

Mount Rushmore

Statue of Liberty

The White House

Hollywood

Grand Canyon

Monarch butterfly

Mississippi River

Kennedy Space Center

The **United States** is home to the remains of more types of **dinosaur** than any other country.

Armadillo

Pico de Orizaba volcano

Baird's tapir

Panama Canal

Every year, 14,000 ships pass through the Panama Canal, which links the Pacific and Atlantic oceans.

Statue of Liberty
This statue towers 305 ft (93 m) over New York Harbor. Completed in 1886, it was a gift from the people of France to the people of the US.

Mississippi River
The Mississippi is a huge river in North America. Ships use it for transporting goods, and tourists ride on its riverboats called paddle steamers.

Numbers

Numbers are symbols that can be used to show amounts, sizes, distances, and times. The ordinary numbers we count with are called "whole numbers" or "natural numbers." All math requires us to use numbers.

SEE ALSO
▶ Clocks p.61
▶ Coding p.65
▶ Codes pp.66-67
▶ Fractions p.112
▶ Measuring p.159
▶ Temperature p.252

Whole numbers

The numbers 0 to 9 are used to build all the bigger numbers. They are called whole numbers because they are not split into smaller amounts.

0 1 2 3

Zero represents nothing.

Whole numbers are also called "positive" numbers.

Negative numbers

Numbers less than zero are called "negative" numbers. They are used to show things less than zero, such as cold temperatures.

-5 -4 -3 -2 -1 0 1 2 3 4 5

Negative numbers are shown with a minus sign.

Zero is neither positive nor negative.

Positive numbers have no symbol in front.

Algebra

Algebra is a type of math that uses letters to stand for numbers or amounts. We can use algebra to work out the value of unknown amounts.

$$2 + a = 5$$

The "a" represents a mystery number. We can work out what it is by taking 2 away from 5.

An equals sign means both sides of the equation have the same value.

Place value

The place where a number is written in a longer number shows how much it is worth. The lowest worth, the unit, is on the right.

4 , 5 6 2

Thousands
This shows how many thousands the number has.

Hundreds
This shows how many hundreds the number has.

Tens
This shows how many tens the number has.

Units
Units are numbers from 0-9.

Oceania

Oceania is a continent made up of Australia, New Zealand, Papua New Guinea, Fiji, and other islands in the tropical Pacific Ocean. It is home to some of the world's most unusual wildlife, including kangaroos, koalas, duck-billed platypuses, and kiwis.

SEE ALSO
▶ Asia p.29
▶ Birds p.39
▶ Coral reefs p.74
▶ Deserts p.78
▶ Mammals p.154
▶ Sports p.239
▶ World p.275

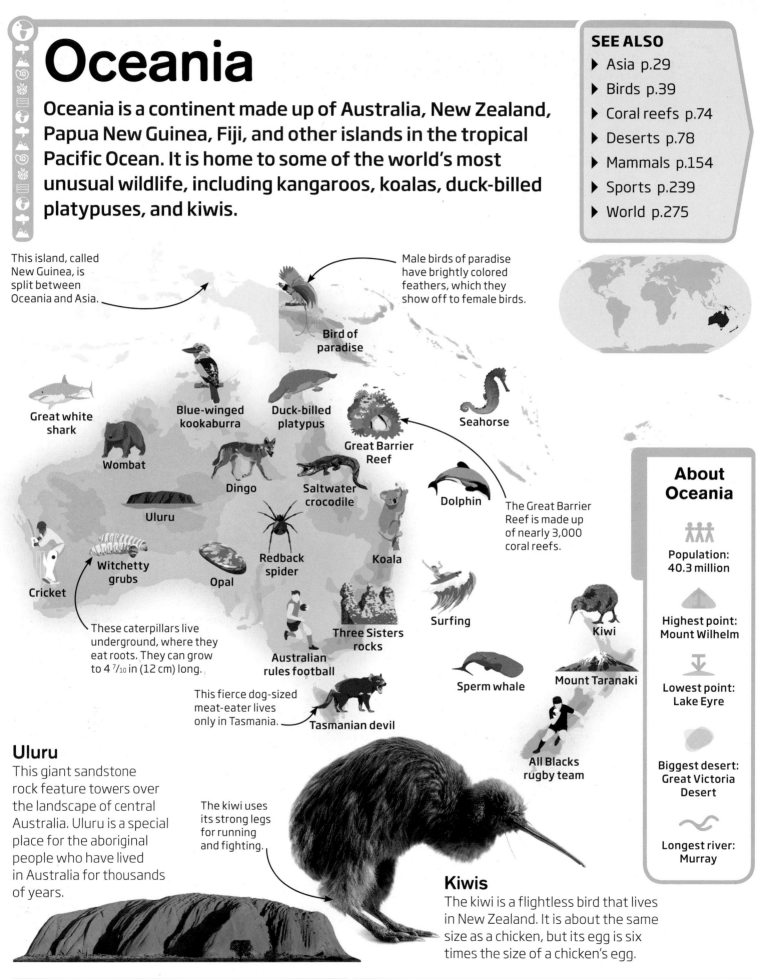

This island, called New Guinea, is split between Oceania and Asia.

Male birds of paradise have brightly colored feathers, which they show off to female birds.

Bird of paradise

Great white shark

Blue-winged kookaburra

Duck-billed platypus

Great Barrier Reef

Seahorse

Wombat

Dingo

Saltwater crocodile

Dolphin

The Great Barrier Reef is made up of nearly 3,000 coral reefs.

Uluru

Koala

Witchetty grubs

Opal

Redback spider

Cricket

These caterpillars live underground, where they eat roots. They can grow to 4 7/10 in (12 cm) long.

Australian rules football

Three Sisters rocks

Surfing

Kiwi

Sperm whale

Mount Taranaki

This fierce dog-sized meat-eater lives only in Tasmania.

Tasmanian devil

All Blacks rugby team

Uluru

This giant sandstone rock feature towers over the landscape of central Australia. Uluru is a special place for the aboriginal people who have lived in Australia for thousands of years.

The kiwi uses its strong legs for running and fighting.

Kiwis

The kiwi is a flightless bird that lives in New Zealand. It is about the same size as a chicken, but its egg is six times the size of a chicken's egg.

About Oceania

Population: 40.3 million

Highest point: Mount Wilhelm

Lowest point: Lake Eyre

Biggest desert: Great Victoria Desert

Longest river: Murray

Oceans and seas

More than two-thirds of our planet is covered by oceans and smaller seas. They contain most of the world's water and are full of life of all shapes and sizes. Some of the deepest parts of the ocean have still not been explored.

SEE ALSO

▶ Coral reefs p.74
▶ Water pp.120–121
▶ Exploration pp.180–181
▶ Seashore p.220
▶ Tides p.254

Ocean depths

Oceans are divided into different zones according to depth. The deepest part is more than 6 miles (10 km) beneath the surface.

Sunlit zone
This zone receives lots of sunlight and is the layer of the ocean that contains most plants and animals.

Twilight zone
Little sunlight reaches the twilight zone. Many creatures that live here have body parts that glow in the dark.

Dark zone
The dark zone is deeper than 3,300 ft (1,000 m). The water is dark apart from some animals that glow with light.

Deep-sea zone
In the deepest part of the ocean, weird creatures live in total darkness.

The world's oceans

The Earth has five oceans. The largest is the Pacific, which holds half of the world's salt water. The smallest is the Arctic Ocean, which is partly frozen.

Ocean smokers

In places, hot water bursts from the seabed, creating chimneylike structures known as smokers. The water that comes out from the smokers can be white or black, depending on what minerals the water around them contains.

Orchestra

An orchestra is a large group of people playing different musical instruments together. Orchestras were created to play classical music, such as complicated pieces called symphonies. Orchestras often create music for films, and sometimes play non-classical pieces, such as pop music.

SEE ALSO
▶ Dance p.76
▶ Film p.100
▶ Musical instruments p.175
▶ Music pp.176–177
▶ Radio p.203
▶ Sound p.235

Classical orchestra

A classical orchestra is split into four sections: strings, woodwind, brass, and percussion. It is led by a person called a conductor.

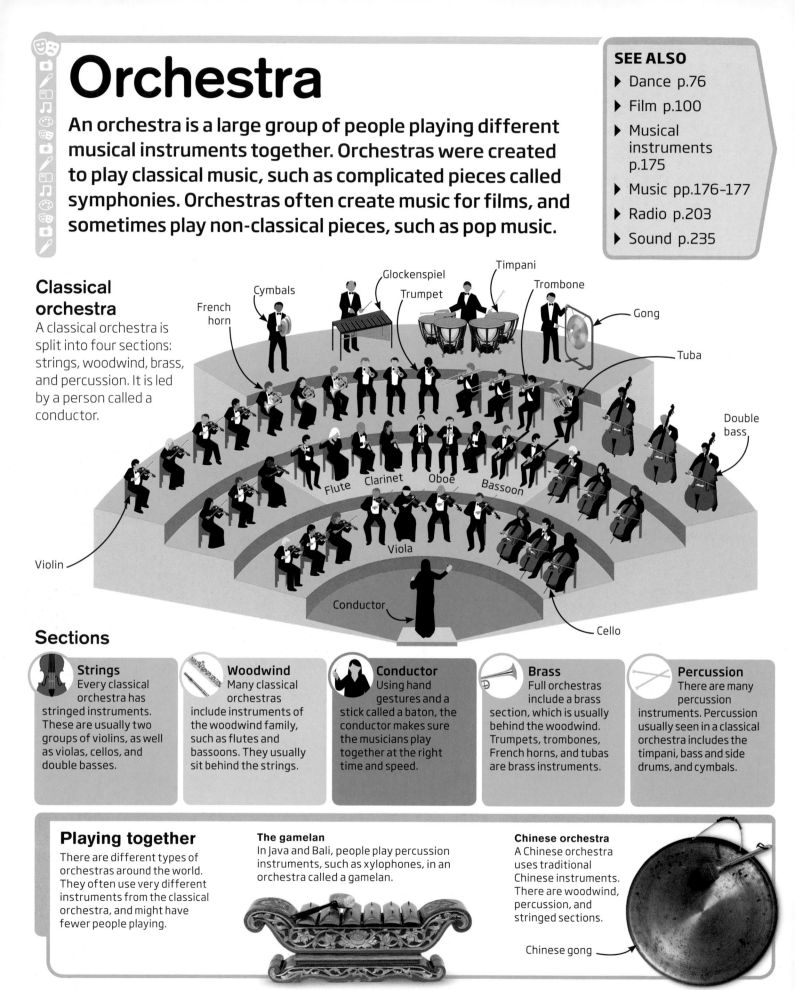

Cymbals

French horn

Glockenspiel

Trumpet

Timpani

Trombone

Gong

Tuba

Double bass

Flute   Clarinet   Oboe   Bassoon

Viola

Violin

Conductor

Cello

Sections

Strings
Every classical orchestra has stringed instruments. These are usually two groups of violins, as well as violas, cellos, and double basses.

Woodwind
Many classical orchestras include instruments of the woodwind family, such as flutes and bassoons. They usually sit behind the strings.

Conductor
Using hand gestures and a stick called a baton, the conductor makes sure the musicians play together at the right time and speed.

Brass
Full orchestras include a brass section, which is usually behind the woodwind. Trumpets, trombones, French horns, and tubas are brass instruments.

Percussion
There are many percussion instruments. Percussion usually seen in a classical orchestra includes the timpani, bass and side drums, and cymbals.

Playing together

There are different types of orchestras around the world. They often use very different instruments from the classical orchestra, and might have fewer people playing.

The gamelan
In Java and Bali, people play percussion instruments, such as xylophones, in an orchestra called a gamelan.

Chinese orchestra
A Chinese orchestra uses traditional Chinese instruments. There are woodwind, percussion, and stringed sections.

Chinese gong

Philosophy

Philosophy is a way of trying to understand things by asking questions and thinking of answers. It was first studied thousands of years ago, when people wanted to find out about the world and their own lives. People who try to find answers to these questions are known as philosophers.

SEE ALSO

▶ Ancient China p.16

▶ Ancient Greece p.18

▶ Governments p.123

▶ Religion p.208

▶ Science p.217

Asking questions
To find out about the world, philosophers ask all sorts of questions. They ask about things such as what is real around us, and what is the best way to live our lives.

Thinking of answers
Philosophers try to come up with answers to these questions. By thinking hard about their answers, they can decide whether they are true or false.

What makes me who I am?

Why do things exist?

How do I know what is true?

Right and wrong
An important part of philosophy is deciding what makes something right or wrong. For example, we all know that stealing is bad. Philosophers ask why it is bad.

Equality
Men and women are often treated differently. For example, men are generally paid more. Philosophers try to explain how everybody should be treated equally (the same).

First philosophers
Western philosophy began in ancient Greece. The Greek city of Athens was home to many of the most important early philosophers, such as Socrates, Plato, and Aristotle.

Statue of Plato

Plato

Photography

A photograph is a still image taken using a machine called a camera. Photographs give us a visual record of who we are and what we have done. These images can capture important people and events in history, or private moments in your own life.

SEE ALSO

▸ Art p.28
▸ Computers p.71
▸ Film p.100
▸ Inventions pp.136–137
▸ Telephones p.250
▸ Television p.251

Cameras
The first photographic cameras were invented in France in the 1800s, but were large and hard to use. Cameras are now small enough to fit inside mobile phones.

Daguerreotype cameras were the first cameras to go on sale to the public in 1839.

Early cameras
The first cameras took pictures on metal sheets that had been made sensitive to light. It took many minutes to take a photo.

These cameras can connect to computers to transfer images.

Digital camera
Modern digital cameras produce images made up of millions of tiny points of color that are displayed on screens.

The film is rolled up inside the camera.

Film camera
Later cameras use strips of light-sensitive plastic film. When the film is exposed to light, a picture forms.

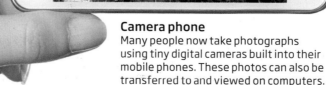

Camera phone
Many people now take photographs using tiny digital cameras built into their mobile phones. These photos can also be transferred to and viewed on computers.

The first photograph was taken in 1816 by French inventor **Nicéphore Niépce.**

Taking pictures
Photographs fall under different categories called genres. Pictures you take of yourself are called selfies, and other genres include animals and travel.

Selfie

Pet portrait

Vacation snap

Photosynthesis

Plants make their own food. They do this by taking in the sun's light energy, as well as water from the ground and gas from the air. Producing energy in this way is called photosynthesis.

SEE ALSO
- Carbon cycle p.49
- Cells p.56
- Gases p.117
- Light p.147
- Plants p.194
- Temperature p.252

How do plants make food?

The plant combines carbon dioxide with water to make sugar. The energy it needs to do this is supplied by the sun's light.

The **oxygen** that plants give out is the same gas that **humans and animals** need to breathe in.

Sunlight
Plants need energy from sunlight to complete photosynthesis. They grow toward the light.

Carbon dioxide
Holes in the plant's leaves take in a gas called carbon dioxide.

Oxygen
Oxygen is released as waste when carbon dioxide, water, and light react together in the plant.

Conditions

Temperature, light, and water need to be just right for a plant to survive. If these conditions change too much and don't suit the plant it will start to die.

Leaves droop.

Leaves turn brown.

Without light   **Without water**

Leaves
A chemical in the leaves called chlorophyll absorbs light energy from the sun. Chlorophyll makes plants look green.

The stem is strong to support the plant and move it toward light.

Water
The plant needs water to survive. Water travels up the stem into the plant.

Roots
The plant roots take in water and minerals from the soil.

Physics

Everything in the universe that weighs something is called "matter." Physics is a science that looks at how matter moves and interacts. This includes energy, forces, magnets, light, heat, waves, and sound.

SEE ALSO

▶ Circuits p.59

▶ Electricity p.87

▶ Energy pp.88–89

▶ Forces p.108

▶ Magnets p.151

▶ The sciences pp.218–219

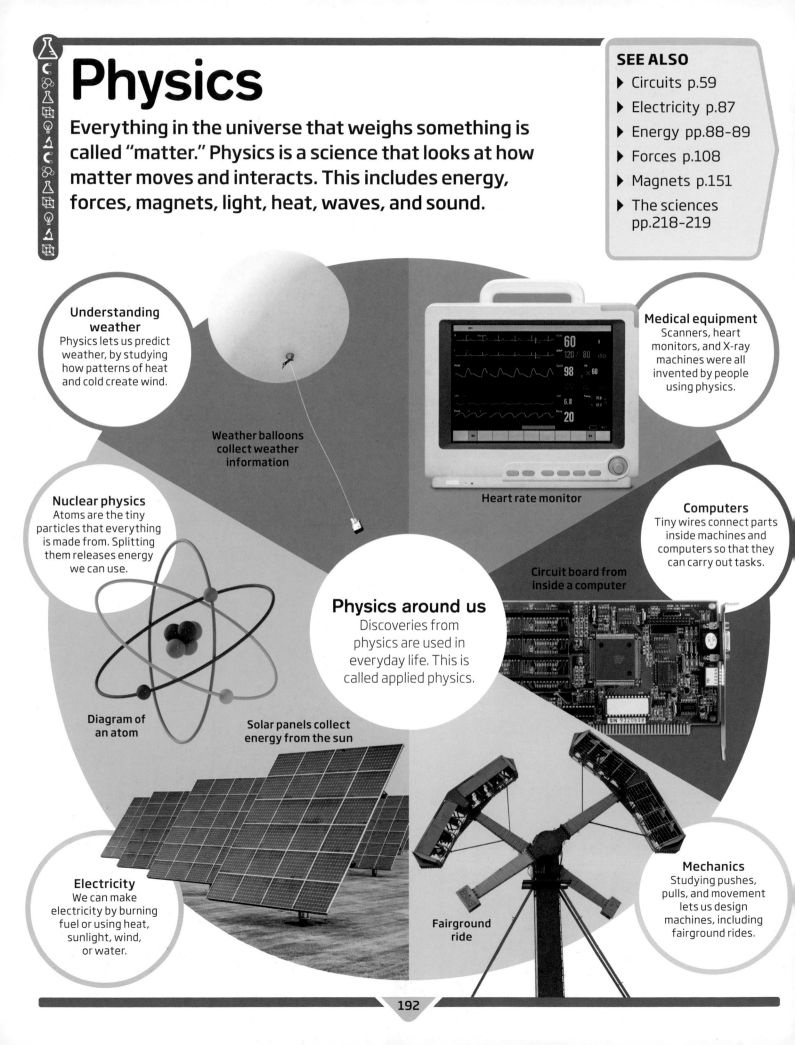

Understanding weather
Physics lets us predict weather, by studying how patterns of heat and cold create wind.

Weather balloons collect weather information

Medical equipment
Scanners, heart monitors, and X-ray machines were all invented by people using physics.

Heart rate monitor

Nuclear physics
Atoms are the tiny particles that everything is made from. Splitting them releases energy we can use.

Computers
Tiny wires connect parts inside machines and computers so that they can carry out tasks.

Circuit board from inside a computer

Physics around us
Discoveries from physics are used in everyday life. This is called applied physics.

Diagram of an atom

Solar panels collect energy from the sun

Electricity
We can make electricity by burning fuel or using heat, sunlight, wind, or water.

Fairground ride

Mechanics
Studying pushes, pulls, and movement lets us design machines, including fairground rides.

Pirates

Pirates were criminals who attacked ships to steal goods, using force and violence to get their way. They are often now remembered as jolly villains who buried treasure and relaxed on tropical islands, but the reality was not so pleasant.

SEE ALSO
▶ Clothing pp.62–63
▶ Explorers p.96
▶ Flags p.102
▶ Maps p.155
▶ Oceans and seas p.187
▶ Ships p.224

Pirate flag

Pirates put symbols of death on their flags to frighten people. These symbols included skulls, bones, and skeletons. This flag was flown by famous pirate Jeremiah Cocklyn.

Pirate ship

Pirate ships had to be fast so they could catch other ships or escape from trouble. They were armed with cannons for fighting. This type of ship is called a sloop.

Large sails helped the ship move quickly.

Large hats kept pirates sheltered from the sun and rain.

Clothes were made of wool, linen, and canvas.

Leather shoes closed with small brass buckles.

Pirate life

Pirates could be at sea for weeks at a time. To keep from getting irritable, which could lead to fights among the crew, they passed the time with music, games, food, and drink.

The years between **1690** and **1725** are known as the **golden age** of **piracy**.

Swords called cutlasses had short, curved blades.

Blackbeard

The most famous pirate of all was nicknamed Blackbeard. He attacked ships on the American coast until he was finally killed in a battle with the British Navy in 1718.

Plants

Plants are living things that make their own food using energy from the sun. Most plants stay in one place, with roots that fix them in the ground.

SEE ALSO
▸ Flowers p.103
▸ Food p.106
▸ Fruit and seeds p.115
▸ Insects p.134
▸ Photosynthesis p.191
▸ Trees p.261

Types of plants

There are four main groups of plants. Some have flowers, like hibiscus. Others don't, such as conifers and mosses.

Conifer
Plants that have seeds in cones are called conifers. They are mainly trees.

Moss
These leafy plants grow where it is damp and dark.

Fern
Ferns don't have flowers. Their leaves start off very small and uncurl as they grow.

Flowers produce seeds, which grow into new plants.

Before a flower opens, it is called a bud.

Leaves make the food that keeps plants alive and helps them grow.

Flowering plant
Most plants have flowers, which make seeds.

The stem helps keep the plant upright. It also transports water and minerals to the leaves.

Plants are **the only living things** that live on **every continent**.

Meat-eating plants

Some plants get extra energy by catching and eating animals, such as insects. Some even catch frogs! The plant shown here is called a Venus flytrap.

The insect's weight makes the trap shut.

The plant squeezes all the juices out of the insect.

Sweet nectar lures the insect into the plant.

Roots anchor the plant in the soil.

Tiny hairs on the plant's roots take in minerals and water from the soil.

Hibiscus plant

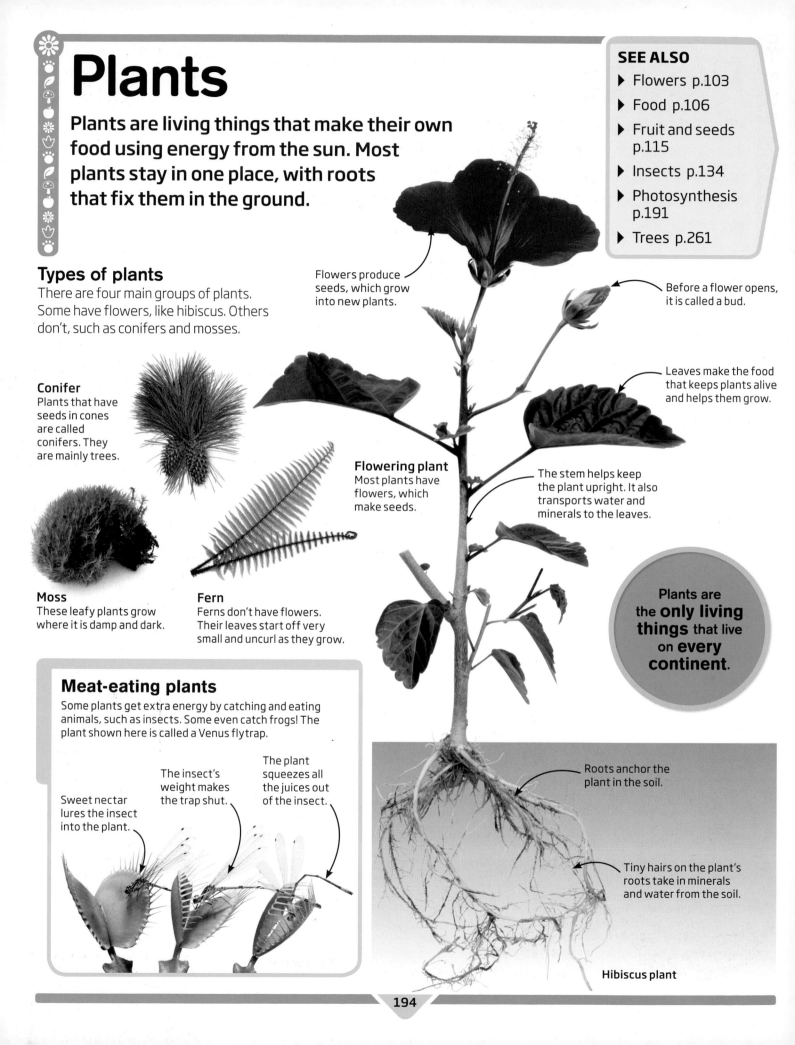

Plastic

Plastic is a useful material that we make, but it can also be found naturally. It can be colored and molded into shapes without breaking. It is waterproof, so it can be used for packaging and to carry liquid. It's also strong enough to make rope.

SEE ALSO
▶ Atoms p.34
▶ Carbon cycle p.49
▶ Electricity p.87
▶ Gases p.117
▶ Liquids p.148
▶ Materials p.157
▶ Recycling p.205

Plastic everywhere

We use plastic to make many everyday objects, including toys, glue, cars, bags, computers, tents, and clothes like fleeces and raincoats. For most items, the plastic is heated to become liquid, then poured into molds to set.

Plastic containers are waterproof to carry liquids.

Liquid plastic can be poured into interesting molds.

Plastic can be see-through, so we know what's inside.

Tough and hard-to-break plastic is useful in toys.

Smooth plastic is used for things we need to hold on to.

Plastic rope is flexible and strong.

Plastic lenses in glasses are harder to break than glass.

Useful plastic

Plastic is a useful material because of how it behaves. For example, it doesn't let electricity through, and is strong and long-lasting.

Electric cable

Insulation
Plastic is an insulator, which means electricity and heat can't flow through it. It keeps electricity inside cables.

Laboratory containers

Hard to break
Plastic containers are harder to break than glass or pottery ones. They are also easier to make and safer to use.

Plastic bags

Long-lasting
Plastic lasts a long time. It can build up in the environment, so we turn it into new plastic by recycling it.

25 plastic bottles can be recycled to make one polyester fleece.

Making plastic

Natural plastic is found in plants, trees, insects, animal horns, and milk. Artificial plastic is made from oil, coal, and natural gas found underground. All plastic contains an element called carbon.

Plastic pellets

Pluto

Pluto is a dwarf planet that travels around the sun at the edge of our solar system, beyond Neptune. It has one giant moon called Charon, and four small moons.

SEE ALSO

▶ Earth's surface p.84

▶ Glaciers p.122

▶ Moon p.171

▶ Neptune p.183

▶ Solar system p.233

▶ Volcanoes p.268

Pluto's surface is covered with ice.

Ex-planet
Pluto used to be considered the ninth planet in our solar system. When other similar small "planets" were discovered, astronomers downgraded Pluto to a dwarf planet.

Ice volcanoes
Pluto may have cryovolcanoes—volcanoes that erupt an icy slush of water and gases.

A feature known as Wright Mons is thought to be a cryovolcano.

Pluto's orbit
Pluto travels around the sun at a different angle to the planets. Its orbit is shaped like an elongated circle. It takes Pluto 248 Earth years to circle the sun.

Pluto

Pluto's orbit

Dwarf planets
Dwarf planets are similar to planets but smaller, which means they share their path around the sun with other objects, such as asteroids and comets.

Ceres   Makemake   Huamea   Pluto   Eris   Moon

Polar habitats

Polar habitats are snow- or ice-covered areas found in the coldest places on Earth—the Arctic in the north and Antarctic in the south. There are no trees and only very few plants. Animals have to survive in freezing temperatures.

SEE ALSO

▶ Animal groups p.22

▶ Antarctica p.24

▶ Arctic p.25

▶ Earth p.83

▶ Habitats p.126

▶ Oceans and seas p.187

Arctic

Around the North Pole at the top of the world is the frozen Arctic Ocean. The Arctic also includes the northern tips of Canada, Russia, Greenland, and Norway.

Antarctic

Around the South Pole at the bottom of the world is the large landmass, or continent, of Antarctica. The Antarctic is the coldest and windiest place on Earth. It has no large land animals.

Arctic skuas often chase other birds to steal their food.

Snowy owls have thick feathers to keep them warm.

Reindeer walk long distances in search of food.

Polar bears have thick fur coats to keep them warm.

Animals use pieces of floating ice to take a rest.

Walruses use their tusks for fighting and pulling themselves onto the ice.

Male narwhals have a long tooth. Narwhals eat squid and large fish.

Arctic Ocean
In the center of the Arctic Ocean is a gigantic piece of ice that never melts. The icy water around it is full of fish and squid.

Wandering albatrosses have the widest wingspan of all birds.

Emperor penguins huddle together for warmth in the winter.

Chinstrap penguins live in large groups, called colonies.

An iceberg is a chunk of floating ice. Most of it is underwater.

Southern elephant seals catch krill, fish, and squid in the cold ocean.

Weddell seals have thick layers of fat to keep them warm in the cold water.

Southern minke whales use their beak to make holes in the ice for breathing air.

Southern Ocean
Around Antarctica, the Southern Ocean is very cold. Huge chunks of ice, called icebergs, float in the water.

Pollution

Pollution happens when dirty or harmful substances are released into the world around us. Pollution kills wildlife, causes health problems for humans, spoils the countryside, and makes the world around us dirty. It is even making our planet warmer.

SEE ALSO

▶ Cars p.52

▶ Climate change p.60

▶ Factories p.97

▶ Farming p.98

▶ Industrial Revolution p.133

▶ Recycling p.205

Air pollution
Cars, trucks, factories, and power stations pump out gases into the air. These can cause illness, poison rivers and oceans, and heat up our world.

Land pollution
Poisons from garbage dumps seep into the ground and then into rivers. Chemicals used in farming kill insects, such as bees, and can make people ill.

Water pollution
Plastic garbage is washed into the sea and swallowed by sea life. Harmful waste from factories and sewage from homes pollute rivers and sea water.

Garbage at sea

When waste plastic is dumped in the sea, it is carried away by currents into gigantic, floating garbage patches. The biggest patch is in the North Pacific Ocean. It is called the Great Pacific garbage patch and is bigger than the US.

Great Pacific garbage patch

Precious metals

Precious metals are rare and worth a lot of money. They are found in the ground as pure metal or combined with other elements in rocks. Silver and gold are the best known and have been treasured for thousands of years. Other precious metals include platinum and beryllium.

SEE ALSO
▶ Aircraft p.13
▶ Elements p.90
▶ Metals p.162
▶ Money p.169
▶ Gold pp.200–201
▶ Rocks and minerals p.214

Gold

Pure gold is a very soft metal. To make it harder–so that we can make useful objects out of it–we combine gold with small amounts of other metals.

A mobile phone contains just a tiny amount of gold–about 0.001 oz (0.025 g).

Gold earrings

The highest quality flutes are made of solid silver.

This ancient Egyptian burial mask is covered in gold foil.

Cutlery

Silver

This precious metal, along with gold and mercury, has been used by humans since prehistoric times.

Silver is used in many of today's batteries.

DVD

The most valuable coins have always been made of gold.

Mirror

Platinum bar

Pieces of jewelry are often made from platinum.

Catalytic converters in cars contain platinum. It makes exhaust fumes less poisonous.

Platinum

Just a few hundred tons of platinum are produced each year. Because it is so rare, it is used in very small amounts.

Platinum is used in pacemakers. These devices can keep a person's heart beating.

Watch

Beryllium

Beryllium is a steel-gray precious metal. It is a vital component of computers, cars, aircraft, phones, medical equipment, and many other hi-tech gadgets.

Fighter aircraft

The **story** of...

Gold

Gold is a precious metal that has been used to make jewelry and decorations since ancient times. It is rare and very expensive. But that's just the start of its story. Gold has a glittering history and is still popular all over the world.

Meteor shower
When Earth first formed, gold and other metals sank deep into the core. Other gold, found near the surface of our planet, arrived later from space. Asteroids rained down in a powerful storm, bringing gold with them.

This gold mask is thought to show the Greek hero Agamemnon.

Digging for gold
In the past, a single nugget could change the life of a gold-digger. When gold was found in the US in the 1800s, it started a "gold rush." Thousands of people, known as prospectors, traveled to the US hoping to find gold and become rich.

Gold nugget

Large gold mines have created huge holes deep into the ground.

25
percent of all the world's gold is stored in a New York City vault.

Gold mine
Pieces of gold found loose on the Earth's surface can be picked up by hand. Bigger quantities deep underground must be dug out in a process called mining. Modern mines use heavy machines to dig chunks of rock that contain traces of gold.

Centuries of sparkle
Gold was the first metal to be discovered and used by humans. It is beautiful and shiny, as well as soft and bendy. This makes it ideal for shaping into jewelry, including delicate rings, bracelets, and necklaces.

Golden money

The first gold coins were made by King Croesus in 564 BCE. All coins used to be made of precious metals, including gold and silver. However, modern coins are usually made of cheaper metals, such as copper, nickel, and zinc.

Sacred manuscripts were decorated with gold leaf.

Gold leaf

For centuries, gold has been used to decorate religious buildings, works of art, and objects. As well as using the solid metal, gold can be thinned down into very fine sheets called gold leaf. Gold leaf is used to decorate books and paintings.

A model of the spacecraft used in the 1969 moon landing.

Golden craft

Space scientists use sheets of gold foil to cover parts of some spacecraft and satellites they send into space. The foil protects them by reflecting the sun's harmful rays during their journey.

The mask was discovered by archaeologists in a burial tomb in 1876.

Prehistoric life

Earth has changed a lot over many millions of years. It has not always been home to plants, animals, and people. Many early living things no longer exist, so we only know about them from their remains. The distant past is known as "prehistory."

SEE ALSO
▶ Dinosaurs p.80
▶ Early humans p.82
▶ Earth p.83
▶ Fossils p.111
▶ Habitats p.126
▶ Oceans and seas p.187

Ammonites were animals with shells that lived in water.

Oceans
The first life was in the oceans. There were underwater plants and early animals.

Forests
As Earth warmed up, plants grew on land and forests provided food for different types of animals.

Dinosaurs were the main land animal in prehistoric forests.

Ice ages
In times when the Earth cooled down, most of it was covered in ice. Animals had to adapt to survive.

Woolly mammoths had thick fur coats to help them keep warm in the ice ages.

Stone Age
After the last ice age, Earth warmed up to how it is today. A great variety of plants and animals live in many different habitats, such as deserts, forests, and polar regions.

Early humans invented ways to hunt and gather food, and survive longer.

Radio

Radios pick up signals and turn them into sounds we can hear. They do this by using invisible waves that carry sound information. Thousands of different radio stations play music, news, and drama to listeners all over the world.

SEE ALSO
▶ Atmosphere p.33
▶ Books p.44
▶ Communication p.69
▶ Hearing p.127
▶ Navigation p.182
▶ Television p.251

How radio works
Radio towers turn sounds into radio waves. Radios pick up these waves and turn them back into sounds that you can hear.

1. Radio tower
Radio towers have antennas on the top of them. These antennas send out radio waves.

2. Radio waves
Invisible radio waves carry sounds from radio towers to radios in the home.

3. Radio antenna
An antenna is a thin metal rod that picks up radio waves.

Radio waves travel at the **speed of light**–about 186,000 miles (300,000 km) a second!

4. Speaker
The radio's speaker plays the waves as sounds.

Radio towers are tall to make sure that radio waves can travel over buildings.

Digital radio
Instead of radio waves, digital radio uses digital signals that don't get broken up like radio waves do. This means they sound better.

Remote control
Wireless gadgets use radio waves to contact each other. For example, a remote control can tell a toy car how to move around.

Controller

Remote control toy car

Rain forests

Rain forests are forests with tall trees and lots of rain. Tropical rain forests are hot places. They are home to nearly half of all animals and plants in the world. The trees are so thick with leaves that very little sunlight reaches the forest floor.

SEE ALSO
▶ Birds p.39
▶ Forests p.109
▶ Habitats p.126
▶ Materials p.157
▶ Plants p.194
▶ Trees p.261
▶ Weather p.271

Amazon rain forest
The world's largest rain forest is the Amazon in South America. This rain forest surrounds the Amazon River. Its trees and plants provide food and shelter for many animals.

This large blue Morpho butterfly is brown on the other side of its wings, so it can hide when resting.

Canopy layer
This is a thick layer of leaves and branches. Most rain forest animals live here.

Emerald tree boas squeeze animals to death before eating them whole.

Understory
Shrubs and new trees grow in this hot, dark layer of the rain forest.

Forest floor
This dark, damp layer is covered in dead leaves that have fallen from above.

This harpy eagle hunts for animals in the treetops.

The leaves of bromeliads catch water that small animals come to drink.

Jaguars hunt other animals and climb trees to rest and eat.

Toco toucans use their long beaks to reach fruit to eat.

A praying mantis waits for other insects to come close, then grabs and eats them.

Capybaras are good swimmers and eat water plants.

This many-legged centipede can kill bigger frogs, spiders, and snakes.

Emergent layer
Only the tallest trees reach this top layer of the rain forest.

Howler monkeys get together and howl each morning.

Some trees have giant buttress roots that help them soak up water quickly.

The bright red leaves surrounding the flowers of the heliconia stricta look like lobster claws.

This long-tongued giant anteater can eat 30,000 ants a day.

Recycling

Recycling means reusing garbage or making it into new things rather than burning it or burying it in the ground. Everything from paper, glass, metal, and plastic to phones and computers can be recycled. The more we recycle our waste, the less we damage our planet.

SEE ALSO

▸ Changing world pp.50-51
▸ Climate change p.60
▸ Computers p.71
▸ Metals p.162
▸ Plastic p.195
▸ Pollution p.198

Paper and cardboard
Old paper and cardboard can be mashed up in water, then rolled flat and dried to make new paper products.

Food waste
Leftover food can be fed to animals, such as pigs or chickens, or used to make compost to help plants grow.

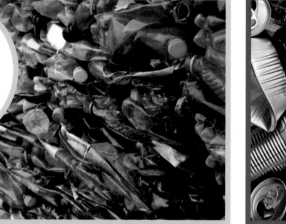

Plastic
Most of the plastic we throw away can be chopped up, melted down, and re-formed into new items.

Metal
Cans can be melted down. They are either remade into more cans or used to make other metal goods.

Glass
Bottles and jars made of glass can be cleaned and used again or melted down to make new glass objects.

Electronics
Devices such as phones and laptops can be repaired or have their valuable metal parts taken out to be reused.

The **story** of...

Festivals

Festivals are celebrated across the world. Some festivals, like Eid or Christmas, mark important religious events. Others, like the Chinese New Year, mark the passing of time. Festivals are often a time of joy. People might put up lights, dance, or give each other presents.

Christmas

Every year at Christmas, Christians celebrate the birth of Jesus Christ. Some go to church and sing carols or special songs about the event. Most people give presents to each other and have a large meal with special food. Many people spend Christmas with friends and family.

Christmas trees are often finished with a star or angel on top.

Presents are placed below a decorated Christmas tree.

The "Elegant Skull" is a symbol of the Day of the Dead.

Day of the Dead

In Mexico, people celebrate the Day of the Dead for three days at the start of November. This ancient festival is held to remember friends and family who have died. People build shrines to the dead and bring gifts of food and drink to their graves.

Elegant Skull statue

A Chinese Dragon puppet that is used in festival celebrations.

Chinese New Year

Celebrations for the Chinese New Year last for 15 days. Families clean their houses to sweep away bad luck, decorate their windows and doors with red paper shapes, and enjoy a big feast together. Some people throw firecrackers to make a big noise, and dragons dance in the streets.

Muslims say the special Eid prayer outside a mosque.

Eid

Muslims celebrate the Eid al-Fitr holiday at the end of Ramadan. During Ramadan, they fast, or go without food during the day. At Eid, Muslims give money to charity, pray together, visit friends and family, and enjoy a feast.

At **New Year,** Chinese parents give their children **money in red packets**.

Passover

Jewish people celebrate Passover to remember the escape of the Jews from slavery in Egypt. The festival lasts for seven or eight days and is marked with the special *seder,* or meal, which includes matzo—a flat, or unleavened, bread that hasn't been given time to rise.

Passover is one of the most important Jewish festivals, and is more than

3,000

years old.

Dancers control the colorful dragons using long sticks.

The special food on the plate tells the story of the Jews' escape from slavery.

Fireworks light up the sky at Diwali, the festival of lights.

Diwali

The Hindu festival of Diwali takes place every fall in the north of the world and every spring in the south. It celebrates the victory of light over darkness and good over evil. People light up their homes and public places and set off fireworks.

Religion

A religion is a set of beliefs. Religions often try to explain the world, such as how it came to exist. Religion is an important part of many people's lives. They agree with their religion's teachings, and try to behave by its rules, for example, about how to treat other people. Many religions have central figures that are prayed to, called gods.

SEE ALSO
▶ Ancient India p.19
▶ Dance p.76
▶ Festivals pp.206–207
▶ Turkish Empire p.262
▶ World p.275

Buddhism
Buddhists follow the teaching of Buddha, who lived in India in the fifth century BCE. They meditate, which involves thinking deeply. They believe that they will be reborn after death.

Buddha statue

Special candlestick called a Menorah

Judaism
Judaism dates back 4,000 years. Jews believe in one God who created the world. They trace their history back to the Hebrew people of what is now Israel.

Sikhism
Sikhs follow the teachings of Guru Granth Sahib. They believe that all people are equally important. Sikhs pray in grand buildings called Gurdwaras.

Gurdwara

World religions
More than 75 percent of believers follow Buddhism, Islam, Christianity, or Hinduism. Judaism and Sikhism also have worldwide followings. There are many other religions, but fewer people follow them.

Islam
The followers of Islam are called Muslims. They believe that the Quran, their holy book, is God's word told through his messenger Muhammad, whose teachings they follow.

Mosque

The Hindu god Shiva

Hinduism
Hinduism began in India more than 2,500 years ago. Hindus pray to many gods and believe that life is a circle of birth, death, and rebirth.

Jesus on the cross

Christianity
Christians have one God. They believe that their God's son Jesus lived on Earth 2,000 years ago. He died nailed to a cross so that Christians could have life after death.

Renaissance

Italy experienced great change in science and art between 1400 and 1600. This movement then spread across Europe. It was called the "Renaissance," which means "rebirth," because it looked at ideas that originally came from ancient Rome and Greece.

SEE ALSO
▶ Aircraft p.13
▶ Ancient Rome p.20
▶ Art p.28
▶ Inventions pp.136–137
▶ Religion p.208
▶ Writing p.280

Buildings

Renaissance builders copied ancient styles to produce larger, more elegant buildings. These buildings often had columns and domes.

The great dome of the cathedral in Florence was built in 1436.

Science

Scientists began to carry out experiments for the first time. They made important discoveries about space, science, and medicine.

This flying machine was designed by Leonardo da Vinci. It never actually flew.

Art

Renaissance artists used a more realistic style than previous artists. They tried to show light and shade and came up with new types of paint and materials.

This painting, by Pietro Perugino, shows Jesus giving the keys of Heaven to St. Peter.

The people at the front of the painting appear larger than those farther away. This is called perspective.

Reptiles

Reptiles are scaly-skinned, cold-blooded animals. Most reptiles lay soft, leathery eggs. A baby reptile grows inside the egg and then, when it's ready, breaks its way out. There are four main groups of reptile.

SEE ALSO
▸ Amphibians p.15
▸ Antarctica p.24
▸ Deserts p.78
▸ Dinosaurs p.80
▸ Eggs p.86
▸ Evolution p.95
▸ Sun p.247

All reptiles have scaly skin.

Some lizards can move their eyes to look in two directions at once.

Lizards

These reptiles have many skills. This chameleon can change the color of its skin. Other reptiles can run up walls, or break off their tails to escape danger.

Tortoises have hard shells.

Crocodiles and alligators

These giant reptiles have existed since before dinosaurs. They hide under water, then spring up to catch their prey and drag it under.

Crocodiles and alligators have strong jaws.

Tortoises and turtles

Turtles live in water and tortoises live on the land. Their shells protect them, but are heavy, so they move very slowly out of the water.

Reptiles live on **every continent** except Antarctica.

Basking

Reptiles are cold-blooded animals. They get the heat their bodies need from the world around them, lying in the sunshine to warm up. They hide in the shade to keep themselves from overheating.

Snakes

All snakes swallow their prey whole. They smell using their tongues. Some snakes have poisonous bites, but most are not dangerous to people.

Rivers

Starting as tiny streams, rivers flow from mountaintops down to the ocean. They provide a home to lots of wildlife. People transport things along rivers, grow crops next to them, and even use rivers for spare-time activities, such as sailing and fishing.

SEE ALSO
▶ Farming p.98
▶ Water pp.120–121
▶ Glaciers p.122
▶ Lakes p.143
▶ Water cycle p.270
▶ Weather p.271

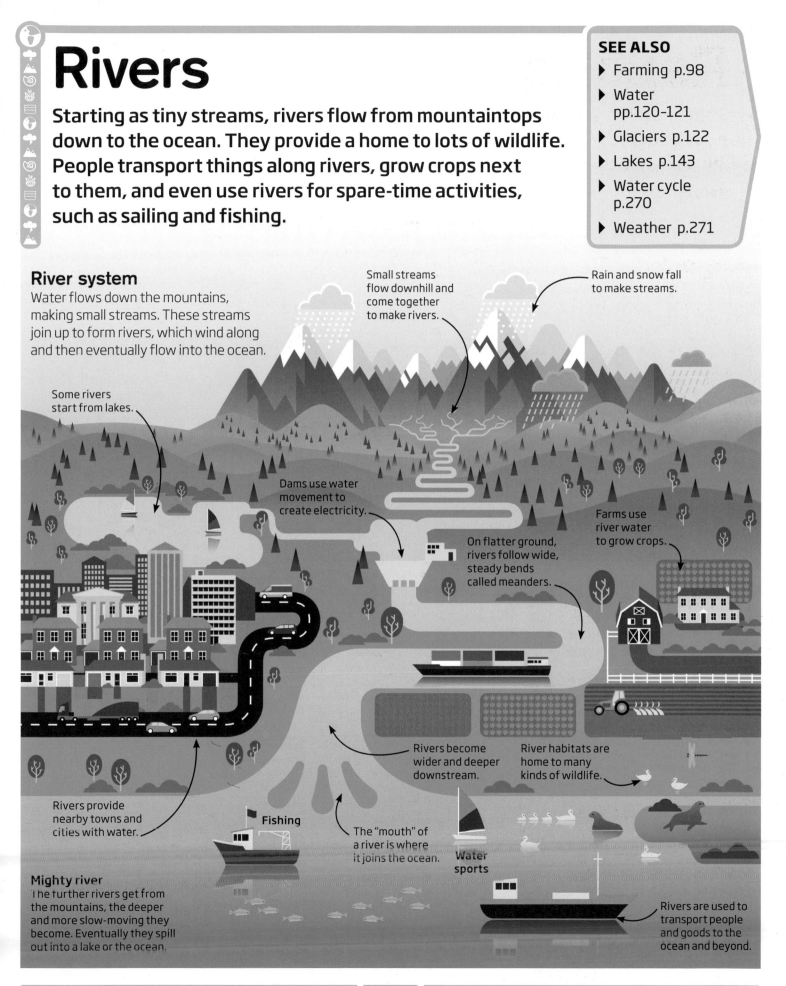

River system

Water flows down the mountains, making small streams. These streams join up to form rivers, which wind along and then eventually flow into the ocean.

Small streams flow downhill and come together to make rivers.

Rain and snow fall to make streams.

Some rivers start from lakes.

Dams use water movement to create electricity.

On flatter ground, rivers follow wide, steady bends called meanders.

Farms use river water to grow crops.

Rivers provide nearby towns and cities with water.

Fishing

Rivers become wider and deeper downstream.

River habitats are home to many kinds of wildlife.

The "mouth" of a river is where it joins the ocean.

Water sports

Mighty river

The further rivers get from the mountains, the deeper and more slow-moving they become. Eventually they spill out into a lake or the ocean.

Rivers are used to transport people and goods to the ocean and beyond.

Robots

Robots are computer-controlled machines that do jobs for us. They can be used in many ways, such as helping doctors, building things, and doing jobs that would be too dangerous for people to do.

SEE ALSO
▶ Computers p.71
▶ Factories p.97
▶ Machines p.150
▶ Medicine p.160
▶ Space travel p.237

Types of robot

Robots are carefully designed to do their jobs. Each type of robot has its own unique look.

Eye sensors allow the robot to "see."

Each "finger" has a different function.

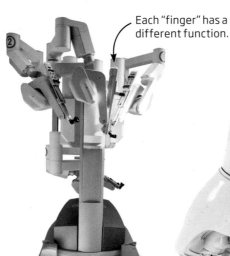

Medical robot
Robots are capable of performing very delicate movements. They can help doctors operate on their patients.

Humanoid robot
Some robots are designed to look a bit like people. This robot is called NAO. It can dance and speak.

Robots can see and feel, but not like humans. Their **sensors use code** to interpret feedback.

Hand sensors allow NAO to "feel" objects.

Robots in space

NASA uses robots to perform dangerous tasks in outer space. This robot mends things on the International Space Station.

Foot sensors are used for walking, climbing stairs, and detecting obstacles.

Factory robot
Robots are strong, and are good at doing the same thing over and over again. This makes them useful in factories.

Motors allow the robot to move up and down.

Rock cycle

Rock may be very hard, but it does not last forever. It is constantly being worn away by wind, water, and ice. At the same time, new rock is being made at the bottom of the sea and by volcanoes. This is called the rock cycle.

Recycled rocks

Tiny pieces of volcanic rock are washed into the sea and settle on the sea bed. They become buried by new layers of rock particles that get squashed together to form new rock. As this new rock is buried deeper, it gets hotter and melts to form magma. Magma rises and cools to form new volcanic rock.

Breaking down
Volcanic rock is broken up by wind, rain, and ice. Tiny particles of the broken rock are washed into the ocean by rain.

Settling
Pieces of volcanic rock settle on the sea bed. They are buried and squashed to make a type of rock called sedimentary rock.

Cooling
Magma erupts from volcanoes. It cools and hardens to form a type of rock called volcanic, or igneous, rock.

Changing
If sedimentary rock is buried deep enough, it is changed by heat and the weight of the rock above it into metamorphic rock.

Melting
Deep in the Earth, where it is extremely hot, rock melts to form magma. In some places, magma rises to the Earth's surface, forming volcanoes.

Heated and squashed

Any rock can be changed into metamorphic rock by the heat and the weight of the rock above it. Slate, which is used to make roof tiles, is a common metamorphic rock.

Lots of layers

Most rocks being formed today are sedimentary rocks. They are made from tiny pieces of older rocks that build up on the sea bed in layers. Sandstone is a common sedimentary rock.

Rocks and minerals

The Earth's surface is made up of hard natural objects called rocks. Rocks are made up of a mixture of substances called minerals. There are many different kinds of rocks and minerals.

SEE ALSO
- Earth's surface p.84
- Elements p.90
- Gemstones p.118
- Metals p.162
- Rock cycle p.213
- Volcanoes p.268

Rocks

Types of rock have different names depending on how they were formed. The three types are called sedimentary, igneous, and metamorphic.

Metamorphic rock
Under great heat and pressure, metamorphic rock is formed deep inside the Earth.

Sedimentary rock
When particles of minerals settle and are squashed together, they slowly become sedimentary rock.

Igneous rock
This type of rock is formed when melted rock cools down and becomes solid.

Minerals

A mineral is a naturally occurring solid. It is made from chemical elements—simple substances that cannot be broken down further. Minerals grow together to form rocks.

There are nearly **4,000** different types of **minerals** on Earth.

Glowing rocks

Some rocks look plain in daylight, but their minerals change color under special "ultraviolet" light. The glowing minerals in this rock are called calcite and willemite.

Serpentine   Amethyst   Garnet   Opal

214

Satellites

Satellites are objects that go around, or orbit, something bigger. There are more than 2,000 artificial satellites orbiting the Earth. They are used for a variety of different jobs. Some track the weather while others let us communicate with each other.

GPS satellite
The global positioning system (GPS) gives us our exact position on the Earth. The system uses more than 20 satellites, working together to pinpoint your location.

Local satellites
Some types of satellite stay over the same area as they orbit the Earth. These are called geostationary satellites. To cover the whole Earth, many satellites are needed.

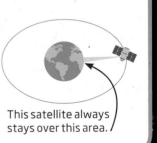

This satellite always stays over this area.

Solar panels collect the sun's rays to power the satellite

Photos of the Earth are sent to weather stations.

When this flap is open, the telescope takes photos.

Communication satellite
These satellites pick up signals and send them to other places in the world. They are used for phone calls and live video communications.

Weather satellite
These satellites take pictures of the clouds and measure land and sea temperatures. This information helps us to study and forecast the weather.

Hubble space telescope
This satellite points away from the Earth and takes detailed images of the universe. It lets us see farther into space than we could from the Earth.

Saturn

Saturn is the second largest planet in the solar system after Jupiter and the sixth farthest planet from the sun. It is a "gas giant," mainly made of hydrogen and helium, and is best known for its rings.

SEE ALSO
▶ Astronomy p.32
▶ Atmosphere p.33
▶ Jupiter p.141
▶ Moon p.171
▶ Exploration pp.180–181
▶ Solar system p.233

Ringed planet

Saturn is surrounded by huge rings that stretch over a vast distance. However, they are only a few hundred feet thick.

Saturn

Icy rings
Saturn's rings are made of chunks of ice, rocks, and dust.

Gaps between rings

The gaps between the rings are areas with less ice and dust.

Moons of Saturn

Like Jupiter, Saturn has more than 60 moons. Titan, the largest moon, has lakes of liquid methane and a thick atmosphere. Enceladus, Saturn's sixth largest moon, shoots out water from its south pole.

The unmanned spacecraft Cassini

Titan

Cassini-Huygens

The Cassini spacecraft explored Saturn between 2004 and 2017. A probe called Huygens, carried by Cassini, landed on the surface of Saturn's moon Titan in 2005.

Huygens probe

Science

Science is the search for truth and knowledge. It's about understanding the world and learning how and why things work the way they do. Science includes doing experiments to test predictions and collect evidence. We divide science into three main areas: chemistry, biology, and physics.

SEE ALSO
▶ Astronomy p.32
▶ Biology p.38
▶ Chemistry p.58
▶ Medicine p.160
▶ Physics p.192
▶ The sciences pp.218-219

Biology
The study of living things and their surroundings is called biology. It includes the human body, plants, and animals.

Chemistry
Looking at what things are made of is known as chemistry. This includes the tiny building blocks of all materials, called atoms.

Physics
Physics studies light, sound, forces, waves, magnets, electricity, energy, and the planets.

Scientists
Scientists are people who investigate the world to answer questions and find solutions to problems. They do experiments to see if ideas are right or wrong, and they share information.

Inventions
Studying science helps us to create new things. For example, if we understand movement, we can design better cars. If we understand the body, we can invent medicines to help fight off sickness.

Copy of Edison's light bulb

Thomas Edison invented the electric light bulb in 1879, while studying electricity.

Science isn't just facts in a book— it's a whole way of **thinking** and **discovering.**

The sciences

For thousands of years, people have been observing the world around them and coming up with ideas to explain why things behave the way they do. Science is about answering questions with ideas, evidence, and experience.

Notches around the edge were lined up with objects in the sky.

Child making a wave in a bottle

Some of the earliest doctors were ancient Egyptian women,

5,000

years ago.

Curing diseases

In 1928, Scottish scientist Alexander Fleming noticed how a mold called penicillin killed bacteria. This discovery led to a type of medicine called antibiotics. They have been killing germs in the human body ever since.

1. Bacteria growing

2. Penicillin introduced

3. Bacteria dies

Experiments

In ancient Greece, a man called Aristotle said that people should look at nature and carry out experiments to find answers to their questions. Scientist do experiments to test their ideas and to make new discoveries.

Renaissance

Starting in the 15th century, the Renaissance was an explosion of ideas that transformed science and art in Europe. Leading experiments, gathering evidence, and sharing ideas became popular—this led to new inventions and discoveries.

Compasses helped explorers to travel the world and discover new ideas.

Early compass

Accidental inventions

Many great scientific discoveries have been made by accident. For example, German scientist Wilhelm Conrad Röntgen accidentally discovered X-rays in 1885. He was sending electricity through tubes of gas when he noticed that he could see what was inside a nearby box. He then used this finding to take pictures of the bones inside his wife.

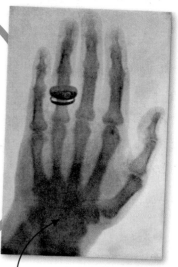

Early X-ray

X-rays pass through skin and flesh but bounce back off bones.

Nebra Sky Disk

The night sky

One of the earliest sciences was studying the movements of the moon, planets, and stars. This is now called astronomy. Moon calendars were first made about 10,000 years ago. Around 4,000 years ago, the Nebra Sky Disk was used to track seasons and the sun's position.

Scientific drawings

Many scientists create beautiful, precise drawings to record their findings. Mary Anning was a famous British fossil hunter who lived in the 1800s. Mary found her first fossils as a child and made drawings of them. Her discoveries helped scientists to understand how life existed in the oceans millions of years ago.

Renaissance artist and scientist **Leonardo da Vinci** sketched pictures of **humans and animals** he had cut up.

The Plesiosaurus's paddles have bones that are also present in legs and feet.

Plesiosaurus drawn by Mary Anning in 1824

Seashore

The area where land meets the sea or ocean is called the seashore. It may be sand, mud, or rock. Animals and plants that live here have to be able to survive crashing waves and the water level changing twice a day.

Shore zones

The seashore has different zones, which are divided by the distance they are from the ocean. Animals in the low tide zone are mostly in the water all the time, while those in the high tide zone have to survive in air when the tide is out.

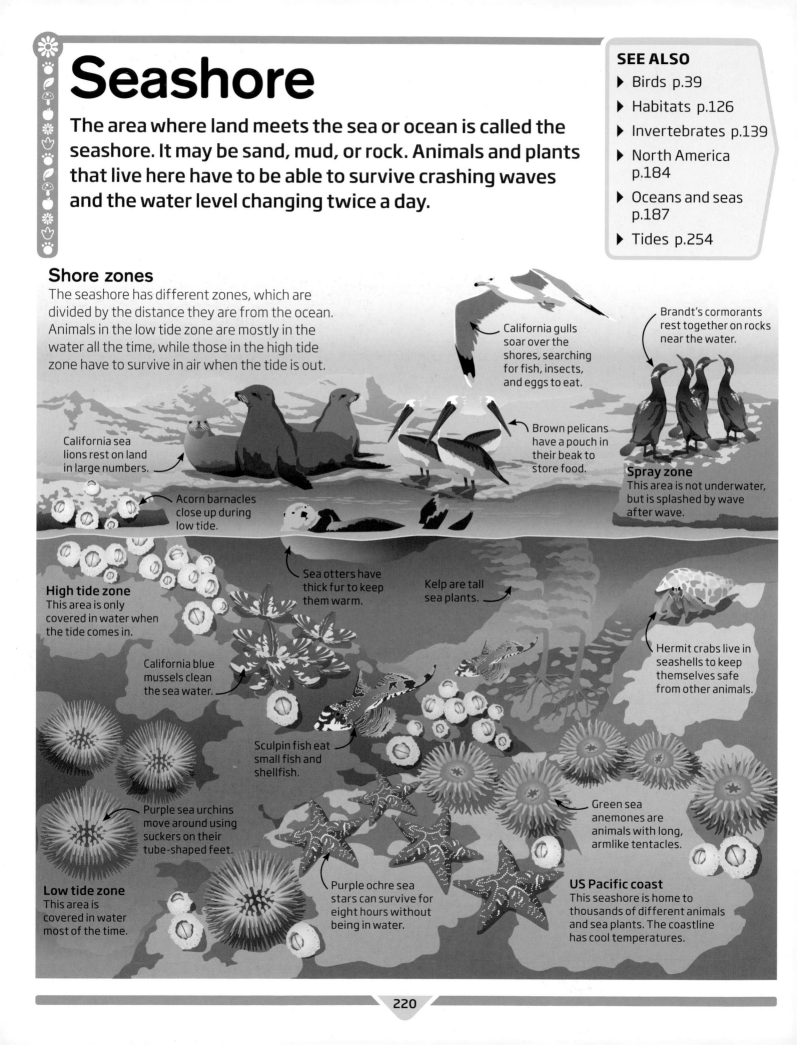

California gulls soar over the shores, searching for fish, insects, and eggs to eat.

Brandt's cormorants rest together on rocks near the water.

California sea lions rest on land in large numbers.

Brown pelicans have a pouch in their beak to store food.

Acorn barnacles close up during low tide.

Spray zone
This area is not underwater, but is splashed by wave after wave.

Sea otters have thick fur to keep them warm.

Kelp are tall sea plants.

Hermit crabs live in seashells to keep themselves safe from other animals.

High tide zone
This area is only covered in water when the tide comes in.

California blue mussels clean the sea water.

Sculpin fish eat small fish and shellfish.

Purple sea urchins move around using suckers on their tube-shaped feet.

Green sea anemones are animals with long, armlike tentacles.

Low tide zone
This area is covered in water most of the time.

Purple ochre sea stars can survive for eight hours without being in water.

US Pacific coast
This seashore is home to thousands of different animals and sea plants. The coastline has cool temperatures.

Seasons

In many parts of the world, the year has four seasons. These seasons are winter, spring, summer, and autumn. The lives of plants and animals, the weather, and the hours of daylight all change from one season to the next. In some hot parts of the world, there are just two seasons.

SEE ALSO
▶ Climate change p.60
▶ Day and night p.77
▶ Hibernation p.129
▶ Solar system p.233
▶ Trees p.261
▶ Weather p.271

Changing seasons

In the cold winter, plants stop growing. In spring, they begin to grow again and baby animals are born. Summer sees the hottest weather, and then in autumn leaves change color and fall off the trees.

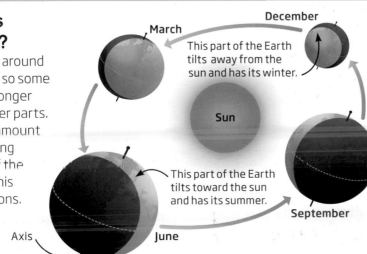

| Winter | Spring | Summer | Autumn |

What causes the seasons?

The Earth travels around the sun. It is tilted so some parts of it get stronger sunlight than other parts. As it moves, the amount of sunlight reaching different parts of the Earth changes. This gives us our seasons.

December

March

This part of the Earth tilts away from the sun and has its winter.

Sun

This part of the Earth tilts toward the sun and has its summer.

September

June

Axis

Monsoons

Tropical parts of the Earth are warm all year round. There are often just two seasons—a dry season and a rainy season, called a monsoon.

221

Shapes

Shapes are areas with different outlines. In math, there are two types of shape. Two-dimensional shapes have length and width, while three-dimensional shapes have length, width, and height. Shapes can be made of straight or curved lines, or a mixture such as in a semicircle.

What makes a shape?

A shape is named depending on the number of sides and angles it has. Regular shapes have sides that are all the same length.

Angle
An angle is the place where two lines meet.

Point
A point is a place on a shape. It is shown with a dot.

Edge
The side of a shape is called an edge.

Line
A straight line is the shortest distance between two points.

Triangles have three sides and three inside angles adding up to 180°.

Circles have one long, round side.

Squares have four equal sides and four right angles.

Angles

Angles are measured in degrees (°) out of 360. Angles have different names depending on how big they are.

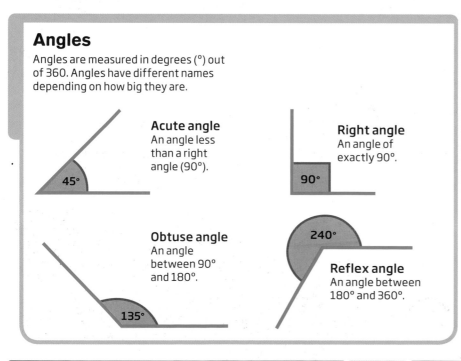

Acute angle
An angle less than a right angle (90°).

45°

Right angle
An angle of exactly 90°.

90°

Obtuse angle
An angle between 90° and 180°.

135°

240°

Reflex angle
An angle between 180° and 360°.

Polygons

"Polygon" is the name for any flat, two-dimensional shape.

Pentagons have five equal sides and five inside angles.

Sharks

Sharks are a type of fish. Almost all of them eat meat. They are found in every ocean and some rivers. There are more than 400 types of sharks. Most are active during the day, but some hunt at night.

SEE ALSO

▸ Conservation p.72

▸ Fish p.101

▸ Food chains p.107

▸ Oceans and seas p.187

▸ Prehistoric life p.202

Sharks have good eyesight even when there isn't much light.

Great white shark

This shark eats other animals. It mainly hunts and feeds on fish, but also eats turtles, dolphins, and seals.

Sharks have been around for more than **400 million years!**

The front fins can be used to slow down the shark.

The tail moves from side to side to power the shark forward.

The pointed nose is used to sniff for food.

The sharp, pointed teeth are perfect for ripping food.

The back fins stop the shark from rolling over.

Whale shark

This is the largest fish in the world. It can travel thousands of miles every year.

Each whale shark has its own pattern of spots.

Hammerhead shark

Hammerhead sharks use their wide heads to pin down stingrays on the ocean floor.

The eyes are a long way apart, letting the shark see far to spot its prey.

Sharks under threat

The number of sharks is getting smaller because they are hunted for their fins, teeth, and fish oil. Scientists try to learn about sharks, so that they can help them.

Ships

Sea transportation comes in all shapes and sizes, from tiny sailing boats to large cruise liners and gigantic container ships. They can be used for sports, to take people on vacation, and to move things from one country to another.

SEE ALSO

▶ Oceans and seas p.187

▶ Sports p.239

▶ Trade p.257

▶ Transportation pp.258–259

▶ Work p.274

Container ship

Some of the largest boats on the oceans are container ships. These giants of the seas can transport more than 15,000 containers full of items such as clothes, toys, and televisions to different countries.

The captain steers the ship from the bridge.

Cranes load containers on and off the ship.

Containers are large metal boxes. Each container can hold around 6,000 shoe boxes.

The hold carries more containers. Some store hundreds of cars.

Sailing boat

This tiny boat doesn't have an engine. It is powered by wind, which is caught in the sail to push the boat across the water.

Cruise ship

A cruise ship is a floating hotel that takes tourists to different countries. On board are swimming pools, theaters, and water slides.

Submersible

This craft doesn't travel on the ocean, but underneath it. It can take scientists deep underwater to look at sea life and study the ocean floor.

Sickness

Tiny living things called germs can make us sick if they get inside our bodies. Germs are all around us—in the air, in our food, and on the things we touch. Our bodies have many different ways to stop them from harming us.

SEE ALSO
▶ Body cells p.41
▶ Human body p.130
▶ Medicine p.160
▶ Microscopic life p.165
▶ Skin p.229
▶ Taste p.249

Body defenses
The body has a defense system to stop germs from getting in. It also kills germs that find a way in.

Mucus (nose and throat)
Mucus traps germs we breathe in. Hairs move the mucus to the mouth, where the germs and mucus get swallowed.

Senses
Sight, smell, and taste help us avoid eating food that has gone bad.

Tears
Watery tears wash dirt out of our eyes. They also kill germs.

Ear wax
Ear wax flows out of our ears, pushing germs and dirt out with it.

Saliva
Also known as spit, saliva protects your mouth by killing germs.

Skin
Skin stops germs from entering the body by forming a protective barrier.

White blood cells
Tiny white blood cells in your blood kill germs in the body.

Acid
Chemicals in the stomach kill most germs we swallow.

Good bacteria
Helpful bacteria in our intestines stops germs from growing.

1,000 germs can fit on the head of a pin. They're tiny!

Avoiding sickness
Covering our nose and mouth when we sneeze or cough stops germs from spreading through the air.

Sight

Sight is seeing the shapes, sizes, and colors of nearby and faraway objects within our surroundings. When we see, colored light is bouncing off objects and into our eyes.

How we see
Tiny sensors at the back of the eye receive light and send signals to the brain to make an image from the light we see.

Glasses
If an eye lens doesn't focus the light in the right place, the image is blurred. Glasses contain lenses that change where the light focuses in the eye, so the image becomes clear.

Some people use glasses to help them read

Eyelid

Eyelashes

Tear duct
Liquid is made here. When we blink, our eyelids wipe our eyeballs with the liquid, to clean out dust.

Pupil

Outer eye

Iris
The iris is the colored part of the eye. It changes the size of the round hole in the middle—the pupil.

Retina
In the retina at the back of the eye, tiny sensors called "cells" collect information about color, light, and shape.

Iris

Cornea
The cornea bends the light entering the eye.

Pupil
The pupil gets bigger to let in more light when it's dark and gets smaller to let in less light when it's bright.

Just **one-sixth** of the eyeball can be **seen from outside**.

Lens
The lens focuses the light at the back of the eye. It makes the picture we see clear.

Eyeball

Optic nerve
The optic nerve sends the light information collected in the eye to the brain.

Muscles

Sinking and floating

When we place objects in water they can float on the surface or sink below it. The heavier and more packed together a material is, the more likely it is to sink. Materials like stone and metal usually sink, while wood and plastics usually float.

Floating

If the downward force of an object's weight is less than the force of the water pushing up on it, it will float. The more air an object contains, the more likely it is to float.

The weight of the duck pushes down.

The duck is full of air, making it light and buoyant.

Salt water has more **buoyancy** than fresh water, so we can **float** more easily in the ocean than in a lake.

Buoyancy

As the duck pushes some of the water out of the way, the water pushes back on the duck. The effect of the upward push of the water is a force called buoyancy.

Buoyancy pushes the duck upward.

The weight of the coin is pushing it down.

The coin sinks because its weight is greater than its buoyancy.

Massive ships

It seems amazing that huge metal ships float while small metal coins sink. Ships float because they are full of air and because they have a large surface area. The force of buoyancy pushing upward is spread out and is greater than the ship's overall weight.

The buoyancy of the coin pushes it up.

Sinking

An object sinks when the force of its weight pushing downward is greater than the force of buoyancy pushing back up on it.

Skeleton

All the bones in the human body fit together in the skeleton. They make up the shape of the human body. The skeleton forms a protective cage around the soft, inner organs like the lungs and the heart.

SEE ALSO
▶ Brain p.45
▶ Heart p.128
▶ Human body p.130
▶ Lungs p.149
▶ Muscles p.173

Our bones
The skeleton is made up of 206 bones. The bones are moved by muscles.

Skull
The skull protects the delicate brain inside.

Ball and socket joint
Ball and socket joints in the shoulder and hip allow a swivel movement.

Ribcage

Humerus

Ulna

Radius

Saddle joint
A saddle joint allows the thumb to move in a circle.

Pelvis

Spine
The spine is made up of 24 bones called vertebrae.

The ends of bones are harder at the joints.

Femur

Tibia

Bone is stronger than wood, concrete, or steel.

The hinge joint lets the arm move up and down.

Hinge joint

Joints
Joints are the places where one bone joins another to allow movement. They let our bones move side to side, up and down, or in circles. Joints have fluid in them to help make movement smooth.

Inside bones
The outer layer of bones is made from a strong substance called calcium. Inside is the bone marrow, which supplies blood cells to the rest of the body.

Spongy bone

Bone marrow

Compact bone

Blood

Types of bone
There are two kinds of bone inside each bone. Hard, compact bone gives the bone strength and protection. Spongy bone is full of little holes that make the bone lighter.

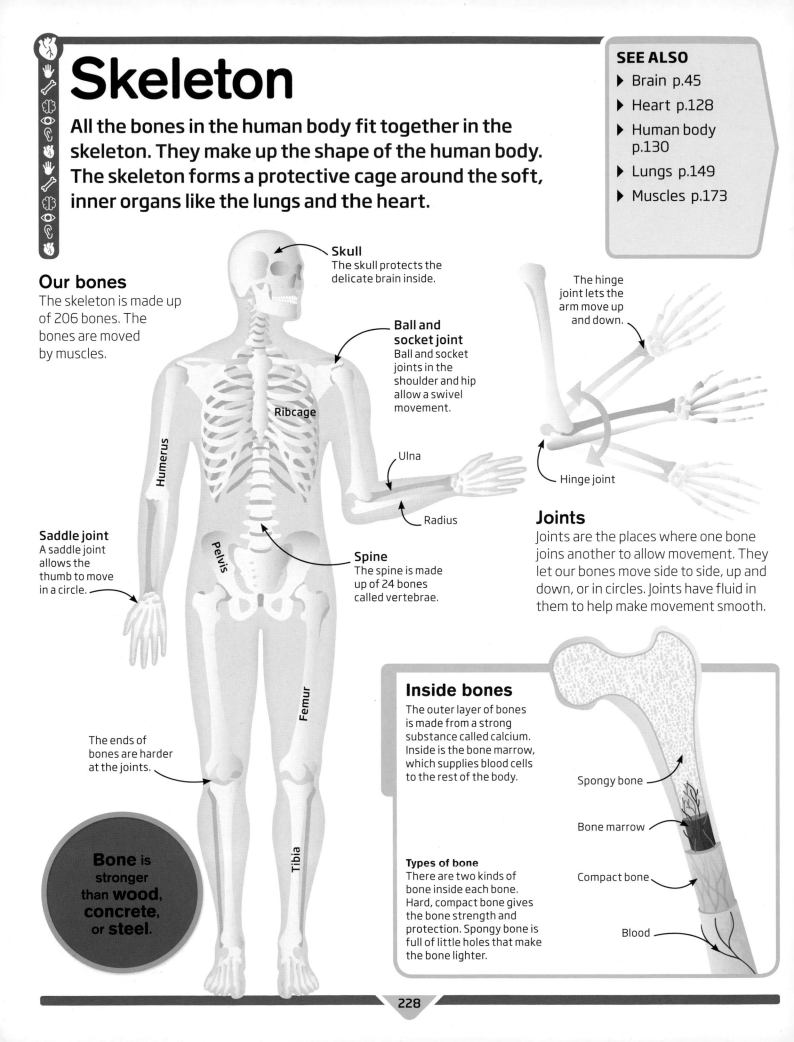

Skin

Skin is the stretchy outer layer of the body. It keeps our inside parts inside and germs outside. It protects us from water and sunshine, and keeps us at the right temperature. The outer layer continually flakes off as new skin is made.

SEE ALSO
▶ Body cells p.41
▶ Cells p.56
▶ Genes p.119
▶ Heart p.128
▶ Human body p.130
▶ Touch p.256

Inside the skin
The skin is split into layers. Below the outer layer that you can see, there is a lot going on.

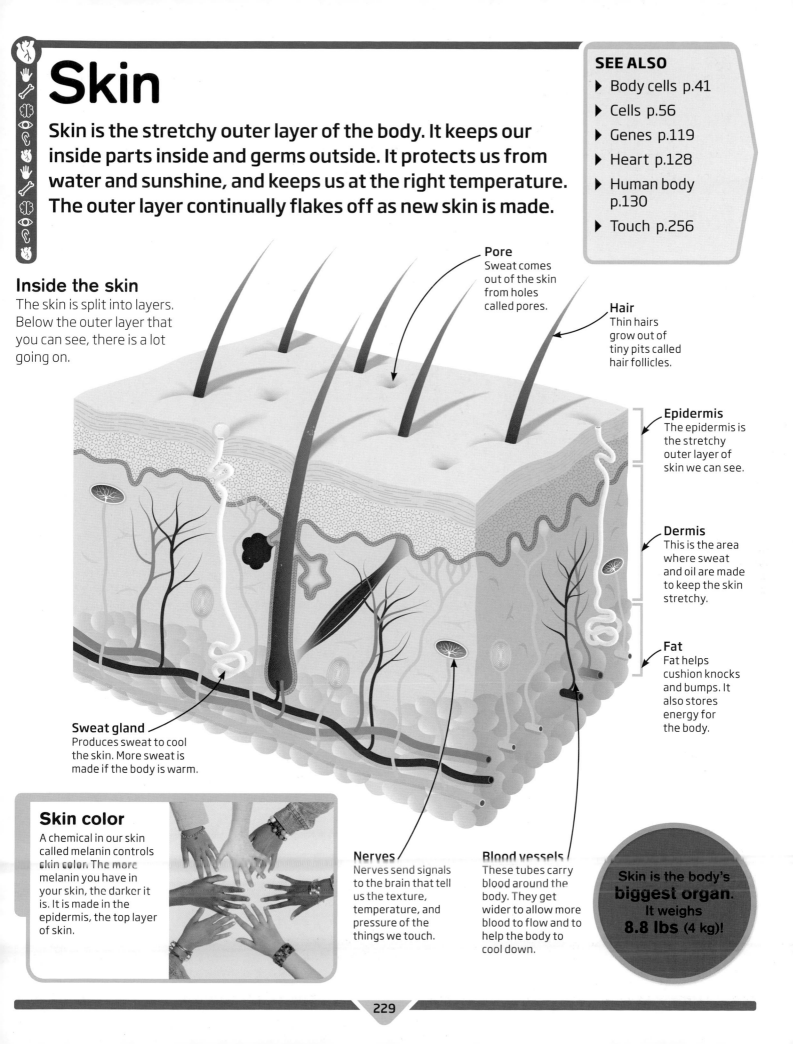

Pore
Sweat comes out of the skin from holes called pores.

Hair
Thin hairs grow out of tiny pits called hair follicles.

Epidermis
The epidermis is the stretchy outer layer of skin we can see.

Dermis
This is the area where sweat and oil are made to keep the skin stretchy.

Fat
Fat helps cushion knocks and bumps. It also stores energy for the body.

Sweat gland
Produces sweat to cool the skin. More sweat is made if the body is warm.

Nerves
Nerves send signals to the brain that tell us the texture, temperature, and pressure of the things we touch.

Blood vessels
These tubes carry blood around the body. They get wider to allow more blood to flow and to help the body to cool down.

Skin color
A chemical in our skin called melanin controls skin color. The more melanin you have in your skin, the darker it is. It is made in the epidermis, the top layer of skin.

Skin is the body's **biggest organ.** It weighs **8.8 lbs** (4 kg)!

Slavery

Slaves are people who have had their rights taken away and are treated like property. They may have been captured in war, owe more money than they can pay, or have parents who are slaves. Slavery has been used throughout history, but today it is against the law in every country in the world.

Slave labor
In the early 1800s, big farms called plantations in the US used slave labor to pick cotton, cut sugar cane, and perform other tasks. Slaves worked long hours in very bad conditions.

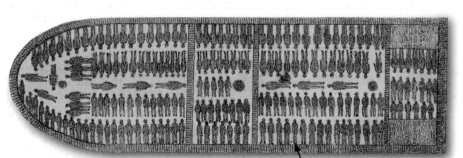

The slave trade
To keep American plantations supplied with workers, ships carried slaves from Africa to America. Between 1450 and 1850, 12 million people crossed the Atlantic Ocean.

People were often chained and packed tightly into slave ships.

Slavery today
Though slavery is now illegal, more than 20 million people are still kept as slaves, mostly in Asia and Africa. Groups around the world are working to solve this terrible problem.

Sleep

Every night we sleep and our bodies rest, repair, and grow. While we sleep our brains sort through the information gathered from our senses and some of it is deleted and some is stored as memories. We need sleep to stay fit and healthy.

SEE ALSO
▶ Brain p.45
▶ Eating pp.104–105
▶ Hibernation p.129
▶ Human body p.130
▶ Sickness p.225

Sleep patterns
Our sleep follows a pattern of different stages. You go through each stage several times every night.

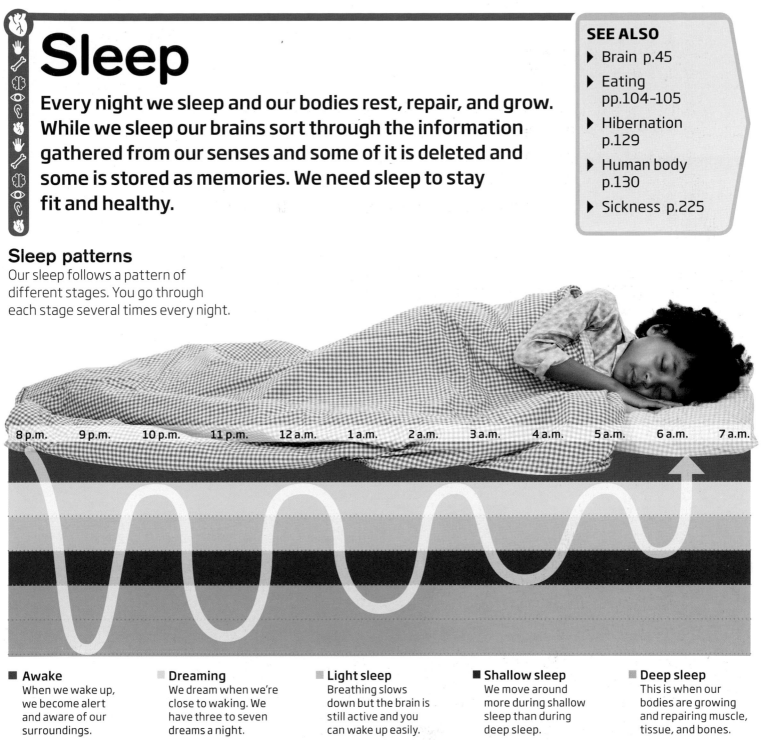

8 p.m. 9 p.m. 10 p.m. 11 p.m. 12 a.m. 1 a.m. 2 a.m. 3 a.m. 4 a.m. 5 a.m. 6 a.m. 7 a.m.

■ **Awake**
When we wake up, we become alert and aware of our surroundings.

■ **Dreaming**
We dream when we're close to waking. We have three to seven dreams a night.

■ **Light sleep**
Breathing slows down but the brain is still active and you can wake up easily.

■ **Shallow sleep**
We move around more during shallow sleep than during deep sleep.

■ **Deep sleep**
This is when our bodies are growing and repairing muscle, tissue, and bones.

Why do we sleep?
Sleep is important because without it our brain and body slowly stop working.

Memory
Our brain deletes useless information and stores more important things while we sleep.

Healing
Our bodies heal better and faster when we get plenty of solid sleep.

Energy
If we don't get enough sleep, we lack energy and want sugary food.

Growth
Our bodies grow and repair muscles and bones while we are in a deep sleep.

You will spend **one-third** of your life asleep. This is around **30 years** in total!

Smell

Smell is one of our senses. When tiny parts of something float through the air and into our nose we identify a smell. The brain tells us what it smells like compared to other things we've smelled before.

SEE ALSO
▶ Brain p.45
▶ Hearing p.127
▶ Human body p.130
▶ Muscles p.173
▶ Skeleton p.228
▶ Taste p.249

How we smell

Anything that smells releases tiny particles into the air. The particles mix with a sticky fluid in our nose called mucus. Sensors in the nose detect the smell and send signals to the brain to identify it.

This area works out what the smell is and sends information to the brain.

These cells are sensors that detect smells.

The brain tells us about the smell.

Mucus
This sticky fluid mixes with the smell to help the sensor cells detect what it is.

Nose bone

We can detect more than **10,000** different smells with our nose!

Nose cavity
This is the main airway for breathing. It is connected to the throat and mouth.

The smell enters the nose.

The tongue has sensors for tasting food.

Taste and smell

Smell and taste are closely linked. If you hold your nose, you will find it harder to figure out what something tastes like.

Solar system

The solar system is made up of our star, the sun, and everything that travels around it. This includes eight planets and their moons, asteroids, and comets. Scientists think the solar system formed 4.6 billion years ago, from a massive spinning cloud of gas and dust.

SEE ALSO
- Asteroids p.30
- Comets p.68
- Earth p.83
- Jupiter p.141
- Neptune p.183
- Sun p.247
- Universe p.263

Sun

Asteroid belt

Orbiting planets

The sun is the center of the solar system. Everything in the solar system travels around, or orbits, the sun.

1. Mercury
Mercury is the smallest planet.

2. Venus
The surface of Venus is super-hot.

3. Earth
Earth has lots of liquid water.

4. Mars
Mars has a red, dusty surface.

5. Jupiter
Jupiter is the largest planet.

6. Saturn
Saturn is famous for the rings around it.

7. Uranus
Uranus is thought to be the coldest planet.

8. Neptune
Neptune has strong winds and giant storms.

Types of planet

There are three types of planet in the solar system. The rocky planets orbit close to the sun, and the gas and ice giants orbit farther away.

Earth

Neptune

Jupiter

Rocky planets
Mercury, Venus, Earth, and Mars are small and rocky with solid surfaces.

Ice giants
Uranus and Neptune are made of a mixture of gas and icy materials.

Gas giants
Jupiter and Saturn are huge planets made of gas.

Kepler-16b

There are many other solar systems in the universe. Scientists have even found a planet, called Kepler-16b, that orbits two suns.

Solids

Solids are materials that keep their shape. They don't flow like water–they stay where you put them. Solids are useful for making many things, from mobile phones to houses. They are usually hard materials, but soft materials that keep their shape are solid, too.

What solids do
Solids can be hard, bendy, strong, squishy, see-through, or magnetic. The behaviors of a solid are called its properties.

Particles
Solids are made from tiny particles that are close together. If enough heat is added, they start to move past each other to become liquid.

Solids make a pile, not a pool or puddle.

Solid rocks become **liquid lava** when heated to very high temperatures.

Solids keep their shape.

Cutting solids
We can cut solids into different shapes. Wood is a solid material that comes from trees. We cut and shape it to make furniture.

Chopped wood

Shaping solids
Metal is a hard solid we can find underground. We heat metal to make it soft, then bend and hammer it into the shape we want. When it cools, metal keeps its shape.

Making new solids
We can make new solid materials by mixing other materials together. For example, gelatin is made by adding hot water to gelatin powder to make a liquid. The liquid then cools into a solid.

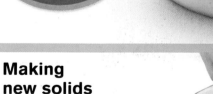

Gets chilled

Liquid gelatin

Solid gelatin

A hot metal horseshoe

Sound

A sound is made when something vibrates. The bigger the vibration, the louder the sound is. The faster something vibrates, the higher pitched the sound is. Sound vibrations travel through things to get to our ears.

Sound vibrates through the air.

The voice box vibrates when we speak, making sound.

Our ears detect the vibration and our brain understands them as sound.

How sounds travel

Sounds travel by vibrating the air until it reaches our ears and we hear the sound. The vibrations are called sound waves. Sound waves can travel through solids, liquids, and gases.

Volume

Volume changes depending on how big a vibration is. The bigger the vibration, the louder the sound. How high or low a sound is depends on how fast something vibrates. The faster the vibration, the higher the sound.

Small, fast vibrations

Big, slow vibrations

Things sound **louder** when they are **close** to us.

Small drum
We can hit a small drum harder to make it louder, but it vibrates at the same speed so it has a constant note.

Big drum
The big drum vibrates more slowly, so it has a lower note compared to the small drum. It's bigger, so it makes bigger vibrations that are louder.

South America

The continent of South America is surrounded by ocean, except at the top where it joins with North America. One-third of the continent is covered by a huge jungle, called the Amazon rain forest. The Andes mountain range stretches all the way down one side of South America.

SEE ALSO
▶ Amphibians p.15
▶ Explorers p.96
▶ Incas p.132
▶ North America p.184
▶ Rain forests p.204
▶ World p.275

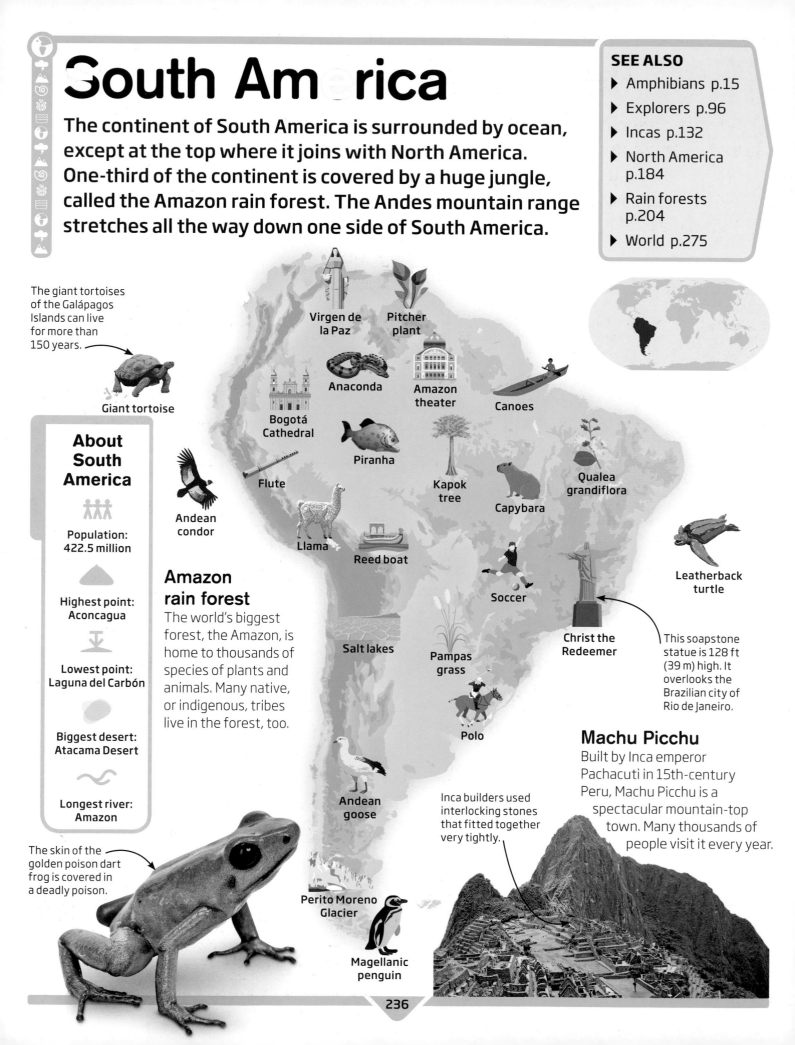

The giant tortoises of the Galápagos Islands can live for more than 150 years.

Giant tortoise

About South America

Population: 422.5 million

Highest point: Aconcagua

Lowest point: Laguna del Carbón

Biggest desert: Atacama Desert

Longest river: Amazon

Andean condor

Virgen de la Paz

Pitcher plant

Bogotá Cathedral

Anaconda

Amazon theater

Canoes

Piranha

Flute

Kapok tree

Qualea grandiflora

Capybara

Llama

Reed boat

Leatherback turtle

Amazon rain forest

The world's biggest forest, the Amazon, is home to thousands of species of plants and animals. Many native, or indigenous, tribes live in the forest, too.

Soccer

Salt lakes

Pampas grass

Christ the Redeemer

This soapstone statue is 128 ft (39 m) high. It overlooks the Brazilian city of Rio de Janeiro.

Polo

Machu Picchu

Built by Inca emperor Pachacuti in 15th-century Peru, Machu Picchu is a spectacular mountain-top town. Many thousands of people visit it every year.

Andean goose

Inca builders used interlocking stones that fitted together very tightly.

The skin of the golden poison dart frog is covered in a deadly poison.

Perito Moreno Glacier

Magellanic penguin

Space travel

Space travel is how we explore the solar system and learn about our place in the universe. Most space travel is done using robot spacecraft called probes. The farthest in space that humans have traveled themselves is to the moon.

Humans in space

To get into space, people use super-powered spaceships. Space shuttles like *Atlantis* were used to take people into space for 30 years. Now people use the Russian *Soyuz* spacecraft.

It takes a robot **spacecraft** about **six months** to travel to **Mars**.

The outside fuel tank is filled with liquid hydrogen and oxygen to power the shuttle's engines.

Astronauts sit in the cockpit.

Solar cells use the sun's power to make the probe work.

Juno probe

Magnetometer measures magnetic fields.

This booster rocket gives extra power.

Launch of the space shuttle *Atlantis*

Robots in space

Probes gather data using cameras, magnetometers, and radars, then send the data back to Earth.

Extreme environment

Space is not an easy place for people to be in. It can be both extremely hot and cold. There are dangerous rays from the sun and there is no air to breathe. Spaceships and stations are carefully designed to keep astronauts safe.

Astronaut Karen Nyberg washes her hair on board the International Space Station.

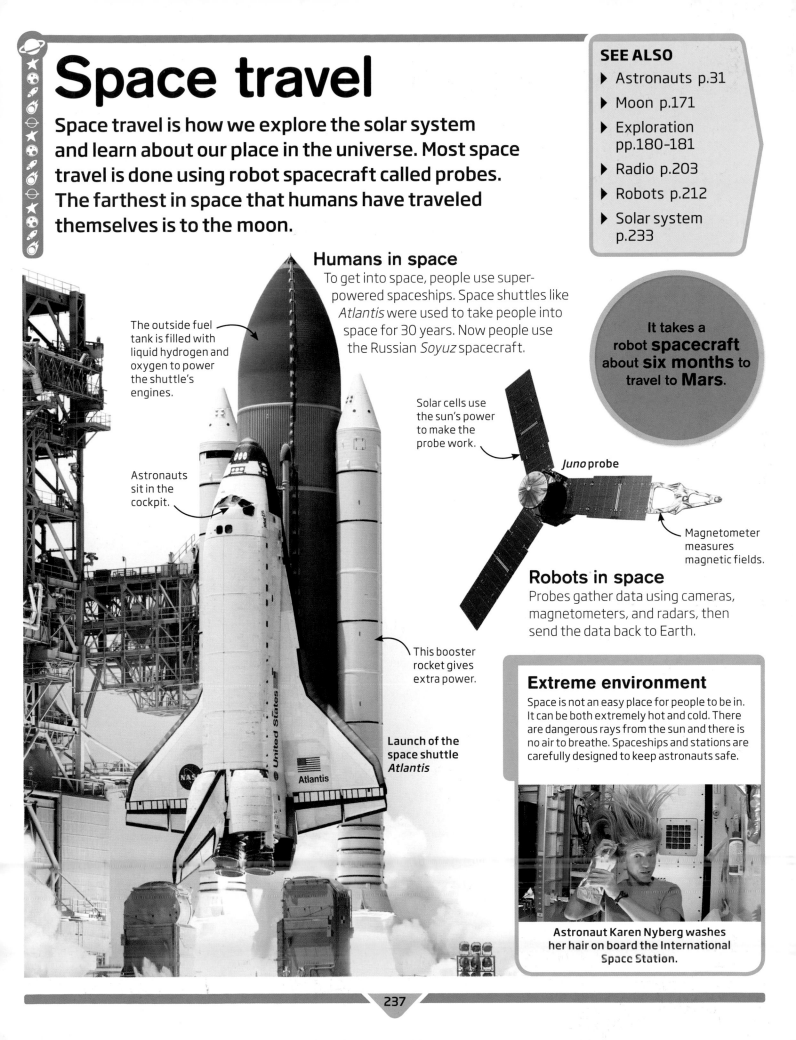

Spiders

Spiders are animals with two body segments and eight legs. They are predators, hunting other small animals to eat. They do not chew their food, but turn it into liquid before sucking it up.

SEE ALSO

▶ Animal groups p.22

▶ Animal homes p.23

▶ Food chains p.107

▶ Insects p.134

▶ Invertebrates p.139

▶ Sight p.226

Tarantula

Some of the world's largest spiders are tarantulas. As they get bigger, their old skin comes off and they grow a new one.

Tarantulas bite with their venomous fangs, but their bite is less harmful to humans than a bee's sting.

Leg hairs help tarantulas feel the vibrations of other animals nearby.

Spiders can **grow back** their legs if they **break off.**

The row of eyes help the jumping spider see all around it.

Jumping spider

Jumping spiders can jump 30 times their body size. They use their good eyesight to spot other animals.

Huntsman spider

These spiders don't build webs, but hunt and forage for insects. Females can go for three weeks without eating.

The body is designed for speed.

Spider webs

Many spiders build webs, using silk that they make in their bodies. Some spiders use their web to trap and store the insects they eat.

Sports

Sports are physical activities performed by individuals or teams of players. There are usually rules to sports, and team sports often take place in a set amount of time. Individuals and teams compete against one another to achieve the best result or the highest score.

Athletics

Athletics is a group of sports that take place around a running track or on a sports field. Big athletic competitions such as the Olympics have lots of events.

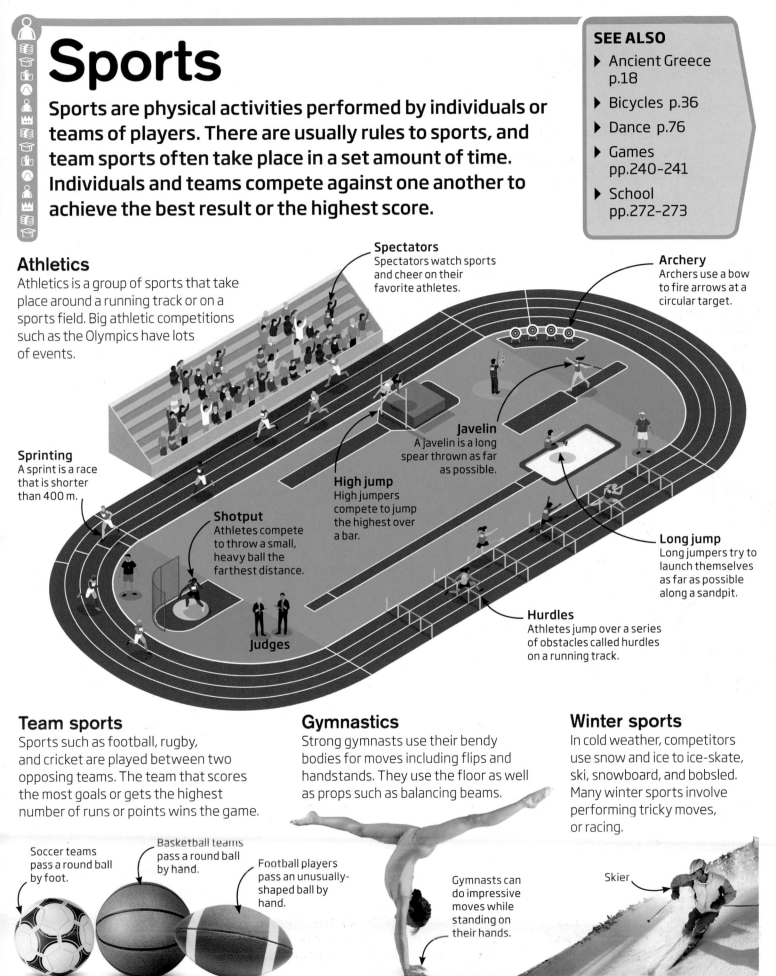

Spectators
Spectators watch sports and cheer on their favorite athletes.

Archery
Archers use a bow to fire arrows at a circular target.

Sprinting
A sprint is a race that is shorter than 400 m.

Javelin
A javelin is a long spear thrown as far as possible.

Shotput
Athletes compete to throw a small, heavy ball the farthest distance.

High jump
High jumpers compete to jump the highest over a bar.

Long jump
Long jumpers try to launch themselves as far as possible along a sandpit.

Judges

Hurdles
Athletes jump over a series of obstacles called hurdles on a running track.

Team sports

Sports such as football, rugby, and cricket are played between two opposing teams. The team that scores the most goals or gets the highest number of runs or points wins the game.

Soccer teams pass a round ball by foot.

Basketball teams pass a round ball by hand.

Football players pass an unusually-shaped ball by hand.

Gymnastics

Strong gymnasts use their bendy bodies for moves including flips and handstands. They use the floor as well as props such as balancing beams.

Gymnasts can do impressive moves while standing on their hands.

Winter sports

In cold weather, competitors use snow and ice to ice-skate, ski, snowboard, and bobsled. Many winter sports involve performing tricky moves, or racing.

Skier

Games

A game is an activity or sport played using a set of rules. Games are played by individuals or by teams of players, who compete against each other. Some games use balls and bats or rackets and are played on special courts; others use boards with specially designed game pieces.

Racket sports

Tennis, badminton, and squash are sports played using a racket on a special court. In tennis, opponents hit the ball across a central net, and in badminton they hit a shuttlecock. In squash, the players hit the ball against a wall.

The tennis racket frame has strings pulled tightly across it.

Board games

Tabletop games, such as chess and backgammon, are played on specially built boards. Each player has a number of pieces, such as chessmen, that they move according to a set of rules. Board games were first played in ancient Egypt 5,500 years ago.

A chessboard has a grid of black and white squares.

The start of a game of chess

Ball and wall games

The ancient Mayans of Central America played a ball game on long, narrow, stone-walled courts. Players used a solid rubber ball, which they had to keep in play by using only their hips and arms—they weren't allowed to touch it with their hands or feet.

Stone ring to hit the ball through.

Stone-walled Mayan ball court

Ping pong ball

Australian rules football

Handball

Baseball

The first **Olympic Games** were held in ancient Greece in 776 BCE.

Olympic sprint relay race

Lacrosse ball

The Olympics
Every four years, athletes compete for their country in the Olympic Games. The Olympics includes lots of different sporting events, including athletics, gymnastics, and team sports.

Football

Golf ball

The first **computer game** was developed in 1947. Players fired a dot at a target.

Volleyball

Soccer ball

Ball sports
Ball sports are among the most popular games of all. Teams of up to 15 players per side play in matches of soccer, rugby, basketball, football, Australian rules football, cricket, and other games. Huge crowds watch these matches, many of which are shown on television.

Computer games
Computer games are played on a computer or through a console on a TV screen. Many games include special effects and music. They can be one-player or multi-player games.

Basketball

Rugby ball

Stars

Stars are balls of very hot gas, deep in space. From Earth, they look like tiny dots but are actually huge. The smallest ordinary star is about the same size as Jupiter. Stars shine because the gases inside them constantly crash together in a process called fusion.

SEE ALSO
▶ Color pp.26–27
▶ Galaxies p.116
▶ Light p.147
▶ Solar system p.233
▶ Sun p.247
▶ Temperature p.252

Sizes and colors

Stars come in different sizes and colors. A star's color depends on how hot its surface is. The hottest stars are blue, and the coolest ones are red.

Blue supergiant
These stars are very young and extremely hot.

Red giant star
Red giants are older stars with cool surface temperatures.

Sun
Our sun is a middle-aged, medium-sized star with a medium surface temperature.

The nearest star

The star closest to the Earth after our sun is Proxima Centauri, a red dwarf with at least one planet. This star is 9,000 times farther away than Neptune, the planet farthest from the sun.

Star deaths

Some stars end their lives in a spectacular explosion called a supernova. Others slowly fade as they run out of energy.

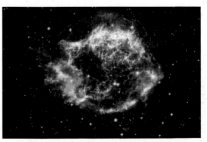

Cloud of material from a supernova explosion

Stone Age

The Stone Age was a period of time that began about 3.3 million years ago and lasted until about 4,000 years ago. In the Stone Age, people made tools out of stone for the first time. They used them to cut meat and plants, to build shelters, and, in the late Stone Age, for farming.

SEE ALSO
▶ Art p.28
▶ Buildings p.48
▶ Caves p.55
▶ Early humans p.82
▶ Farming p.98
▶ Food p.106

Stone tools

Stone Age people began making stone tools to do different tasks. Using tools meant people could get food or do work more quickly and easily.

A stone axe helped to chop wood and dig into dirt.

People made handaxes to help them cut meat and chop hard plants.

Finding food

Finding food was the most important part of life for people in the Stone Age. They ate wild plants, and animals from land and sea.

Blueberries

Salmon

Bison
Hunting for big animals, such as bison, could be dangerous.

Cave painting

Some Stone Age people made beautiful artwork on cave walls, often showing the animals they would hunt. These paintings are still being found today.

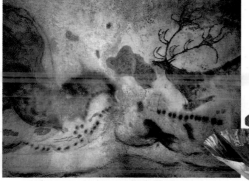

Paint could be made from powdered fats and minerals.

Lascaux cave paintings in France

Buildings

The first Stone Age buildings were made of wood and animal skins. By the end of the Stone Age, people had begun building large stone structures called megaliths.

Stonehenge in England is a famous Stone Age megalith that is still standing today.

Homes

A home is a house or building in which you live. That home might be built of canvas, stone, bricks, wood, or ice. It could even be carved out of solid rock. Homes can be built separately as single, detached houses or built together as row houses or terraces. Some homes are built on top of each together in blocks called apartments.

Grand palaces
The kings and queens of Europe were very rich and lived in magnificent palaces and castles. They feasted in great halls and received visitors in grand throne rooms.

Neuschwanstein Castle in Germany

Early homes
Some early people made their homes in caves or holes dug into sides of mountains and hills. Others cut down trees to build simple wooden huts, which they draped with animal skins.

Some early people built simple **grass shelters**. The layering of grasses is called **thatching**.

Caves were easy to turn into homes, as they didn't have to be built!

Caves in Cappadocia, Turkey

Eco homes
Today, some homes are specially built to work with the natural world, or environment. They don't use up as much energy as ordinary homes.

Solar panels on the roof make energy from sunshine.

Rainwater is collected for reuse.

Walls have added layers to save heat (this is called insulation).

Plan for 3D-printed houses on the planet Mars

Future homes

What will homes of the future look like? Some might be built using a method called "3D printing." With this method, robots add material layer upon layer to create a three-dimensional shape.

Igloo

Extreme homes

In the cold Arctic, some Inuit people build shelters called igloos out of blocks of ice. Igloos keep out the wind and are warm inside.

House designed by Antoni Gaudí

Houseboat in India

Moving homes

Some people live in homes that can move from place to place. They float in houseboats on water or live in wheeled caravans towed by cars or horses.

Architecture

Architecture is the art of designing and making buildings. In Barcelona in Spain, architect Antoni Gaudí was inspired by nature and decorated his buildings with different materials and colorful patterns.

Storms

Storms are powerful winds that often bring rain, thunder and lightning, snow, hail, dust, or sand. Storms can cause serious damage if they have very high wind speeds or heavy rain that leads to flooding. Tornadoes, hurricanes, and thunderstorms are all types of storm.

SEE ALSO

▶ Climate change p.60

▶ Clouds p.64

▶ Electricity p.87

▶ Erosion p.93

▶ Water cycle p.270

▶ Weather p.271

Tropical giants

The biggest and most destructive storms, called hurricanes or typhoons, happen in tropical areas, above warm water. They begin when groups of smaller storms spin together into a spiral shape.

The hurricane's eye, or center, is calm, with very little wind.

The strongest winds surround the storm's eye.

Hurricanes are given **people's names**, such as Alex, Matthew, and Patricia.

Thunderstorms

Storms with thunder and lightning are common in summer. They often have heavy rain or hail that can break things and cause floods.

Tornadoes

Tornadoes are fast-spinning columns of air that form during massive thunderstorms. A tornado can destroy everything in its path.

Sun

The sun is the star at the center of our solar system. It is one of at least 100 billion stars in our Milky Way galaxy. The sun gives off light and heat, making it possible for life to exist on Earth.

Massive explosions send jets of gas out from the surface.

Dark sunspots are the cooler regions on the sun's surface.

Yellow dwarf
Astronomers describe the sun as a yellow dwarf, although it is a medium-sized star. It is a hot ball of gases that are constantly on the move, creating energy.

These bright bursts of energy are called solar flares.

Loops of gas are called prominences.

The sun is **1.3 million** times bigger than Earth.

Auroras
Toward the top and bottom of the Earth (at its poles), particles from the sun meet Earth's magnetic field. This colorful glow is called an aurora.

Final stages of the sun
In about 5 billion years time, the sun will have used up most of the gases that keep it shining. It will collapse into a small, very hot white dwarf. It will then slowly cool down and eventually fade away.

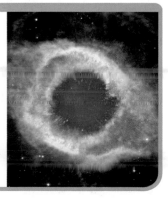

Symmetry

There are two types of symmetry. Reflective symmetry is when lines can be drawn to divide a shape into identical parts. Rotational symmetry is when a shape can be turned around (rotated) and still look the same.

SEE ALSO
▶ Art p.28
▶ Flowers p.103
▶ Human body p.130
▶ Shapes p.222
▶ Sight p.226
▶ Games pp.240–241

Reflective symmetry

Lines of symmetry are like folding a shape in half. If a shape is symmetrical, both sides of the fold will look the same. Shapes can have more than one line of symmetry.

Diamonds have two lines of symmetry. Each one splits the diamond into two equal parts.

This triangle has three lines of symmetry, one through each side.

A regular octagon has eight lines of symmetry, through its sides and angles.

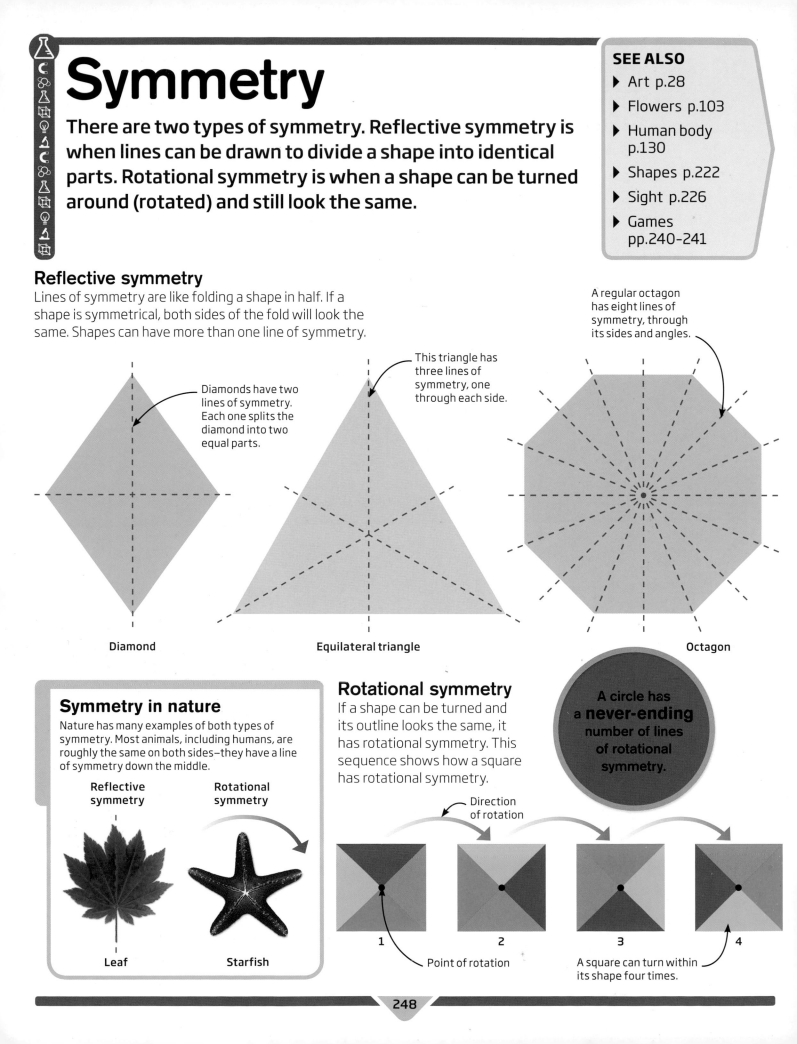

Diamond

Equilateral triangle

Octagon

Symmetry in nature

Nature has many examples of both types of symmetry. Most animals, including humans, are roughly the same on both sides–they have a line of symmetry down the middle.

Reflective symmetry

Rotational symmetry

Leaf

Starfish

Rotational symmetry

If a shape can be turned and its outline looks the same, it has rotational symmetry. This sequence shows how a square has rotational symmetry.

A circle has **a never-ending** number of lines of rotational symmetry.

Direction of rotation

1

2

3

4

Point of rotation

A square can turn within its shape four times.

Taste

When we eat food, tiny bumps in our mouth sense if it tastes sweet, sour, salty, savory, or bitter. The mouth sends information to our brain, which works out the flavors of what we are eating and drinking.

Taste and smell
The sense of taste from the tongue and the sense of smell from the nose work together to tell us how our food tastes.

Bitter
Bitter-tasting foods include olives, coffee beans, and cocoa beans.

Sour
Lemons, limes, and grapefruit taste sour. A sour taste can also be a warning that food has gone bad.

Salt
Salt is added to dishes to help them to taste better. Our bodies need a small amount of salt to stay healthy, but too much salt is bad for us.

Savory
Savory flavors include soy sauce and parmesan cheese.

The body regrows all of our taste buds every **two weeks**.

Taste buds

The little bumps in our tongue and mouth have tiny taste sensors in them called taste buds. We have around 10,000 taste buds.

Sweet
Foods such as honey and fruit taste sweet because of the natural sugar they contain.

Telephones

Telephones allow people to speak to each other from anywhere in the world. They turn the sound of our voices into signals, which are sent through radio waves or cables to another phone. That phone then changes the signals back into sound.

SEE ALSO
▶ Codes pp.66-67
▶ Communication p.69
▶ Computers p.71
▶ Electricity p.87
▶ Hearing p.127
▶ Internet p.138

Where does your voice go?

When you speak into a phone, the sound of your voice is turned into electrical signals. A network of telephone lines and cell towers let us speak to people over long distances.

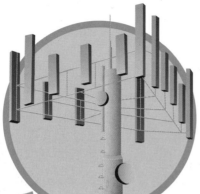

Cell tower
These towers send and receive signals between mobile phones and a telephone exchange.

Telephone lines
Phone lines carry phone signals long distances by holding the wires up above the ground. For longer distances, cables can even go underwater.

Mobile phones
Mobile phones send and receive signals as radio waves. They don't work if they are too far away from a cell tower.

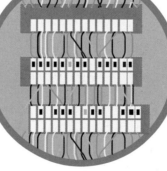

Telephone exchange
This place connects telephone calls using computers. It sends incoming signals to the right phone.

Wired phones
Landline phones have a cable that plugs into a wall. They send a signal through a network of wires.

Past and present

The way that phones send and receive signals has changed since they were first invented. Early telephones sent sounds short distances through pipes or tubes. From the 1800s, telephones sent electrical signals through wires. Mobile phones use radio waves to pick up signals.

First telephone
The telephone was invented in 1876 by Alexander Graham Bell, a Scottish music teacher.

Smartphone
A smartphone is a pocket computer that can be used to make phone calls, record videos, and play games.

Television

Television lets people watch the news, documentaries, films, cartoons, and game shows without leaving the house. It is one of the world's most popular forms of entertainment.

Sounds and pictures are recorded, using a video camera.

2. Television satellite
The recorded program is sent as signals to machines in space, called satellites. The signals are then sent back to many places on Earth.

3. Broadcast tower
These towers pick up satellite signals and send them out to areas nearby. This can be done using special cables or small satellite dishes.

1. Filming
Television programs are recorded using video cameras. When a program is ready, the production company sends, or transmits, it.

Satellite dishes send signals to and from Earth.

Televisions pick up the signals from their nearest tower.

Sending signals
The pictures and sounds of a television program are sent, or transmitted, around the world as signals. Televisions pick up the signals and change them back into moving images.

John Logie Baird invented the **first television** in **1926**, using cookie tins, hat boxes, bicycle lights, and needles.

4. Television
The signals are turned back into pictures and sounds using electricity. We can then watch the television program.

Early television
The first television sets were big boxes with small screens. They showed programs in black and white. By the 1950s, color televisions became more common in homes.

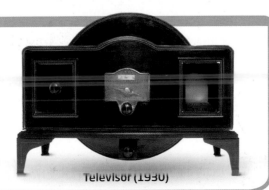
Televisor (1930)

The picture on the screen is made up of thousands of tiny colored squares, called pixels.

Temperature

Temperature is a measurement of how hot or cold something is. We measure temperature in degrees of Fahrenheit (°F) or Celsius (°C). We can use a thermometer to measure the temperature of the air, liquids, or the human body.

SEE ALSO
▸ Changing states p.57
▸ Gases p.117
▸ Human body p.130
▸ Liquids p.148
▸ Measuring p.159
▸ Solids p.234

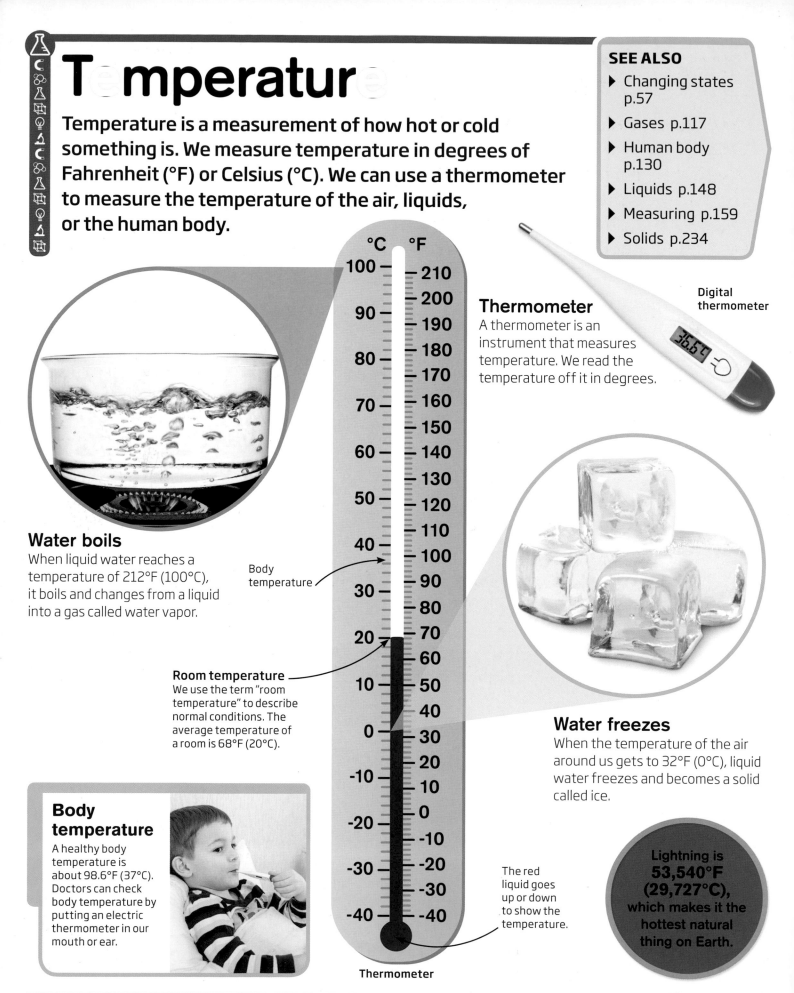

Thermometer
A thermometer is an instrument that measures temperature. We read the temperature off it in degrees.

Digital thermometer

Water boils
When liquid water reaches a temperature of 212°F (100°C), it boils and changes from a liquid into a gas called water vapor.

Body temperature

Room temperature
We use the term "room temperature" to describe normal conditions. The average temperature of a room is 68°F (20°C).

Water freezes
When the temperature of the air around us gets to 32°F (0°C), liquid water freezes and becomes a solid called ice.

Body temperature
A healthy body temperature is about 98.6°F (37°C). Doctors can check body temperature by putting an electric thermometer in our mouth or ear.

The red liquid goes up or down to show the temperature.

Lightning is **53,540°F (29,727°C)**, which makes it the hottest natural thing on Earth.

Thermometer

Theater

People have acted out stories for thousands of years. These stories are plays, and the theater is the exciting place in which they are performed. Theater performers try to make you believe that the characters in a play are real, and that the events they show are actually happening.

SEE ALSO
- Ancient Greece p.18
- Books p.44
- Buildings p.48
- Clothing pp.62–63
- Film p.100
- Music pp.176–177

On stage
The area where plays are performed in a theater is called the stage. Many actors can be on stage at the same time. Music, sounds, and lighting on stage make the play more exciting.

British author Agatha Christie's play **The Mousetrap** has been performed more than **25,000** times!

Actor
The people in plays who pretend to be characters are called actors.

Costume
The clothing an actor wears is called their costume.

Stage
The stage is usually in front of the audience.

Prop
Props are things used in plays to make them more lifelike, such as weapons.

Ancient plays
The first plays were written in ancient Greece, around 700 BCE. Greek playwrights mainly wrote sad plays, called tragedies, and funny plays, called comedies.

Tragedy mask

Comedy mask

Greek theater masks

Puppets
Models controlled by strings or rods are called puppets. They are given voices by performers and tell stories on small stages. Puppet shows have been performed for at least 3,000 years.

These Chinese puppets cast shadows onto a screen.

Tides

Tides are daily changes in the level of the sea on the coast. They are mainly caused by the moon's gravity, which is an invisible force that pulls on the Earth. When the water is high up the coast, it is called high tide, and when it falls it is low tide.

Low tide
When the pull of the moon is weak, water levels fall and the tide goes out.

High tide
When the pull of the moon is strong, water levels rise and the tide comes in.

The moon and tides
The moon pulls the Earth's oceans on the side facing it. This makes sea levels rise, creating a high tide. Because the Earth turns, tides rise and fall as parts of Earth turn toward and then away from the moon.

A high tide happens around the parts of Earth closest to the moon.

Earth

Moon

High tides happen on both sides of the Earth at the same time.

Low tide occurs where the moon's pull is at its weakest.

Living between tides
The part of the coast that is covered up and then uncovered between the tides is called the intertidal zone. Many living things are found here. They have to be tough to cope with battering waves at high tide, and air and sunlight at low tide.

Mussels live on rocks. They shut their shells when the tide is out.

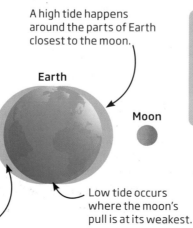

Time zones

Clocks do not show the same time all over the world. If they did, it would be dark at noon and light at midnight in some places. To avoid this, the world is divided into 24 areas called time zones. There is a difference of one hour between time zones that are next to each other.

Times around the world

Time zones are based on the time in Greenwich, in London, which is known as Greenwich Mean Time. The time in the zones to the west of Greenwich are earlier, and the times in the zones to the east are later.

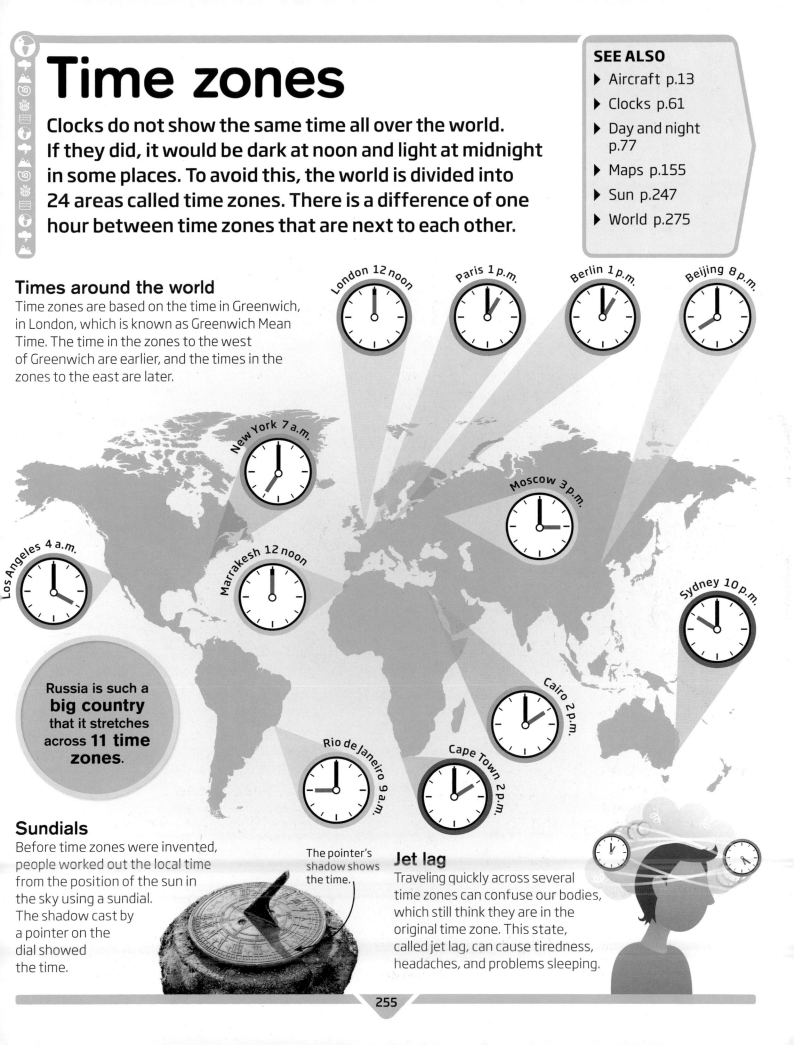

London 12 noon

Paris 1 p.m.

Berlin 1 p.m.

Beijing 8 p.m.

New York 7 a.m.

Moscow 3 p.m.

Los Angeles 4 a.m.

Marrakesh 12 noon

Sydney 10 p.m.

Cairo 2 p.m.

Rio de Janeiro 9 a.m.

Cape Town 2 p.m.

Russia is such a **big country** that it stretches across **11 time zones**.

Sundials

Before time zones were invented, people worked out the local time from the position of the sun in the sky using a sundial. The shadow cast by a pointer on the dial showed the time.

The pointer's shadow shows the time.

Jet lag

Traveling quickly across several time zones can confuse our bodies, which still think they are in the original time zone. This state, called jet lag, can cause tiredness, headaches, and problems sleeping.

255

Touch

Touching is how we feel the world around us. When we touch something, sensors in our skin send information to our brain. We can tell if things are rough or smooth, hot or cold, and how much something pushes against us.

SEE ALSO

▶ Body cells p.41
▶ Brain p.45
▶ Human body p.130
▶ Muscles p.173
▶ Skin p.229
▶ Temperature p.252

Feeling things

There are tiny sensors in our skin called cells or neurons. These neurons collect information about what we touch and send electrical signals to the brain.

Hot and cold

We can detect if things are hot or cold. If something is too hot, our skin tells us to move away quickly.

Hard and soft

We can feel how hard things are by how much they push back against our touch.

Blind people can read by touching a series of tiny bumps on a page called **braille**.

Smooth and rough

We are able to feel very small bumps and differences in texture.

Pain

The neurons in your skin can also detect damage. If we cut or burn ourselves, the neurons send a message to our brain that we feel as pain.

Wet and dry

We can tell the difference between wet, sticky, and dry things just by touching them.

Trade

Trade is buying and selling. We trade raw materials, like metal, to make things, as well as trading the things they are made into, like phones. Everything we eat, wear, and use is the result of trade. You can also buy and sell services, which are jobs people do, such as computer coding.

SEE ALSO
- Farming p.98
- Governments p.123
- Materials p.157
- Money p.169
- Transportation pp.258–259
- Work p.274

Vegetables, fruit, animals for meat, and other products are farmed to be sold.

Aircraft carry some products overseas quickly.

Factories turn raw materials, such as iron and copper, into finished products, such as computers.

Products are sold in stores and markets.

Trucks transport things that are ready to be sold.

At the port, containers of goods are loaded onto ships to be sent abroad.

Border controls check what goes in and out of the country.

Clothes

Rice

Computers

Furniture

Exports

Goods and raw materials that are sent overseas are known as exports. Most exports go by boat. Some go by plane, train, or road.

Imports

Goods and raw materials coming into a country are known as imports. These are often items that cannot be made or grown in that country.

Pineapples

Cocoa beans

Cars

Lemons and limes

Bananas

Steel

International trade

Countries all over the world send goods to one another. They can make money by charging the other country tax (money) for the right to sell its goods within their borders.

Coastguards make sure that ships make it to land safely.

Spice trade

One of the oldest trades in the world is the spice trade. Cinnamon, turmeric, and other spices are grown in Asia and used around the world to flavor food. When the trade began, spices were carried by land across Asia.

Cinnamon

The **story** of...

Transportation

Humans have been inventing new ways of moving from one place to another for thousands of years. At first, people used animals for transportation on land. Later, the wheel was invented, then engines. People started crossing water using rafts and simple dugout canoes, while air travel began with hot-air balloons. We have even traveled into space!

Green travel
The bicycle is one of the most environmentally friendly (green) forms of transportation, because it has no engine to release harmful gases into the air. Other forms of green travel include electric cars and buses that run on clean hydrogen gas.

Horse and cart

Animals
Animals were our first type of transportation other than walking. At first, people rode on them. In 3500 BCE the wheel was invented, and carts and carriages were pulled by horses, oxen, and other animals.

Cyclists and their passengers wear a helmet to keep their head protected if they fall.

Ancient boats were powered by people using oars.

Model of a boat, from ancient Egypt

Crossing water
The first boats were log boats, carved out of tree trunks, and basic rafts made from reeds and sticks. People used them to travel around and also for fishing.

Turning the pedals makes a bicycle's wheels go around.

Model T Ford

Air travel
A few decades after the first powered flight in 1903, aircraft were developed to take people around the world faster than ever before. Today, the longest nonstop flight takes 17 hours and 27 minutes from New Zealand to Qatar.

Poster for Korean Air Lines

Cars for all
In 1908, the Model T Ford became the first car that was cheap enough for many people to buy. More than 15 million were built. Most cars at the time cost nearly $3,000, but the Model T Ford was only $850.

Video camera records moving color images of the moon.

Only three **lunar rovers** were built. They are all still on the surface of the moon.

There are more than **one billion** bikes on the planet.

Moon buggy

Lunar Rover
The Lunar Roving Vehicle was designed to transport astronauts on the moon's surface. Three of these battery-powered craft drove on the moon. They could transport two astronauts at speeds of up to 8 mph (13 kph).

Trains

Trains are vehicles that move along tracks. The first trains were powered by steam, but modern trains use diesel, electricity, or even magnets. They are a fast way for passengers to travel and for goods to be transported.

SEE ALSO

▶ Asia p.29
▶ Engines p.92
▶ Inventions pp.136–137
▶ Magnets p.151
▶ Trade p.257
▶ Transportation pp.258–259

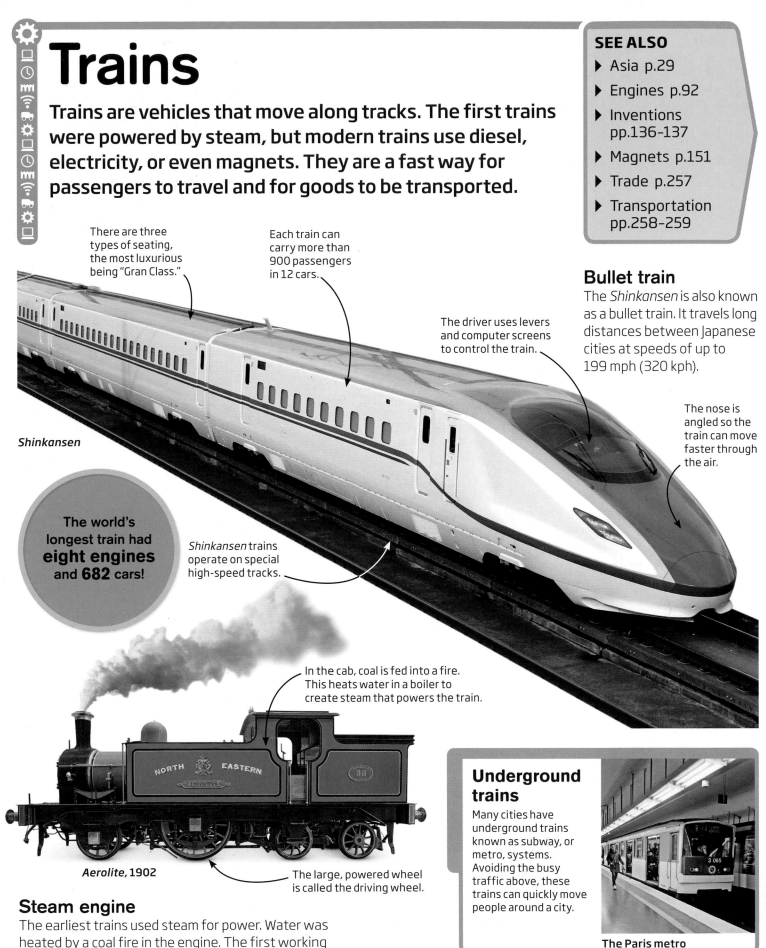

There are three types of seating, the most luxurious being "Gran Class."

Each train can carry more than 900 passengers in 12 cars.

The driver uses levers and computer screens to control the train.

Shinkansen

Bullet train

The *Shinkansen* is also known as a bullet train. It travels long distances between Japanese cities at speeds of up to 199 mph (320 kph).

The nose is angled so the train can move faster through the air.

The world's longest train had **eight engines** and **682** cars!

Shinkansen trains operate on special high-speed tracks.

In the cab, coal is fed into a fire. This heats water in a boiler to create steam that powers the train.

NORTH EASTERN
AEROLITE
36

Aerolite, 1902

The large, powered wheel is called the driving wheel.

Steam engine

The earliest trains used steam for power. Water was heated by a coal fire in the engine. The first working train, Stephenson's *Rocket*, was built in 1829.

Underground trains

Many cities have underground trains known as subway, or metro, systems. Avoiding the busy traffic above, these trains can quickly move people around a city.

The Paris metro

Trees

A tree is a plant with a woody stem called a trunk. Trees are found all over the world, except in Antarctica. The two main types of tree are deciduous and evergreen.

SEE ALSO
▶ Forests p.109
▶ Fruit and seeds p.115
▶ Habitats p.126
▶ Materials p.157
▶ Photosynthesis p.191
▶ Plants p.194

Deciduous trees
These trees have leaves that die and drop off in the autumn. In the spring, their leaves grow back again.

Leaves
Leaves make the food a tree needs to grow. They come in all shapes and sizes depending on the type of tree.

Needles
Needles are leaves that are curled up into a tough pointed shape.

Evergreen trees
These trees keep their leaves all year round. They have flat, hard leaves called needles or scales.

Sicilian fir

Oak tree

Bark
The tree trunk is covered in bark, a rough covering that protects the tree.

Tree rings
You can tell how old a tree is by counting the rings in its trunk. Each ring shows a year in the tree's life.

261

Turkish Empire

For hundreds of years, the Ottoman Turks ruled one of the largest empires the world has ever seen. It stretched from North Africa across the Middle East to the Indian Ocean. The Ottomans were Muslims, but they ruled over many different people.

SEE ALSO

▶ Africa p.12
▶ Asia p.29
▶ Buildings p.48
▶ Crafts p.75
▶ Europe p.94
▶ Flags p.102
▶ Religion p.208

Ottoman leader

In 1299, a Turkish leader, Osman I, founded what was to become a new Turkish empire–the Ottoman Empire. The same family of sultans ruled this empire for 600 years.

Osman I led the Turks from 1299 to 1323.

The famous Blue Mosque in Istanbul, Turkey, was completed in 1616.

Religious empire

The Ottomans were Muslims, which means they followed the religion of Islam. They built grand buildings called mosques to pray in. Many of their mosques are still in use today.

The capital of the Ottoman Empire was **Constantinople**, which is now known as **Istanbul.**

Flower patterns were often used to decorate Iznik pottery.

Turkish art

The Turks made beautiful pottery in the town of Iznik in northwest Turkey. They also wove wool carpets and tapestries.

The republic

The Ottoman Empire ended in 1922, and the sultans were no longer in charge. The next year, Turkey became a republic, with its people voting to choose the leaders.

Flag of Turkey

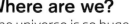

Universe

The universe is everything around us: matter, energy, and space. This means the Earth, the solar system, the Milky Way, and other galaxies are part of the universe. The universe is very big and is always changing.

Where are we?

The universe is so huge that it is hard to understand. This diagram shows how Earth fits with the rest of the universe.

The **universe** has **no center**, and is filled with galaxies in all directions—it **goes on forever**.

Universe

The universe is made up of billions of galaxies that cluster together, with huge empty spaces between them.

The Milky Way

The solar system orbits the center of our home galaxy, which is known as the Milky Way.

Scientists thought the Milky Way was the only galaxy until the early 20th century.

The solar system

The sun and its family of planets are known as the solar system.

The Earth

Our planet is one of eight planets that move around the sun.

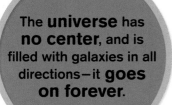

Earth was thought to be the center of the universe until the 16th century.

City landscape

Our planet is home to 7 billion people living in towns, cities, and the countryside.

Dark matter

Scientists think that dark matter is made of particles smaller than atoms. Dark matter is invisible to us, but we know it exists because its force of gravity pulls nearby space objects toward it.

Visible matter 20 percent

Dark matter 80 percent

Uranus

Uranus is the third largest planet in the solar system, after Jupiter and Saturn. It is the second farthest planet from the sun. From Earth, Uranus looks like a very faint star.

SEE ALSO
▶ Atmosphere p.33
▶ Elements p.90
▶ Gases p.117
▶ Mixtures p.168
▶ Neptune p.183
▶ Solar system p.233

Ice giant

Uranus is an "ice giant"–it has a rocky core that is surrounded by a mixture of liquid ices. Uranus has no solid surface.

The atmosphere of Uranus is mostly made of hydrogen and helium gas. It is very cold.

Rolling planet

Most planets spin like tops on their axis, but Uranus spins on its side like a rolling ball. Its tilt was probably caused by a giant crash with another planet-sized body.

Earth is slightly tilted and spins from west to east.

Earth

Uranus

Uranus is very tilted and spins from east to west.

Few features

The spacecraft *Voyager 2* visited the Uranus system in 1986. Images sent back to Earth revealed 10 new moons and two new rings but few other features.

Voyager 2

Uranus has thin, dark rings that are hard to see.

Uranus is the **coldest planet** in the solar system, with temperatures as low as **−371°F (−224°C).**

Venus

Venus is a rocky planet that is only slightly smaller than Earth. It is the second planet away from the sun, and sits between Mercury and Earth. Venus spins very slowly and has the longest day of all the planets in the solar system.

Harsh planet

Venus's rocky surface is extremely hot. Temperatures can reach more than 878°F (470°C), which is hot enough to melt metal.

Maat Mons is the biggest volcano on Venus. It is 245 miles (395 km) wide.

Venus has thousands of volcanoes on its surface.

Atmosphere

Venus is surrounded by a thick layer of poisonous gases. This atmosphere makes it hard for scientists to see Venus's surface.

Sulphur gas in the clouds makes Venus appear yellow.

Much of Venus's surface is covered with solid rock that used to be liquid.

Transit of Venus

Venus is closer to the sun than the Earth is. We sometimes see Venus moving in front of the sun. It looks like a small, dark disk moving across the bright Sun. This is called the transit of Venus.

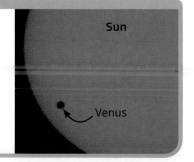

Sun

Venus

Vertebrates

Vertebrates are animals that have a backbone. The skeleton is a frame that helps the body move around. Mammals, amphibians, reptiles, fish, and birds are all vertebrates.

SEE ALSO
▶ Amphibians p.15
▶ Birds p.39
▶ Fish p.101
▶ Invertebrates p.139
▶ Mammals p.154
▶ Reptiles p.210
▶ Skeleton p.228

The skull protects the soft brain inside.

The small, linked-up bones in the back are called vertebrae.

Mammals

All mammals have a similar skeleton. Only mammals have a lower jawbone that is joined to the skull by a hinge.

Having lots of little bones in the tail means it can be moved around easily.

The ribcage holds the tiger's lungs in place.

Tiger skeleton

Strong bones in the legs let the tiger jump a long way.

Frog skeleton

Amphibians

Frogs and toads don't have ribs. They have strong leg bones for jumping.

Fins let the fish swim smoothly through water.

Fish skeleton

Fish

Only some fish have bony skeletons. Others, such as sharks, have skeletons made from a bendy substance called cartilage.

Birds

Most birds have light bones, to let them fly. Penguins have heavier bones so they can dive deep in the water.

Bird skeletons are full of holes. This helps them to be as light as possible.

The jaw have extra bones.

There are more rib bones.

Lizard skeleton

Reptiles

Reptiles have more bones in their skeletons than other animals. This makes them very bendy.

Penguin skeleton

Vikings

Starting in the year 800, people from Norway, Sweden, and Denmark set out to travel long distances and explore the world. We call these people Vikings. At home they had been farmers and craftspeople. On their travels, Vikings traded with or sometimes stole from others.

SEE ALSO

▶ Crafts p.75
▶ Europe p.94
▶ Explorers p.96
▶ Myths and legends p.178
▶ Oceans and seas p.187
▶ Ships p.224

Viking longship

Longships were fast ships Vikings used to travel across the Atlantic Ocean and up rivers in Europe. They were powered by oars and a sail.

In 1004, Viking woman Gudrid Thorbjarnardóttir **led a voyage** from Greenland to Canada.

Viking longhouse

Vikings built houses using wood. The roofs were either wooden or thatched (woven using straw or other soft materials). Inside were several different rooms for the family, slaves, and animals.

Roof decorations helped to identify the owner.

Straw or wool filled gaps in the planks.

Some Viking warships had an animal head carved on the front.

The square sail was rolled up in shallow waters.

The mast could be taken down in a storm.

The strong keel was made from oak wood.

Overlapping planks made a strong, light ship.

Oars could change the direction of the ship.

Ropes controlled the sail.

Shields protected the crew from spray.

Helmets were worn by most Viking warriors.

Swords were expensive weapons.

A belt pouch was a good place to keep coins.

Volcanoes

A volcano is a mountain or crater that forms when melted rock, called magma, breaks through the Earth's surface. As soon as the magma breaks through, or erupts, from a volcano, it is known as lava. Every year around the world, between 50 and 70 volcanoes erupt.

SEE ALSO
▶ Earth's surface p.84
▶ Earthquakes p.85
▶ Inside Earth p.135
▶ Rock cycle p.213
▶ Rocks and minerals p.214

Volcanic eruption

Volcanoes erupt in different ways. In some eruptions, lava gently flows out or spurts like a fountain. In other eruptions, gas, ash, and rocks explode out of the volcano.

Gas in the magma can make it blast high into the sky, forming a lava fountain.

Small pieces of lava fall around the crater, forming a cone-shaped mountain.

About **80 percent** of **volcanic eruptions** take place under the sea.

Lava flows are slow-moving rivers of melted rock that can bury or destroy everything in their path.

Types of volcano

Volcanoes come in all shapes and sizes. Some are small, cone-shaped hills formed in a single eruption. Others are giant mountains built up by many eruptions.

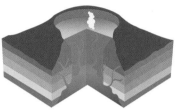

Caldera
The biggest volcanic eruptions leave behind an enormous crater known as a caldera. Some craters fill with water and become lakes.

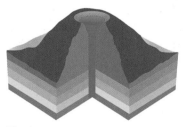

Cinder cone
Built of fragments of cooled lava called cinders, cinder cones are the smallest and most common type of volcano.

Stratovolcano
This type of volcano is made up of layers of ash and lava from many eruptions. Stratovolcanoes are steep-sided and cone-shaped.

Volume

In math, volume is the amount of space inside a shape. The volume of a shape is measured in "cubed" units, such as cubic inches (in^3) or cubic centimeters (cm^3).

SEE ALSO

▶ Ancient Greece p.18

▶ Human body p.130

▶ Measuring p.159

▶ Numbers p.185

▶ Science p.217

▶ Shapes p.222

3-D shapes

Three-dimensional (3-D) shapes have length, width, and height. While 2-D shapes such as squares are flat, 3-D shapes have volume.

Cone
Cones have a circular base and a curved side that ends in a point.

Cylinder
A cylinder has circular ends and a long middle section.

Cuboid
These shapes have six flat, rectangular sides of any size.

Sphere
A sphere is shaped like a ball. If you cut it in half, the sliced face would be circular.

Cube
Cubes have six equal-sized, square sides.

Finding volume

The volume of any object can be found by putting it in water. The volume of the water is measured first. The object is added, then the water is measured again.

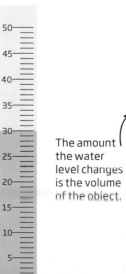

Carefully measure the volume of the water. Then add your object.

The amount the water level changes is the volume of the object.

Eureka!

An ancient Greek mathematician called Archimedes realized that the amount of water he pushed out when he got in the bath was the same volume as his body. He shouted "Eureka!," which means "I have found it!"

Archimedes in the bath

Water cycle

The Earth always has the same amount of water, but it is constantly moving between the oceans, rivers, underground reservoirs, ice caps, and the atmosphere. This continuous movement is called the water cycle.

SEE ALSO

▶ Clouds p.64
▶ Water pp.120–121
▶ Glaciers p.122
▶ Lakes p.143
▶ Oceans and seas p.187
▶ Rivers p.211

Moving water

The amount of water in the atmosphere, the oceans, and on land is always changing.

Water in the atmosphere comes together in masses of tiny droplets to form clouds.

When clouds contain enough water they produce rain, snow, or hail that falls down to Earth.

Some rainwater and snowmelt soak into the ground, forming underground lakes known as aquifers.

Water evaporates from the sea into the atmosphere. Plants release water in a process called transpiration.

Rainwater and snowmelt find their way into rivers, which eventually carry them to the sea.

Water of life

Without water there would be no life on Earth. Even plants and animals that live in very dry places, such as deserts, need some water to stay alive.

Breaking the cycle

Humans break the water cycle in several ways. We dam rivers, suck up water from underground, and use water for washing and drinking.

Weather

The weather is what is happening in the atmosphere, or air and sky, outside. It could be sunny or cloudy, windy or calm, rainy or dry, or foggy or clear. In tropical parts of the world, it is hot and sunny most of the time. Further north or south, the weather can be different every day.

Sunny
When there is bright sunshine, it is often warm with clear blue skies. Plants grow well in this kind of weather. If it is too hot and dry, however, they might die.

Windy
The wind is the movement of the air. Winds may be warm or cold, depending on the direction they blow in from. Very strong winds can damage buildings and blow down trees.

Rainy
Water droplets that fall from clouds are called rain. Plants need rain to grow, but too much rain can cause floods. When it is very cold, rain falls as snow.

Foggy
Fog and mist are made up of water droplets. They are clouds at ground level. Fogs are thicker than mists. People driving in fog need to be very careful as it is hard to see ahead.

The **story** of...

School

A school is where children go to learn subjects, such as reading and writing, that help them to understand the world. Going to school gives us the knowledge and skills that help us to get a job.

Madrasa
In parts of the Islamic world, children go to a school known as a madrasa. Here they learn more about their religion by studying the Quran.

Students take **ten billion trips** every year on **school buses** in the United States and Canada.

Extra flashing lights help children see that the school bus is coming.

First schools
Boys first started to go to school in ancient Greece, Rome, China, and India. Later, in Europe, church schools were set up. Girls were not always sent to school.

A school in ancient Rome

School buses have extra mirrors to help the driver spot children.

Education for all
Today, both boys and girls go to school from around the age of five. They learn math, reading, and writing. Older children study other subjects, too.

College

A college or university is where people over 18 can study a subject in great detail for three or four years. They are awarded a degree when they graduate.

Graduation cap

Degree certificate

Almost **two million** children are home-schooled in the US.

CHOOL BUS

INTERNATIONAL

Getting to school

Many students walk to school, others are taken there in special school buses or by car or train. In the US, school buses are painted bright yellow.

Home school

Some children stay at home during the day and are given lessons by their parents. They get to study all the subjects they would learn at school. Children that live a long way from the nearest school join in lessons over the Internet.

Victorian desktop blackboard

Tools for school

In the past, children wrote out their lessons using chalk on a small blackboard. Today, some schools use computers and tablets, although tests and homework usually have to be written out on paper.

Work

Work provides people with money to pay for the things they need, such as food and somewhere to live. There are lots of different types of work you can do. Many jobs need special skills that you must train for. Some people stay doing the same work all their lives. Others learn new skills and change jobs.

SEE ALSO
▶ Farming p.98
▶ Inventions pp.136–137
▶ Law p.145
▶ Medicine p.160
▶ Money p.169
▶ School pp.272–273

Jobs

The type of work a person does is called their job. Different jobs require different skills. People might work on a building site, in a hospital, or at a school.

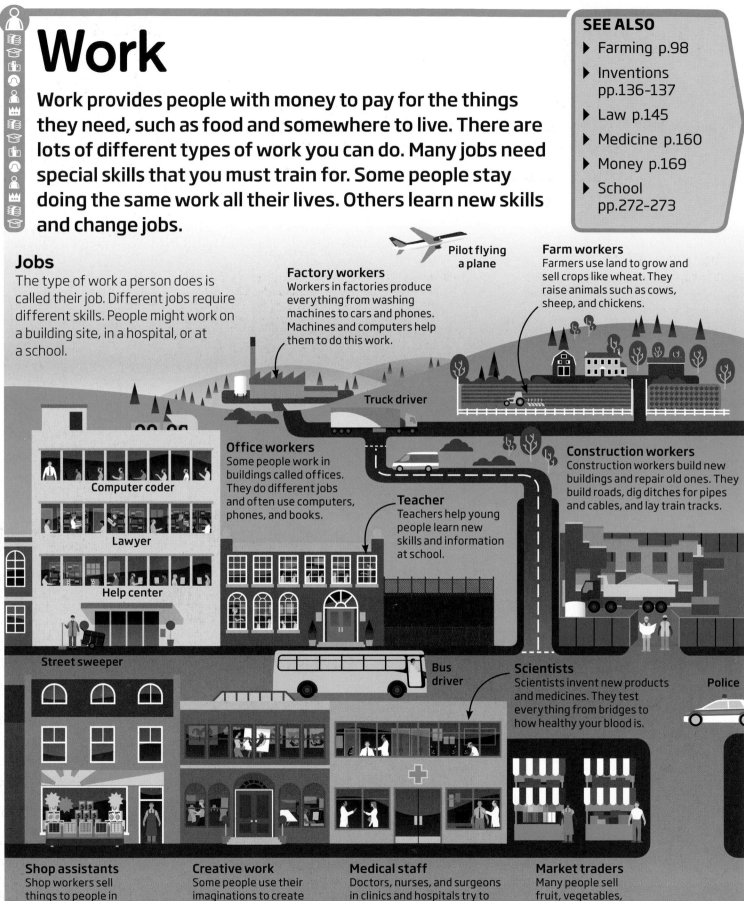

Pilot flying a plane

Factory workers
Workers in factories produce everything from washing machines to cars and phones. Machines and computers help them to do this work.

Farm workers
Farmers use land to grow and sell crops like wheat. They raise animals such as cows, sheep, and chickens.

Truck driver

Computer coder

Lawyer

Help center

Office workers
Some people work in buildings called offices. They do different jobs and often use computers, phones, and books.

Teacher
Teachers help young people learn new skills and information at school.

Construction workers
Construction workers build new buildings and repair old ones. They build roads, dig ditches for pipes and cables, and lay train tracks.

Street sweeper

Bus driver

Scientists
Scientists invent new products and medicines. They test everything from bridges to how healthy your blood is.

Police

Shop assistants
Shop workers sell things to people in stores, such as food, clothes, shoes, books, and music.

Creative work
Some people use their imaginations to create websites, design books and posters, and make music and films.

Medical staff
Doctors, nurses, and surgeons in clinics and hospitals try to cure you if you're ill. Carers look after people who need extra help.

Market traders
Many people sell fruit, vegetables, plants, flowers, and household goods in market stalls.

World

The Earth and everything that lives on it make up the world. We often show the world as a map. Just over one-quarter of it is land, which is divided into seven huge areas, called continents. The rest of the world is covered in water, or oceans.

SEE ALSO
▶ Changing world pp.50–51
▶ Climate change p.60
▶ Earth p.83
▶ Earth's surface p.84
▶ Maps p.155

Where we live

We live on all of the world's seven continents. Apart from Antarctica, the continents are divided into areas called countries.

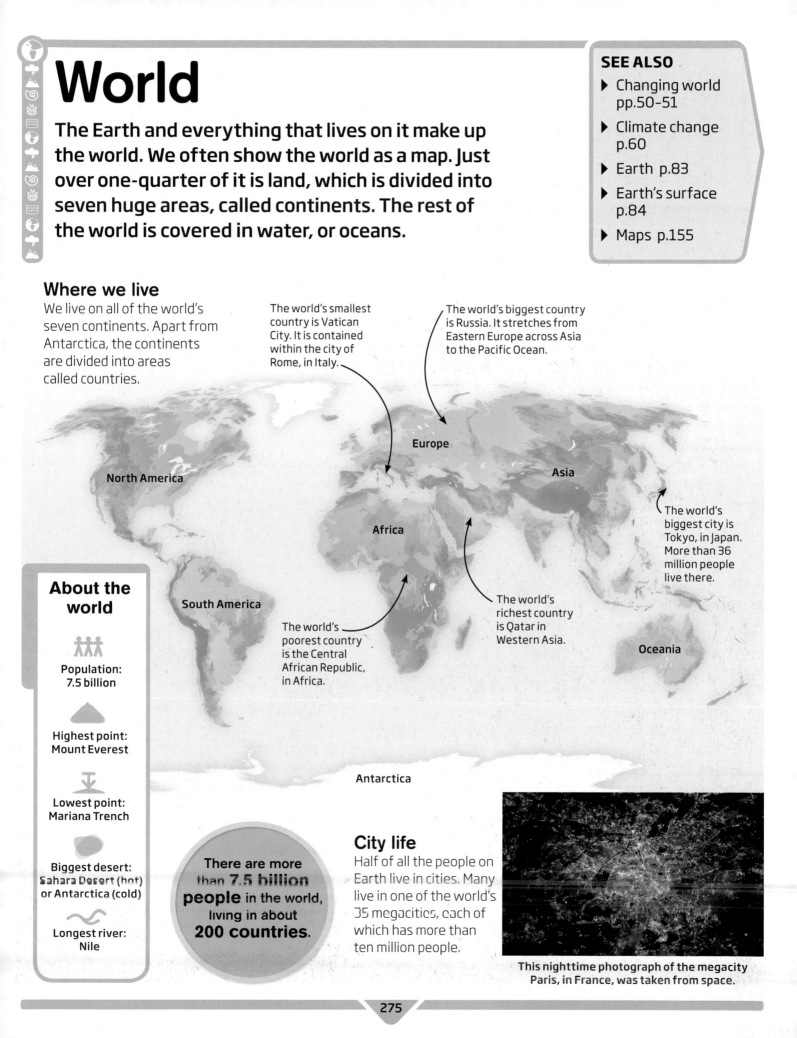

The world's smallest country is Vatican City. It is contained within the city of Rome, in Italy.

The world's biggest country is Russia. It stretches from Eastern Europe across Asia to the Pacific Ocean.

Europe

North America

Asia

Africa

The world's biggest city is Tokyo, in Japan. More than 36 million people live there.

South America

The world's poorest country is the Central African Republic, in Africa.

The world's richest country is Qatar in Western Asia.

Oceania

Antarctica

About the world

👥 Population: 7.5 billion

🔺 Highest point: Mount Everest

⚓ Lowest point: Mariana Trench

Biggest desert: Sahara Desert (hot) or Antarctica (cold)

〜 Longest river: Nile

There are more than **7.5 billion people** in the world, living in about **200 countries**.

City life

Half of all the people on Earth live in cities. Many live in one of the world's 35 megacities, each of which has more than ten million people.

This nighttime photograph of the megacity Paris, in France, was taken from space.

World War I

In 1914, war broke out in Europe and spread across the world. In this war, planes and tanks were used for the first time. The fighting lasted for four years and millions of soldiers were killed. Peace was declared in 1918.

Trench warfare

In Western Europe, the opposing armies defended the land they held by digging lines of deep trenches. Trenches protected the soldiers from enemy fire but were dangerous and very dirty.

Soldiers went over the top of the trench to fight the enemy.

Sand bags protected against rifle fire.

Barbed wire kept enemy soldiers out.

A bayonet on the end of a gun was used to stab the enemy.

Heavy-duty boots were worn.

Rats ran everywhere in the trenches, spreading disease.

Trenches were very muddy and often filled with water.

Gas masks could be worn if the enemy attacked using poisonous gas.

THESE WOMEN ARE DOING THEIR BIT

LEARN TO MAKE MUNITIONS

Women at war

With the men away fighting, women worked in factories to make weapons and ammunition (bullets and shells). They also worked on farms.

Allies and Central Powers

The warring countries formed two groups, with the Allies fighting the Central Powers.

Allies:

Britain   France   Italy

Russia   USA

Central Powers:

Germany   Austria-Hungary   Ottoman Empire

World War II

In 1939, Germany invaded Poland and a war broke out in Europe. Fighting spread across the world, with massive battles on land, at sea, and in the air. The war lasted six years and was the most violent conflict in history, with more than 60 million people killed. Peace was restored in 1945.

Kindertransport

Almost 10,000 mainly Jewish children who were threatened with persecution were brought to safety in Britain from mainland Europe. This was called the *Kindertransport*, or "children's transport."

A single pilot sat in the cockpit. He also fired the guns.

British fighter plane
British Spitfire fighter aircraft brought down many German planes during the Battle of Britain in 1940.

The turret rotated to point the main gun at the enemy.

German tank
Germany made thousands of powerful, well-armed tanks to attack both Western Europe and the Soviet Union (Russia).

Aircraft were kept on the deck ready to take off.

The ship was painted in different colors to confuse the enemy.

US ship
The US Navy fought a series of fierce battles in the Pacific Ocean against the Japanese Navy.

Allies and Axis

The four main Allies faced the three Axis nations of Germany, Italy, and Japan. Fighting between them took place in Europe, Africa, Asia, and Oceania.

Main Allies:

Britain France USA Soviet Union

Axis:

Germany Italy Japan

The **story** of...

War

Throughout history, people have fought each other for land, money, and power. They have fought to defend a religion or overthrow a ruler or a government. Wars are expensive and kill thousands of people. They can last for years. Many don't agree with war, believing it is always wrong to kill people.

A full suit of armor weighed up to **90 lb (40 kg)**, which is about the same as **40 dictionaries**.

Early warfare
Men fought the first wars armed with battle-axes, wooden clubs, knives, spears, and shields. They didn't have uniforms, so it was sometimes difficult for them to know if they were fighting their enemies or their friends.

Horses wore armor to protect their head, neck, and sides.

Knight on horseback

The **Trojan War** ended when Greek soldiers tricked their way into the city of Troy, by hiding inside a **wooden horse**.

Long wars
War can last a long time. The Trojan War lasted for ten years, while the Greeks and Persians fought each other for 50 years in the 400s BCE. The Hundred Years' War between England and France lasted for 116 years, from 1337 to 1453, although fighting did not take place every day.

Knights in armor
In medieval Europe, knights rode into battle on horseback, wearing suits of metal armor. The armor protected them from arrows and spears, but was heavy to wear and meant they couldn't see very well.

The Spanish Armada was made up of **130 ships** that carried **2,500 guns** and **30,000 soldiers and sailors**.

A painting of the Spanish Armada in 1588.

War at sea
Many battles take place at sea. Sea battles can be very dangerous as ships can quickly sink, killing everyone on board. If rival boats get close together, soldiers can scramble across onto an enemy ship.

This flag was used by the rebel states during the Civil War.

Civil wars
Most wars are fought between countries, but wars can also break out between groups within a country–these are known as civil wars. The US fought a war against Britain to win its independence in 1783, and then fought a bitter civil war from 1861 to 1865.

The first official flag of the USA had 13 stars and 13 stripes to represent each of the colonies in 1777.

A modern submachine gun can fire
1,200 bullets
a minute, which is 20 every second.

War graves

Gunpowder
Gunpowder is an explosive material that was first invented in China in the 800s. It can be used in guns to propel bullets and shells very fast and over long distances against an enemy army.

Cost of war
Soldiers are killed or die of their wounds, and civilians caught up in the fighting can be killed by accident. If a person refuses to fight in a war because they don't believe in killing people, they are known as a conscientious objector.

Prussian soldier

Writing

Writing is putting the words we speak down on paper or on a screen. We do this using sets of characters, such as the letters in an alphabet. Characters represent the different letters or words of a language. The many different languages in the world have different systems of writing.

Writing systems

Written characters can be joined together to form words, or sometimes form words on their own. Different systems are written left to right, right to left, or downward.

Writing tools

The first words were carved into soft clay using a hard reed or piece of wood. Today we write with pencils, crayons, and pens. Brushes can be used to paint beautiful characters.

Calligraphy brush

Fountain pen

Pencil

Cuneiform
Used in ancient Iraq, this was one of the first writing systems. Cuneiform means "wedge-shaped."

Have a

nice day

English
The English alphabet has 26 letters. These letters are used by many languages across the world.

Have a nice day

Chinese
These characters are formed of pictures that often show an object. A character forms one word or part of a word.

祝你过一个好天

Have a nice day

Cyrillic
This alphabet is used to write Russian and other Eastern European and Central Asian languages.

Хорошего дня!

Have a nice day

Hindi
The Hindi language of India is written in the beautiful Devanagari alphabet. It has 47 different letters.

आप का दिन अच्छा बीते!

Have a nice day

Some Chinese dictionaries list more than 40,000 characters!

Emojis
Emoji means "picture character" in Japanese. Emojis are used on mobile phones and computers as a quick way to show feelings or words.

Zoo

Zoos are home to animals from all over the world. Scientists work in zoos to learn about the animals, and how animals live in the wild. The oldest zoos have been around for hundreds of years. Millions of people visit zoos to see animals and learn more about them.

SEE ALSO
- Animal families p.21
- Conservation p.72
- Farming p.98
- Pets pp.152–153
- Mammals p.154
- Work p.274

Natural spaces
Zoos try to keep animals in spaces that are like where they would be in the wild. This is good for the animals and helps people learn about these places.

Zoo people
Lots of different people work in zoos. Zookeepers look after the animals every day; zoologists are scientists that study the animals; and vets keep the animals healthy.

Conservation
Zoos protect animal numbers in the wild and work to stop animals from becoming extinct. For example, California zoos have set up breeding programs to save the endangered California condor.

Bad zoos
Not all zoos are good. Some don't look after their animals properly or keep them in the right spaces. Good zoos are part of zoo organizations that make sure they keep animals safe and healthy.

Zoo visit
Here are some things to bear in mind if you visit a zoo.

Don't feed the animals
Feeding animals food that is not part of their diet can make them sick.

Don't make loud noises
Loud noises scare the animals, so try not to shout.

Listen to the zookeepers
The keepers know a lot. You can learn about animals by listening to them and reading the signs.

Reference

In this section you'll find a useful collection of lists and diagrams packed with helpful information.

Artists

An artist is someone who creates art by painting, sculpting, or making. Even early humans made cave paintings. Many artists are famous for inventing new styles of art and ways of painting.

Giotto (around 1266-1337)
Italian painter who started painting in a more lifelike way. His pictures mark the start of the Renaissance style of painting, which was more realistic than what had been before.

Jan van Eyck (around 1390-1441)
The first great painter to develop the use of oil paints. He came from what is now Belgium.

Leonardo da Vinci (1452-1519)
Italian painter, inventor, and thinker who painted people with natural expressions. His most famous works are the *Mona Lisa* and the wall painting *The Last Supper.*

Michelangelo Buonarroti (1475-1564)
Italian painter, sculptor, architect, and poet, often called simply "Michelangelo." His large religious paintings on the ceiling and walls of the Sistine Chapel in Rome are among the most famous of all artworks.

Raphael (Raffaello Sanzio, 1483-1520)
Italian painter of religious works and portraits. He used Leonardo's and Michelangelo's techniques to make paintings that influenced art for hundreds of years.

Titian (around 1488-1576)
Painter from Venice, Italy, whose works include mythological scenes and realistic portraits of people, and are well known for their bright colors.

Peter Paul Rubens (1577-1640)
Artist and diplomat who lived in what is now Belgium. He was the most famous painter of the Baroque style, which came after the Renaissance and features dramatic situations and emotions.

Claude Lorrain (around 1600-1682)
French landscape painter who mainly worked in Italy. His landscapes often include ancient ruins, and inspired the fashion for landscape gardening, where people tried to make their land look like his paintings.

Rembrandt (Rembrandt van Rijn, 1606-1669)
Dutch painter whose great skill as an artist helped him paint people's emotions. Many of his best paintings are self-portraits.

Francisco Goya (1746-1828)
Spanish artist who became official painter to the King of Spain, but whose works also include nightmare scenes and paintings of the horrors of war.

Katsushika Hokusai (1760-1849)
Japanese artist who excelled in painting scenes from everyday life and landscapes. Many of his works feature the snow-capped Japanese volcano, Mount Fuji.

J. M. W. Turner (1775-1851)
English landscape painter whose works show his interests in travel, the sea, history, and literature. In his later paintings the scenes are sometimes almost completely hidden by mist, rain, or snow.

John Constable (1776-1837)
English landscape painter known for his everyday countryside scenes. His famous paintings include *The Hay Wain* and *The Cornfield.*

Eugène Delacroix (1798-1863)
French painter of the Romantic period, when art, writing, and music focused on emotions. He chose dramatic subjects, deliberately painting so that his individual brushstrokes could be seen.

Paul Cézanne (1839-1906)
French painter, sometimes called the father of modern art. He mainly painted landscapes and still lifes (objects like flowers and fruits), building up his pictures with large blocks of color.

Claude Monet (1840-1926)
French landscape painter who invented the Impressionist style of art, which tried to paint the overall effect of a moment in time.

Vincent van Gogh (1853-1890)
Dutch painter who developed a unique style featuring bright colors and dramatic brushstrokes. He was not well known until after he died.

Edvard Munch (1863-1944)
Norwegian painter who had a tragic childhood and painted many works expressing fear and anxiety. His most famous painting is *The Scream.*

Qi Baishi (1864-1957)
Popular Chinese artist whose many works include a variety of subjects such as paintings of individual animals and plants.

Henri Matisse (1869-1954)
French painter. His brightly colored, usually cheerful works are sometimes abstract, but usually he painted recognizable objects in a simplified style.

Abanindranath Tagore (1871-1951)
Indian painter and author who helped develop Indian art that was less dependent on British influence (Britain ruled India at the time). His uncle was the poet Rabindranath Tagore (see "Writers" list).

Pablo Picasso (1881-1973)
Spanish artist, probably the most famous painter of the 20th century. He painted in a variety of modern art styles and helped invent Cubism, which includes lots of geometric shapes such as squares and triangles.

Edward Hopper (1882-1967)
American painter of realistic scenes, often city streets or buildings, either deserted or with lonely-looking people in them.

Diego Rivera (1886-1957)
Mexican painter best known for his colorful, action-packed wall paintings which often have a political message. Husband of Frida Kahlo.

Mark Rothko (1903-1970)
American abstract artist whose work features rectangular blocks of color painted without sharp edges.

Salvador Dalí (1904-1989)
Spanish painter and sculptor who belonged to the art movement called Surrealism, which created made-up subjects. His work features dreamlike impossible scenes, painted in a highly realistic way.

Frida Kahlo (1907-1954)
Mexican painter known for her self-portraits. She had a complex life, affected by an accident and illness as a child. Wife of Diego Rivera.

Jackson Pollock (1912-1956)
American painter best known for his "action paintings"—abstract works created by dribbling swirls of paint on a canvas.

Andy Warhol (1928-1987)
American founder of Pop Art, which takes everyday images such as soup cans or celebrities' faces and uses them as the basis for artworks.

Antony Gormley (born 1950)
British sculptor whose works include the huge outdoor winged figure the *Angel of the North* near Newcastle upon Tyne, UK.

Writers

People have written things down for thousands of years. Writing can include books, poems, or plays. It can tell a story or record facts.

Homer (around 800 BCE)
Legendary blind author of the Greek epic poems the *Iliad* and the *Odyssey*, set at the time of the Trojan War.

Sappho (around 630 BCE)
Greek poet famous for her passionate love poetry. Only a small amount of her work now survives.

Qu Yuan (around 340-278 BCE)
Ancient Chinese poet and public servant. His most famous poem is called *The Lament*.

Virgil (70-19 BCE)
Roman author of the epic poem the *Aeneid*, which tells the legendary story of the creation of the city of Rome.

Imru' al-Qais (around 500)
Arabian poet whose works are full of passionate feeling. He is sometimes called the father of Arabic poetry.

Dante Alighieri (1265-1321)
Italian author of the *Divine Comedy*, a three-part epic poem describing hell, heaven, and purgatory (a place in between heaven and hell).

Geoffrey Chaucer (around 1343-1400)
English author of *The Canterbury Tales*, entertaining stories told in the voice of different pilgrims (people traveling to a sacred place).

Miguel de Cervantes (1547-1616)
Spanish writer whose comic book *Don Quixote*, about the adventures of a well-meaning but silly knight, is often described as Europe's first novel.

William Shakespeare (1564-1616)
English playwright and poet whose many famous plays include *Hamlet*, *Macbeth*, *Romeo and Juliet*, and *A Midsummer Night's Dream*.

Molière (1622-1673)
Famous French actor and author of funny comic plays. Molière was his stage name, his real name was Jean-Baptiste Poquelin.

Matsuo Bashō (1644-1694)
Japanese poet, a master of the short type of Japanese poem called a haiku, which contains just 17 syllables (single sounds in words).

Voltaire (1694-1778)
French writer and thinker, whose real name was François-Marie Arouet. He attacked old-fashioned ideas in his funny and controversial writings.

Johann Wolfgang von Goethe (1749-1832)
German writer, poet, and thinker, whose wide-ranging works include *Faust*, a long drama finished just before his death.

Robert Burns (1759-1796)
Scotland's national poet. He wrote or revised the words for hundreds of Scottish songs including *Auld Lang Syne*.

William Wordsworth (1770-1850)
English poet who used nature as a source of inspiration.

Sir Walter Scott (1771-1832)
Scottish writer and poet. He was the first great historical novelist, with works including *Ivanhoe*, *Old Mortality*, and *The Heart of Midlothian*.

Jane Austen (1775-1817)
English author whose funny and clever novels, including *Emma* and *Pride and Prejudice*, are still popular today.

Hans Christian Andersen (1805-1875)
Danish writer best known for his children's stories including *The Ugly Duckling*, *The Little Mermaid*, and *The Snow Queen*.

Charles Dickens (1812-1870)
English author of many famous novels including *Oliver Twist*, *David Copperfield*, and *A Tale of Two Cities*.

Charlotte Brontë (1816-1855)
English author of *Jane Eyre* and other novels. Her sisters Emily (1818-1848, author of *Wuthering Heights*) and Anne (1820-1849) are also well-known writers.

Charles Baudelaire (1821-1867)
French poet whose subjects include city life and the unhappy side of emotions. He was a big influence on later poets.

Leo Tolstoy (1828-1910)
Russian author of the famous novels *Anna Karenina* and *War and Peace*.

Emily Dickinson (1830-1886)
American poet whose deeply felt, personal poems only became well known after her death.

Lewis Carroll (1832-1898)
English author and mathematician. His real name was Charles Lutwidge Dodgson. He wrote the stories *Alice's Adventures in Wonderland* and *Through the Looking-Glass*.

Mark Twain (1835-1910)
American author, whose real name was Samuel Langhorne Clemens. His many works include the novels *The Adventures of Tom Sawyer* and *The Adventures of Huckleberry Finn*.

Oscar Wilde (1854-1900)
Irish author whose works include the play *The Importance of Being Earnest* and his only novel, *The Picture of Dorian Gray*.

Rabindranath Tagore (1861-1941)
Indian poet, novelist, composer, and thinker who wrote mainly in the Bengali language. He won the Nobel Prize for Literature in 1913.

H. G. Wells (1866-1946)
English author and thinker. He wrote works of science fiction such as *The Time Machine* and *The War of the Worlds*.

James Joyce (1882-1941)
Irish author of famous novels including *Ulysses* and *Finnegans Wake*.

Virginia Woolf (1882-1941)
English novelist whose works feature a style of writing called stream-of-consciousness where you read a person's thoughts as they think them.

T. S. Eliot (1888-1965)
American-English poet whose works include *The Waste Land*. His humorous poems about cats became the inspiration for the musical *Cats*. He won the Nobel Prize for Literature in 1948.

Ernest Hemingway (1899-1961)
American author whose books include *A Farewell to Arms* and *For Whom the Bell Tolls*, both set in wartime. He won the Nobel Prize for Literature in 1954.

George Orwell (1903-1950)
English novelist and essay writer. He wrote the famous political novels *Animal Farm* and *Nineteen Eighty-Four*.

Gabriel García Márquez (1927-2014)
Colombian author whose novels, originally written in Spanish, include *One Hundred Years of Solitude* and *Love in the Time of Cholera*. He won the Nobel Prize for Literature in 1982.

Wole Soyinka (born 1934)
Nigerian playwright, poet, and novelist whose works often deal with African political and social issues. He won the Nobel Prize for Literature in 1986.

J. K. Rowling (born 1965)
British author of the hugely successful *Harry Potter* series of books about a young wizard.

Alphabets and writing systems

An alphabet is a set of marks that each means a sound. It is used to write down the words of a language.

Ancient Greek letters
The ancient Greeks used an alphabet with 24 letters. The Latin alphabet is based on it.

Ancient Greek

Aα	Bβ	Γγ	Δδ	Eε	Zζ	Hη	Θθ
alpha	beta	gamma	delta	epsilon	zeta	eta	theta
Iι	Kκ	Λλ	Mμ	Nν	Ξξ	Oo	Ππ
iota	kappa	lambda	mu	nu	ksi	omicron	pi
Pρ	Σσς	Tτ	Υυ	Φφ	Χχ	Ψψ	Ωω
rho	sigma	tau	upsilon	phi	chi	psi	omega

Latin letters
The Latin alphabet is still used today in many European languages. Three letters have been added since ancient times: J, U, and W.

Latin (Roman)

Aa	Bb	Cc	Dd	Ee	Ff	Gg	Hh	Ii	Jj	Kk	Ll	Mm
Nn	Oo	Pp	Qq	Rr	Ss	Tt	Uu	Vv	Ww	Xx	Yy	Zz

Arabic letters
The Arabic alphabet has 28 letters. It reads from right to left and does not have separate capital letters. Some vowels have their own letters, but some are added to the consonants.

Arabic

ص	ش	س	ز	ر	ذ	د	خ	ح	ج	ث	ت	ب	ا
ي	و	ه	ن	م	ل	ك	ق	ف	غ	ع	ظ	ط	ض

Chinese characters
Chinese writing does not have an alphabet; instead, symbols called characters represent whole words. More than one language is spoken in China. Mandarin is the most common.

Chinese (Mandarin)

女	男	子	头	手	脚	日	月
woman	man	child	head	hand	foot	sun	moon
土	水	火	金	木	山	云	龙
earth	water	fire	metal	tree	mountain	cloud	dragon
狗	猫	马	鸟	北	南	大	小
dog	cat	horse	bird	north	south	big	small
刀	叉	辣	冷	春天	夏天	秋天	冬天
knife	fork	hot	cold	spring	summer	autumn	winter

Scientists

For thousands of years, scientists have made all sorts of important inventions and discoveries. Today, they are still answering important questions about the universe.

Aristotle (384-322 BCE)
Ancient Greek philosopher and scientist. His ideas on physics are out of date but he was a good biologist, pointing out many facts about animals for the first time.

Aristarchus of Samos (around 310-230 BCE)
Greek astronomer who first suggested that the Earth goes around the sun, instead of the other way round, as was thought before. Copernicus came up with the same idea much later on.

Zhang Heng (78-139 CE)
Chinese scientist and mathematician who invented a device that would detect earthquakes up to 310 miles (500 km) away.

Galen (around 129-200)
Greek doctor who studied the parts of the human body. Although many of his ideas were later proved to be wrong, people treated his writings on medicine very seriously for more than 1,300 years.

Alhazen (around 965-1039)
Arab mathematician, astronomer, and physicist. He was probably the best scientist of medieval times, writing a major work on the theory of light and vision.

Nicolaus Copernicus (1473-1543)
Polish astronomer who showed both that the Earth was not standing still, but instead spinning on its axis once a day, and that it orbits the sun once a year, instead of the sun orbiting the Earth.

Galileo Galilei (1564-1642)
Italian physicist and astronomer. He was the first person to use a telescope in astronomy, discovering among other things that Jupiter had moons.

Johannes Kepler (1571-1630)
German astronomer who improved Copernicus's theory that the Earth and other planets moved around the sun, by showing that their orbits are ellipses (oval shapes), not circles.

William Harvey (1578-1657)
English doctor who discovered that the heart pumps blood around the body, pushing it outward through arteries and back through veins.

Isaac Newton (1642-1727)
English physicist and mathematician who explained gravity for the first time. In physics, he introduced his famous "three laws of motion," which explain how objects move and interact with each other.

Carl Linnaeus (1707-1778)
Swedish biologist who introduced the idea of naming living things by giving them a name in Latin, for example Homo sapiens for humans.

James Hutton (1726-1797)
Scottish geologist whose work showed that the Earth's rocks formed over a huge time period as a result of very slow changes.

Antoine Lavoisier (1743-1794)
French chemist, often called the father of modern chemistry. He introduced the idea of a chemical element, and named the gas oxygen.

Alessandro Volta (1745-1827)
Italian physicist who in 1800 invented the electric battery, which first allowed a steady electric current to be produced. The unit of electricity, the volt, is named in his honor.

Michael Faraday (1791-1867)
English physicist and chemist. He showed that a moving magnet creates an electric current in a wire and invented the theory of electric and magnetic fields to explain his discoveries.

Charles Darwin (1809-1882)
English biologist whose 1859 book *On the Origin of Species* argued that new species can evolve from existing ones by natural selection.

Ada Lovelace (1815-1852)
English mathematician who put together the world's first computer program. She wrote it for a never-completed mechanical computer built by the inventor Charles Babbage.

Gregor Mendel (1822-1884)
Austrian science teacher and monk. He carried out careful experiments on plants to show how features such as flower color and seed shape are passed on to the next generation.

Louis Pasteur (1822-1895)
French chemist who proved that tiny living things cause rotting and decay. He also showed how people could be protected from diseases by immunizing them.

Dmitri Mendeleev (1834-1907)
Russian chemist who created the first periodic table of elements. He arranged the elements in increasing size of their atoms and whether they have similar properties.

Marie Curie (1867-1934)
Polish-French physicist. Along with her husband Pierre, she was one of the first people to research radioactivity, and discovered the radioactive elements radium and polonium. She won Nobel prizes in 1903 and 1911.

Ernest Rutherford (1871-1937)
New Zealand physicist who discovered that all atoms have a tiny central nucleus containing most of their mass (weight). He won the Nobel Prize for Chemistry in 1908.

Albert Einstein (1879-1955)
German-born physicist best known for his theories of relativity, including that matter and energy can be turned into each other (described by his famous equation $E = MC^2$). He won the Nobel Prize for Physics in 1921.

Alfred Wegener (1880-1930)
German weather scientist who suggested that the Earth's continents slowly move over time (continental drift).

Neils Bohr (1885-1962)
Danish physicist who added to Ernest Rutherford's ideas to suggest that electrons move around an atom in fixed orbits. He won the Nobel Prize for Physics in 1922.

Dorothy Hodgkin (1910-1994)
English chemist who worked out how to discover the shapes of complicated molecules in the body, such as penicillin and insulin. She won the Nobel Prize for Chemistry in 1964.

Alan Turing (1912-1954)
English mathematician and founder of computer science. During World War II he helped crack German military codes, and later he was involved with some of the first practical computers designed for general use.

Francis Crick (1916-2004) and James Watson (born 1928)
Crick (an English physicist) and Watson (an American biologist) co-discovered the spiral (double helix) shape of DNA in 1953. With a third scientist, they won the Nobel Prize for Medicine in 1962.

Rosalind Franklin (1920-1958)
English chemist who provided much of the evidence that Francis Crick and James Watson used in discovering the spiral shape of DNA.

Lynn Margulis (1938-2011)
American biologist who developed the theory that the complicated cells of animals and plants came from smaller bacteria-sized cells that started to live inside each other.

Stephen Hawking (born 1942)
English physicist who has helped us to understand black holes, the origin of the Universe, and the nature of time.

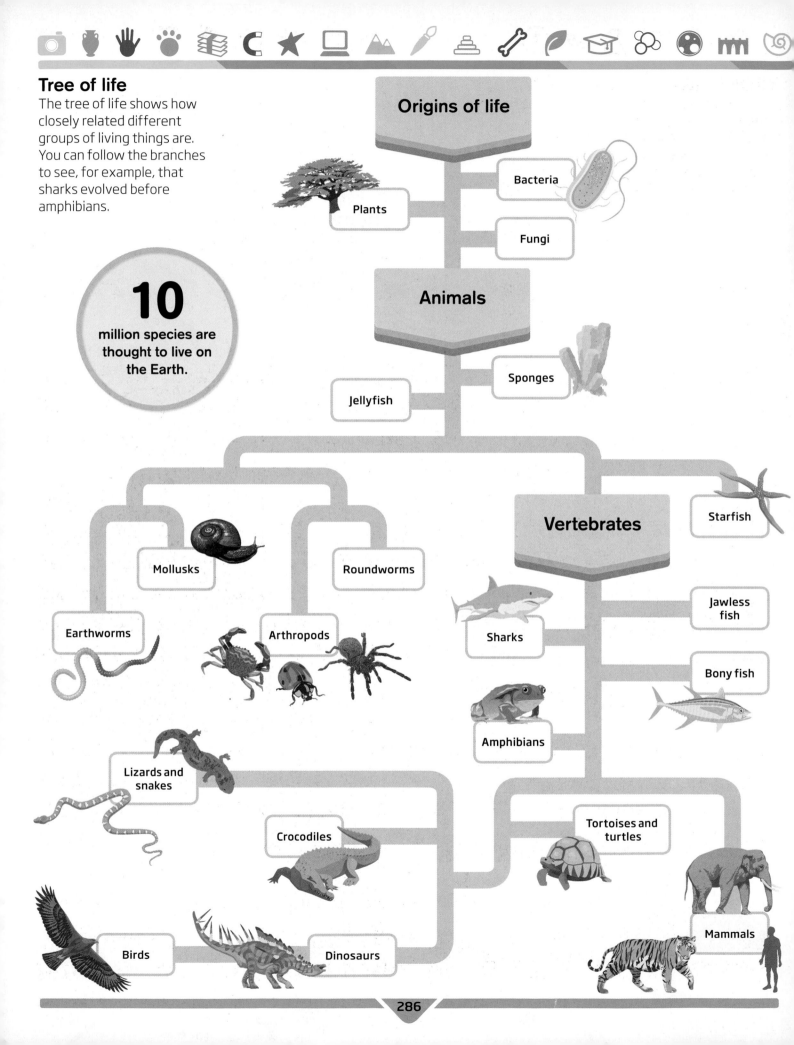

Tree of life

The tree of life shows how closely related different groups of living things are. You can follow the branches to see, for example, that sharks evolved before amphibians.

Origins of life

Plants

Bacteria

Fungi

10 million species are thought to live on the Earth.

Animals

Sponges

Jellyfish

Mollusks

Roundworms

Vertebrates

Starfish

Earthworms

Arthropods

Sharks

Jawless fish

Bony fish

Amphibians

Lizards and snakes

Tortoises and turtles

Crocodiles

Mammals

Birds

Dinosaurs

Multiplication

If you times two numbers together you are multiplying them. You can use this table to quickly work out the answer to multiplying any two numbers between 1 and 20.

Find the second number (2) on the top row and follow the column down to where it meets the row for the first number.

	1	2	3
1	1	2	3
2	2	4	6
3	3	6	9

To work out what 3 x 2 equals, find the first number (3) on the lefthand column.

By following down the column across from 3 and down from 2, you can see that 3 x 2 = 6.

When we multiply a number by itself, we say it has been "squared."

	1	2	3	4	5	6	7	8	9	10	11	12	13	14	15	16	17	18	19	20
1	1	2	3	4	5	6	7	8	9	10	11	12	13	14	15	16	17	18	19	20
2	2	4	6	8	10	12	14	16	18	20	22	24	26	28	30	32	34	36	38	40
3	3	6	9	12	15	18	21	24	27	30	33	36	39	42	45	48	51	54	57	60
4	4	8	12	16	20	24	28	32	36	40	44	48	52	56	60	64	68	72	76	80
5	5	10	15	20	25	30	35	40	45	50	55	60	65	70	75	80	85	90	95	100
6	6	12	18	24	30	36	42	48	54	60	66	72	78	84	90	96	102	108	114	120
7	7	14	21	28	35	42	49	56	63	70	77	84	91	98	105	112	119	126	133	140
8	8	16	24	32	40	48	56	64	72	80	88	96	104	112	120	128	136	144	152	160
9	9	18	27	36	45	54	63	72	81	90	99	108	117	126	135	144	153	162	171	180
10	10	20	30	40	50	60	70	80	90	100	110	120	130	140	150	160	170	180	190	200
11	11	22	33	44	55	66	77	88	99	110	121	132	143	154	165	176	187	198	209	220
12	12	24	36	48	60	72	84	96	108	120	132	144	156	168	180	192	204	216	228	240
13	13	26	39	52	65	78	91	104	117	130	143	156	169	182	195	208	221	234	247	260
14	14	28	42	56	70	84	98	112	126	140	154	168	182	196	210	224	238	252	266	280
15	15	30	45	60	75	90	105	120	135	150	165	180	195	210	225	240	255	270	285	300
16	16	32	48	64	80	96	112	128	144	160	176	192	208	224	240	256	272	288	304	320
17	17	34	51	68	85	102	119	136	153	170	187	204	221	238	255	272	289	306	323	340
18	18	36	54	72	90	108	126	144	162	180	198	216	234	252	270	288	306	324	342	360
19	19	38	57	76	95	114	133	152	171	190	209	228	247	266	285	304	323	342	361	380
20	20	40	60	80	100	120	140	160	180	200	220	240	260	280	300	320	340	360	380	400

Flat shapes

Flat, or 2-D, shapes have length and width but no depth. Triangles have three straight sides, and quadrilaterals have four straight sides.

KEY
- ⌒ Equal angles
- ⌐ Right angle
- = Equal sides
- — Equal sides

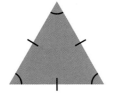

Equilateral triangle
All three sides and all three angles in an equilateral triangle are equal.

Scalene triangle
All three sides and all three angles in a scalene triangle are different.

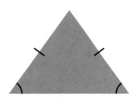

Isosceles triangle
An isosceles triangle has two sides of equal length and two angles of equal size.

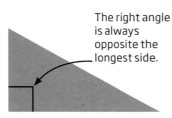

The right angle is always opposite the longest side.

Right-angled triangle
A right-angled triangle has one right angle, but the other angles and sides vary.

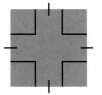

Square
All four sides in a square are of equal length and all four angles are right angles.

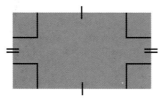

Rectangle
A rectangle has two pairs of sides that are the same length and four right angles.

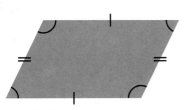

Parallelogram
A parallelogram has two pairs of sides that are equal length and two pairs of angles that are the same size.

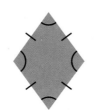

Rhombus
All the sides in a rhombus are equal length and it has two pairs of angles of equal size.

Solid shapes

Solid, or 3-D, shapes have depth as well as length and width.

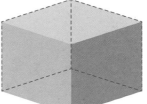

Cube
A cube has 12 edges of equal length and six faces of equal size.

Pyramid
A pyramid can have a triangular base, as seen here, or a square base. A triangular-based pyramid has four faces and six edges.

Cone
Cones have two faces and only one edge. The point is above the center of the circular base.

Cylinder
A cylinder has three faces and two edges. The two circular faces are opposite each other.

Time

We divide time into hours, minutes, and seconds. A clock or watch is used to tell what time of day it is.

The clock face is divided into 12 hours. There are 24 hours in a full day.

The hour hand shows what hour of the day it is.

The minute hand shows how many minutes in an hour have passed. It is longer than the hour hand.

The hands move down on the right and up on the left. We call this direction "clockwise."

Each hour is divided into 60 minutes.

O'clock
When the minute hand points to 12, the time is exactly the hour shown by the hour hand.

Half past
When the minute hand points to 6, we know it is half past the hour.

Minutes past
When the minute hand is on the right of the clock, we say how many minutes are past the hour.

Quarter past
When the minute hand points to 3, we know it is quarter past the hour.

Quarter to
When the minute hand points to 9 we know it is quarter to the hour.

Minutes to
When the minute hand is on the left of the clock, we say how many minutes are to the hour.

The planets

There are eight planets in our solar system, but they are all very different. Here you can compare them—the days and hours given are equal to the time they take on Earth.

243

Earth days in a single day on Venus.

Planet name	Distance from the sun	Width	Orbit time around the sun	Day length	Number of moons
Mercury	36 million miles (58 million km)	3,032 miles (4,879 km)	88 days	59 days	0
Venus	67 million miles (108 million km)	7,521 miles (12,104 km)	225 days	243 days	0
Earth	93 million miles (150 million km)	7,926 miles (12,756 km)	1 year	24 hours	1
Mars	142 million miles (228 million km)	4,220 miles (6,792 km)	1 year 322 days	25 hours	2
Jupiter	484 million miles (778 million km)	88,846 miles (142,984 km)	11 years 315 days	10 hours	At least 67
Saturn	887 million miles (1,427 million km)	74,898 miles (120,536 km)	29 years 163 days	11 hours	At least 62
Uranus	1,784 million miles (2,871 million km)	31,763 miles (51,118 km)	84 years 6 days	17 hours	At least 27
Neptune	2,795 million miles (4,498 million km)	30,775 miles (49,528 km)	163 years 289 days	16 hours	At least 14

US presidents

The president is the head of state and head of government for the United States of America. Alongside the name of each president is the party (political group) that they belong to.

George Washington	Federalist	1789–1797
John Adams	Federalist	1797–1801
Thomas Jefferson	Democratic-Republican	1801–1809
James Madison	Democratic-Republican	1809–1817
James Monroe	Democratic-Republican	1817–1825
John Quincy Adams	Independent	1825–1829
Andrew Jackson	Democrat	1829–1837
Martin Van Buren	Democrat	1837–1841
William H. Harrison	Whig	1841 •
John Tyler	Democrat	1841–1845
James K. Polk	Democrat	1845–1849
Zachary Taylor	Whig	1849–1850 •
Millard Fillmore	Whig	1850–1853
Franklin Pierce	Democrat	1853–1857
James Buchanan	Democrat	1857–1861
Abraham Lincoln	Republican	1861–1865 □
Andrew Johnson	Democrat	1865–1869
Ulysses S. Grant	Republican	1869–1877
Rutherford B. Hayes	Republican	1877–1881
James A. Garfield	Republican	1881 □
Chester A. Arthur	Republican	1881–1885
Grover Cleveland	Democrat	1885–1889
Benjamin Harrison	Republican	1889–1893
Grover Cleveland	Democrat	1893–1897
William McKinley	Republican	1897–1901 □
Theodore Roosevelt	Republican	1901–1909
William H. Taft	Republican	1909–1913
Woodrow Wilson	Democrat	1913–1921
Warren G. Harding	Republican	1921–1923 •
Calvin Coolidge	Republican	1923–1929
Herbert Hoover	Republican	1929–1933
Franklin D. Roosevelt	Democrat	1933–1945 •
Harry S. Truman	Democrat	1945–1953
Dwight D. Eisenhower	Republican	1953–1961
John F. Kennedy	Democrat	1961–1963 □
Lyndon B. Johnson	Democrat	1963–1969
Richard Nixon	Republican	1969–1974
Gerald Ford	Republican	1974–1977
Jimmy Carter	Democrat	1977–1981
Ronald Reagan	Republican	1981–1989
George H. W. Bush	Republican	1989–1993
Bill Clinton	Democrat	1993–2001
George W. Bush	Republican	2001–2009
Barack Obama	Democrat	2009–2017
Donald Trump	Republican	2017–

Assassinated □
Died in office •

Timeline of the Civil War

The Civil War was a major conflict in American history. It began when 11 southern states, unhappy that Abraham Lincoln had been elected president and concerned he would outlaw slavery, seceded (broke away) from the Union. They created their own Confederate States of America, also known as the Confederacy. The war between the North and the South that followed lasted four years and caused the deaths of more than 600,000 soldiers. When it ended in April 1865, the Union was restored, and more than four million slaves were freed.

1850
Compromise of 1850: New states are allowed to decide for themselves whether to be slave states or free states.

1857
The Supreme Court rules that slaves are not US citizens and are not protected by the Constitution.

October 1859
John Brown and his men raid a military arsenal at Harpers Ferry, Virginia, hoping to arm a slave uprising. Brown is caught and hanged.

November 1860
Republican candidate Abraham Lincoln wins the US presidential election, but without any support from the southern states.

December 20, 1860
South Carolina secedes (breaks away) from the Union.

February 1861
Representatives from Alabama, Florida, Georgia, Louisiana, Mississippi, and South Carolina meet to form the Confederate States of America, with Jefferson Davis as president. Later they are joined by Virginia, Texas, North Carolina, Tennessee, and Arkansas.

April 12, 1861
Confederate forces attack and capture Union-held Fort Sumter in South Carolina. The Civil War begins.

July 21, 1861
First Battle of Bull Run (Virginia): Confederate victory.

April 6–7, 1862
Battle of Shiloh (Tennessee): Union victory under Ulysses S. Grant, but with heavy losses.

February 6, 1862
Fall of Fort Henry (Tennessee): Union victory.

February 16, 1862
Battle of Fort Donelson (Tennessee): Union victory.

March 9, 1862
Battle of the *Monitor* and the *Virginia*: Draw.

April 25, 1862
Union forces take New Orleans.

May 31–June 1, 1862
Battle of Seven Pines (Virginia): No clear winner.

June 26–July 2, 1862
The Seven Days Battles (Virginia): Confederate victory. This is a hard-fought victory for the Confederates.

August 29–30, 1862
Second Battle of Bull Run (Virginia): Confederate victory.

September 17, 1862
Battle of Antietam/Sharpsburg (Maryland): No clear winner.

September 22, 1862
The Union's Emancipation Proclamation declares all slaves in the rebelling Confederate areas to be free.

December 13, 1862
Battle of Fredericksburg (Virginia): Confederate victory.

December 31, 1862-January 2, 1863
Battle of Stones River (Tennessee): No clear winner.

May 1-6, 1863
Battle of Chancellorsville (Virginia): Confederate victory.

May 18-July 4, 1863
Siege of Vicksburg (Mississippi): Union victory.

July 1-3, 1863
Battle of Gettysburg (Pennsylvania): Union victory. This battle is a turning point in the war.

September 19-20, 1863
Battle of Chickamauga (Georgia): Confederate victory.

November 19, 1863
Lincoln delivers the Gettysburg Address. This famous speech was given at the dedication of a national cemetery for Union soldiers, close to the site of the Battle of Gettysburg.

November 23-25, 1863
Battle of Chattanooga (Tennessee): Union victory.

May 5-6, 1864
Battle of the Wilderness (Virginia): No clear winner.

May 8-12, 1864
Battle of Spotsylvania (Virginia): No clear winner.

May 11, 1864
Battle of Yellow Tavern (Virginia): Union victory.

June 3, 1864
Battle of Cold Harbor (Virginia): Confederate victory. This is the last major Confederate victory.

June 18, 1864
Siege of Petersburg (Virginia) begins: Union victory.

August 5, 1864
Battle of Mobile Bay (Alabama): Union victory.

September 2, 1864
Fall of Atlanta (Georgia): Union victory.

November 8, 1864
Lincoln is reelected as US president.

November 15, 1864
The Union's Savannah Campaign, or the "March to the Sea," begins.

November 30, 1864
Battle of Franklin (Tennessee): Union victory.

December 15-16, 1864
Battle of Nashville (Tennessee): Union victory.

February 1, 1864
The Thirteenth Amendment, outlawing slavery, is proposed.

April 2, 1864
Fall of Petersburg and Richmond (Virginia): Union victory.

April 9, 1864
Robert E. Lee surrenders to Grant at Appomattox, Virginia. This marks the effective end of the Civil War, although fighting continues for a few weeks afterward.

December 1865
The Thirteenth Amendment is ratified (made law). Slavery is outlawed.

Major religions

Religion is a set of beliefs and ideas about a god or many gods. There are lots of different religions and they are practiced all over the world.

Baha'i
Founded in Iran in the 19th century, the Baha'i religion seeks to achieve peace and togetherness for all humankind.

Buddhism
Buddhism was developed around 500 BCE by an Indian prince who later became called the Buddha (the "Enlightened One"). It teaches the need for a spiritual journey to free people from wants and pain.

Cao Dai
A modern religion founded in Vietnam in 1926 which believes in peace and non-violence.

Christianity
A faith centered on the belief that Jesus Christ, who preached in Palestine around 2,000 years ago, is the son of God and came down to Earth to rescue people from sin (doing wrong).

Confucianism
An ancient Chinese religious philosophy that began with the teachings of the philosopher Confucius, who lived around 500 BCE.

Hinduism
An ancient Indian religion that includes a belief that every person goes through a cycle of life, death, and then rebirth in a future life. Hinduism features many different gods and goddesses.

Islam
Followers of the Islamic faith are called Muslims. They believe that the true word of Allah (God) was revealed to the Prophet Muhammad around 607 CE and written down in the sacred text called the Quran.

Jainism
Jainism is an ancient Indian religion that emphasizes non-violence toward people and animals.

Judaism
The religion of the Jewish people, Judaism also influenced the development of Christianity and Islam. Jews worship one God and their sacred text is called the Torah.

Shamanism
A system of belief common in small traditional societies. Shamans are individuals who believe they have special access to the spirit world, often by going into a dream, which they use to help their community.

Shinto
The traditional religion of Japan, followers of Shinto believe that there are spirits called *kami* everywhere in the world.

Sikhism
A faith that developed in northern India around 1500 and encourages tolerance between religions. Sikhs worship one God and Sikh men traditionally wear a turban to cover their hair, which they leave uncut.

Taoism
An ancient Chinese religion and philosophy that involves accepting, and following, the natural power of the Universe.

Zoroastrianism
Zoroastrianism is an ancient religion of Persia (modern-day Iraq) that features the idea of an unending struggle between good and evil. It is only a small religion today.

The world

Land covers about a third of the Earth's surface. The land is broken up into seven large blocks called continents. The continents are divided into smaller areas called countries.

Europe

This map shows Europe in more detail, as there is not enough space to show all the European countries on the main map.

ARCTIC OCEAN

Greenland
(DENMARK)

Alaska
(UNITED STATES)

C A N A D A

**NORTH
AMERICA**

U N I T E D   S T A T E S

ATLANTIC
OCEAN

ICE

M E X I C O

Hawaii
(UNITED STATES)

PACIFIC
OCEAN

BAHAMAS

DOMINICAN
REPUBLIC

Puerto Rico (UNITED STATES)
ST KITTS & NEVIS
ANTIGUA & BARBUDA
DOMINICA
ST LUCIA

C U B A

HAITI

JAMAICA

BELIZE

GUATEMALA   HONDURAS
EL SALVADOR   NICARAGUA
COSTA RICA
PANAMA

GRENADA

BARBADOS
ST VINCENT & THE GRENADINES
TRINIDAD & TOBAGO

VENEZUELA

SURINAME

Western S
(disp

CAPE
VERDE

SEN
THE GAMBIA
GUINEA-BISSA

SIERRA LE

Galápagos Islands
(ECUADOR)

COLOMBIA

GUYANA

French
Guiana
(FRANCE)

ECUADOR

PERU

B R A Z I L

**SOUTH
AMERICA**

BOLIVIA

PARAGUAY

CHILE

ARGENTINA

URUGUAY

ATLANTIC
OCEAN

Falkland Islands
(UNITED KINGDOM)

ICELAND

Faroe Islands
(DENMARK)

ATLANTIC
OCEAN

NORWAY

SWEDEN

FINLAND

ESTONIA

RUSSIAN
FEDERATION

LATVIA

DENMARK

Kaliningrad
(RUSS. FED.)

LITHUANIA

UNITED
KINGDOM

IRELAND

NETHERLANDS

BELGIUM

LUXEMBOURG

GERMANY

POLAND

BELARUS

CZECH
REPUBLIC

UKRAINE

SLOVAKIA

FRANCE   EUROPE

AUSTRIA   HUNGARY

LIECHTENSTEIN
SWITZERLAND

SLOVENIA

CROATIA

SERBIA

ROMANIA

MOLDOVA

SAN
MARINO

MONACO

BOSNIA &
HERZEGOVINA

ANDORRA

MONTENEGRO

KOSOVO

BULGARIA

ALBANIA

MACEDONIA

VATICAN
CITY

I T A L Y

PORTUGAL   SPAIN

GREECE

TURKEY

Gibraltar
(UNITED KINGDOM)

MALTA

Glossary

abstract
Art that does not copy real life exactly, but may only look a bit like an object, or represent a feeling

adaptation
Way in which an animal or a plant becomes better-suited to its habitat

algebra
Type of math that uses letters to stand for numbers or amounts

amphibians
Cold-blooded vertebrates that start life in water before moving between land and water when fully grown

ancestor
Ancient relative

ancient
Very old

antenna
One of two feelers found on an insect's head with which they can sense their surroundings

appliance
Machine used for a certain job that is usually electrical, such as a toaster

aqueduct
Channel or bridge built to carry water

architect
Person who plans and designs buildings

armor
Hard covering that provides protection

army
Organized group of soldiers

artificial
Object that is made by humans and is not found naturally

asteroid
Small, rocky object that orbits the sun

asteroid belt
Area of the solar system between Mars and Jupiter containing a large number of asteroids

astronaut
Someone who is trained to travel and work in a spacecraft

astronomy
Study of space

atmosphere
Layer of gas that surrounds a planet

atom
Smallest part of an element that can take part in a chemical reaction

attract
When two things pull toward each other

avalanche
Sudden movement of a large amount of snow or rock down a mountainside

axis
Imaginary line that passes through the center of a planet or star, around which it rotates

bacteria
Tiny organisms that live everywhere on Earth, such as inside food, soil, or even in the human body

BCE
Before Common Era, or all the years before year 0

beliefs
Set of views that people hold about the world, life, and the afterlife

biology
Study of living things and their relationship with their habitat. Someone who studies biology is called a biologist

birds
Warm-blooded vertebrates with a beak and feathers that can usually fly. They lay hard-shelled eggs to produce young

black hole
Object in space with such a strong force of gravity that nothing can escape it, not even light

boil
When a liquid is heated to a temperature at which it bubbles and turns into a gas or vapor

boundary
The point where one area ends and another begins.

breed
Variety of a pet or farmed animal; for example, a pug is a breed of dog

burrow
Hole or tunnel dug in the ground by an animal, to live in

calendar
Breakdown of the year into days and months; used to work out the date

camouflage
Colors or patterns that help something appear to blend in with its environment

carnivore
Animal that eats only meat

cartilage
Tough but flexible material found in animals that, among other things, makes up the human nose and ears, and the skeletons of sharks

catapult
Ancient war machine used to hurl rocks over long distances

CE
Common Era, or all the years after year 0

chemical
Substance used in, or made by, a reaction between particles such as atoms

chemistry
Study of chemicals and their reactions. Someone who studies chemistry is called a chemist

chrysalis
Hard casing, often camouflaged, that a caterpillar wraps itself in during metamorphosis

circuit
Loop that an electric current travels around

circulation
Path that blood travels around the body, out from the heart through arteries and back to the heart through veins

citizen
Someone who lives in a certain city or country is a citizen of that place

civil war
War between people who belong to the same country

civilization
Society where people have built a complex city or country

climate
Weather that is usual for an area over a long period of time

code
Written commands, or language, used in a computer program

cold-blooded
Animal with a body temperature that goes up and down to match the surrounding air or water temperature

colony
Large group of animals that live together

comet
Object made of dust and ice that orbits around the sun, developing a tail as it gets close to the sun

competition
Contest between two or more people, groups, or living things where one is trying to win a prize or resource

computers
Machines that can perform difficult tasks by following programs

condensation
When a gas cools and becomes liquid. Often seen as droplets of water that form on cold surfaces, such as windows

conductor
Substance that allows heat or electricity to pass through it easily

coniferous tree
Type of evergreen tree, usually with needlelike leaves

conquer
Act of one country taking over another country

conservation
Trying to stop a plant or animal from becoming extinct

consumer
Animal that eats a producer or other consumers

continent
One of seven large areas of land into which the world is divided: Africa, Antarctica, Asia, Europe, North America, Oceania, and South America

coral
Hard outer skeleton of tiny sea animals, which can build up into large coral reefs

core
Center part of a planet, star, or moon

country
Area of Earth that is governed by the same leaders and has the same flag

court
Place where it is decided if someone has broken the law

crater
Bowl-shaped dent on the surface of a planet or other body in space, caused by a collision with a rock

crime
Activity that is against the law

crop
Group of plants that are grown as food

crust
Outer layer of a planet

culture
Way of life and beliefs of the people of a region or country

deciduous tree
Type of tree that loses all its leaves at the same time during the winter or the dry season

decomposer
Living thing, often a fungus, that breaks down dead matter to create nutrients

deforestation
Destruction of forests

democracy
System of government where people outside the government have a say in how the country is run, usually by voting

desert
Dry region that gets 10 in (25 cm) or less of rainfall in a year. Deserts can be hot or cold

dictator
Ruler with total power

dinosaur
Group of reptiles, often very big, that lived millions of years ago

diplomat
Person from one country who travels to another to make sure the two countries have a good relationship

direction
Way in which an object is traveling, such as up or down, or right or left

disability
Something that makes certain activities difficult or impossible for a person to do

disease
Condition that makes a person ill, often caused by germs

drought
Period when there is little or no rainfall

earthquake
Shaking of the Earth's surface caused by moving tectonic plates or volcanic activity

eclipse
When an object in space passes into the shadow of another object

election
Event where people vote to decide who will be part of the government

electricity
Type of energy that can be used to power appliances such as lights. It is also found naturally as lightning

element
One of 118 chemical substances that are made of the same type of atom, such as gold, oxygen, and helium. The elements are arranged on the periodic table

emperor
Ruler of an empire

empire
Large area with different peoples, ruled by a single government or person

endangered
When an animal or plant species is in danger of becoming extinct

energy
Source of power such as electrical energy or heat energy

environment
Surroundings in which something lives

equality
Equal rights for all people

equator
Imaginary line around the center of the Earth that is an equal distance from the North and South poles

erosion
Gradual wearing away of rocks due to water and weather

eruption
When lava, ash, rock, or gas shoots or flows out of a volcano

ethical
Something that is done the right way, with thought as to how it will affect others

evaporation
When a liquid is heated and turns into a gas or vapor

evolution
Process where living things change, over many generations, to become new species

exoplanet
Planet that orbits a star other than the sun

exoskeleton
Hard outer casing of animals such as arthropods that do not have an inside skeleton

experiment
Test to see how something works

explorer
Someone who travels to unmapped places to find out what is there

extinction
When all of a particular animal or plant species dies out and there are none left in the world

factory
Building where products are made

fertilize
Process by which cells from a male and female join to create offspring, such as male plant pollen and a female plant ovum joining to create a seed

fins
Flattened limbs found on animals that live in water that help them swim

fish
Cold-blooded vertebrates that live underwater and have scales

flexible
Bendy

float
Stay at the surface of a liquid, rather than sinking

forage
Searching for food in the wild

force
Push or pull that causes things to start moving, move faster, change direction, slow down, or stop moving

foreign
Something or someone from a different country or place

fossil
Remains of a dead dinosaur, other animal, or plant, which has been preserved in rock over time

fossil fuels
Fuels made from animals and plants that died millions of years ago, such as coal and oil

friction
Force created when two surfaces rub or slide against each other

fuel
Substance that is burned to create heat or power

fungi
Group of living things, including mushrooms and molds, that break down dead plants and animals to make their food

galaxy
Huge group of stars, gas, and dust held together by gravity

gas
State of matter with no fixed shape, such as air, that fills any space it is in

generation
Group of living things that are of a similar age, and usually related; for example, brothers and sisters are one generation and their parents are another

genetics
Study of the genes in DNA that cause characteristics like hair color to be passed from one generation to the next. Someone who studies genetics is called a geneticist

geometry
Type of math that deals with solids, surfaces, lines, angles, and space

germs
Tiny life forms, such as bacteria or viruses, that cause disease

gills
Organs of fish and some amphibians that allow them to breathe underwater

glacier
Huge, thick sheet of ice moving very slowly, either down the side of a mountain or over land. Glaciers help to shape and form the landscape

government
Group of people who run a country

grasslands
Open land covered in grass and sometimes a few small bushes

gravity
Invisible force that pulls objects toward each other

habitat
Natural home environment of an animal or plant

hardware
Physical parts of a computer, such as the keyboard and screen

hatch
Process by which an animal breaks out of an egg

hemisphere
Top or bottom half of the Earth

herbivore
Animal that eats only plants

herd
Group of animals, particularly hoofed mammals

hibernation
Period of inactivity that some animals go through in the winter

holy
Something or somewhere sacred to a religion

hurricane
Violent storm with extremely strong winds that can cause a great deal of damage

identical
Two or more people or things that look exactly the same

imports
Goods or services bought from another country

incubation
Keeping an egg warm until it hatches

instruction
Command that tells something or someone what to do

insulator
Substance that does not allow heat or electricity to pass easily through it

interact
When two or more things communicate or do something that affects the other

Internet
Network that links computers across the world

invertebrate
Animal that does not have a backbone

jewel
A precious gemstone that has been cut and polished

joint
Place in the body where two bones meet, such as the knee or elbow

king
Man who rules a country

knowledge
Understanding of a topic

laboratory
Place where scientific experiments are done

lake
Large body of water surrounded by land

landfill
Place where garbage is buried in the ground

landslide
Sudden movement of a large amount of earth down a hill or mountainside

latitude
Horizontal line around the Earth that tells you how far up or down the globe a place is

lava
Hot, melted rock on the Earth's surface

light
Type of energy that allows humans and other animals to see, and plants to make food

light year
Distance traveled by light in a year, equal to about 5.9 trillion miles (9.5 trillion km)

liquid
State of matter that flows and takes the shape of any container it is in, such as water

longitude
Vertical line around the Earth that tells you how far east or west around the globe a place is

lungs
Breathing organs found inside the body of vertebrates

luxury
Expensive activity or item that is not neccessary but wanted

machine
Something that is powered by energy and carries out a task

magma
Hot, melted rock below the Earth's surface

magnetic field
Area of magnetism surrounding a magnet or a planet, star, or galaxy

magnetism
Invisible force that is created by magnets, which pull certain metals toward them

magnify
Make something appear larger than it is

mammals
Warm-blooded vertebrates that have skin covered in hair and feed their young milk

mantle
Thick layer of hot rock between the core and the crust of a planet or moon

manuscript
Handwritten book, poem, or other document

mate
When a male and female animal produce young together

material
Substance that can be used to make or build things. It can be natural or made by humans

mathematics
Study of numbers and equations. Someone who studies mathematics is called a mathematician

matter
Stuff that all things are made of

melt
When a solid is heated and becomes a liquid

memory
Ability to remember things that have happened, or where computers store their information

merchant
Person whose job is buying and selling things, often from a foreign country

metamorphosis
Process by which some animals transform themselves into a different form from youth to adulthood

meteor
Streak of light caused by a meteoroid burning up as it enters Earth's atmosphere, sometimes called a "falling star"

meteorite
Rock from space that lands on a planet or moon's surface

microscope
Instrument that magnifies things and is used to look at tiny objects

microscopic
Very small and only able to be seen with a microscope

migration
Regular movement of animals over long distances, often to feed or breed

Milky Way
Galaxy we live in

mine
Place where naturally occurring resources such as coal, iron, copper, or gold, and gemstones such as diamonds and rubies are dug out of the ground

mineral
Natural substance that grows in crystals, such as salt. Minerals can be polished to make gemstones. All rocks are made from minerals

mixture
Combination of more than one type of thing

monument
Statue put up to remember a person or event

moon
Object made of rock, or rock and ice that orbits a planet or an asteroid

navigation
Way of finding a path from one place to another

Nobel Prize
Special prize given to people for different subjects in both science and the arts, once a year

novel
Story book

nucleus
Central part of an atom or cell

nutrients
Food or substance that gives a living thing the energy or chemicals that it needs to live, grow, and move

omnivore
Animal that eats both plants and meat

orbit
Path an object takes when traveling around another object when pulled by its gravity

orchestra
Group of muscians and their instruments playing together

organ
Body part that has a certain job; for example, the heart, which pumps blood

organism
Living thing

particle
Extremely small part of a solid, liquid, or gas

periodic table
Set arrangement of elements into a grid

persecution
Bad treatment of people because of their beliefs

philosophy
Study of how we live, such as whether things are wrong or right. Someone who studies philosophy is called a philosopher

photosynthesis
Process that green plants use to make food from sunlight

physics
Study of the universe and forces. Someone who studies physics is called a physicist

planet
Large, round object that orbits a star

poisonous
Substance that may be deadly if touched or eaten

pollen
Powder that comes from flowering plants and is used in pollination

pollination
Transfer of pollen from one plant to another so those plants can reproduce

pollution
Harmful substances in the air, soil, or water

power source
Energy that is used to make a machine work, such as electricity

predator
Animal that hunts other living animals for food

prehistoric
Time before written history

prey
Animal that is hunted for food

primate
Type of mammal, which includes monkeys and humans

prison
Building where people who have broken the law are locked up as a punishment

probe
Unmanned spacecraft designed to study objects in space and send information back to Earth

producer
Living thing such as a plant that makes its own food and is eaten by animals

program
Set of instructions a computer follows to complete a task

queen
Woman who rules a country

recycle
Use something old to make something new

renewable
Type of energy that will not run out, such as solar power

reptiles
Cold-blooded vertebrates with scaly skin that usually reproduce by laying eggs

republic
State ruled by elected officials instead of a royal family or emperor

robot
Machine that is programmed by a computer to do different tasks

rock
Naturally occuring solid made from different minerals, such as granite. Rocks make up the surface of planets and moons

rover
Robot used to explore the surface of a rocky planet or moon

reaction
Effect when two chemicals cause a change in each other

reflect
When light or sound bounces off a surface

repel
When two objects push away from each other

reproduce
Have young

reservoir
Large store of something, usually water

satellite
Any object that goes around a planet, usually a moon or a human-made machine

scavenger
Animal that feeds on the leftover meat of another animal that has already died

shadow
Area of darkness formed when light rays are blocked by a solid object

shield
Object that protects something from damage or attack

society
Organized group of people with a shared culture

software
Programs and instructions that are used by a computer

solar system
The sun and all the objects that orbit it, including the planets

solid
State of matter that holds its shape

solidify
When a liquid cools and becomes a solid

solution
Mixture that is created when a solid dissolves in a liquid and disappears

sound
Form of energy that is produced when objects vibrate, or shake

space
Place beyond Earth's atmosphere

spacecraft
Vehicle that travels in space

species
Specific type of an animal or plant that can mate and produce young together

spectrum
Range of something; for example, the range of colors in a rainbow

stalactite
Piece of rock that hangs down from the roof of a cave and looks like an icicle

stalagmite
Piece of rock that points upward, slowly growing from the floor of a cave

star
Huge, hot sphere of gas in space that releases energy from its core and gives off heat and light

sustainable
Able to be supported for a long time

tame
Animal that is used to people, such as a pet dog or cat

technology
Using scientific knowledge to create machinery and devices, such as computers

tectonic plate
Large, slow-moving piece of the Earth's crust

telescope
Instrument used to look at distant objects

temperature
Measure of how hot or cold things are

temple
Home for a god or gods and a place for worshipping them

traditional
When something has been done in the same way for a long time

transmit
Pass something, such as information, between two places

tropical
Area or climate with hot temperatures

tsunami
Giant wave created by an earthquake or a volcanic eruption

turbine
Wheel or rotor that is turned to make power

universe
All space and everything in it

venomous
Substance that may be deadly if injected by an animal or plant, through a sting or fangs

vertebrate
Animal that has a backbone

vibrate
Moving back and forth small amounts very quickly

volcano
Opening in the Earth's crust, usually in the shape of a mountain, out of which lava, ash, rock, and gas erupt, sometimes explosively

voyage
A journey, often over water

warm-blooded
Animal that keeps a constant body temperature

weight
Amount of the force of gravity that acts on an object, making it feel heavy. The more mass something has, the larger the force of gravity on the object, and the heavier it feels

wildlife
Animals found in a certain area

womb
Organ in which baby animals develop

worship
Praying to a god or gods

X-ray
Radiation used to create shadows of bones and other organs in the body. Images on an X-ray photo can reveal internal damage and disease

young
Babies, or not very old

zoo
Place where wild animals are kept, so people can see and study them

Index

Acknowledgments

The publisher would like to thank the following people for their help in the production of this book: Patrick Cuthbertson for reviewing the earliest history pages, Dr Manuel Breuer for reviewing the evolution page, and Patrick Thompson, University of Strathclyde, for reviewing the pages on cells, chemistry, and genes. Stratford-upon-Avon Butterfly Farm www.butterflyfarm.co.uk for allowing us to photograph their butterflies and other insects, and ZSL Whipsnade Zoo for allowing us to photograph their animals. Caroline Hunt for proofreading and Helen Peters for the index. Additional editorial: Richard Beatty, Katy Lennon, Andrea Mills, Victoria Pyke, Charles Raspin, Olivia Stanford, David Summers. Additional design: Sunita Gahir, Emma Hobson, Clare Joyce, Katie Knutton, Hoa Luc, Ian Midson, Ala Uddin. Illustrators: Mark Clifton, Dan Crisp, Molly Lattin, Daniel Long, Maltings Partnership, Bettina Myklebust Stovne, Mohd Zishan. Photographer: Richard Leeny

Picture credits

The publisher would like to thank the following for their kind permission to reproduce their photographs:

12 Alamy Stock Photo: Robertharding (br). **Fotolia:** StarJumper (bl). **13 Dorling Kindersley:** Royal Airforce Museum, London (crb). **iStockphoto.com:** RobHowarth (c). **14 Alamy Stock Photo:** Granger Historical Picture Archive (c); Rick Pisio\RWP Photography (br). **Getty Images:** Print Collector (bl). **15 Dorling Kindersley:** Twan Leenders (ca). **16 123RF.com:** Liu Feng / long10000 (b). **Dorling Kindersley:** University of Pennsylvania Museum of Archaeology and Anthropology (ca). **Getty Images:** Danita Delimont (bc). **17 Dorling Kindersley:** The Trustees of the British Museum (br). **18 Alamy Stock Photo:** Lanmas (br). **Dorling Kindersley:** The Trustees of the British Museum (cr). **Getty Images:** Independent Picture Service / UIG (cl). **19 Dorling Kindersley:** Durham University Oriental Museum (clb). **Getty Images:** Universal History Archive / UIG (r). **20 Alamy Stock Photo:** Jam World Images (bc). **21 Alamy Stock Photo:** FLPA (b). **Dreamstime.com:** Wrangel (cb). **Getty Images:** Frank Krahmer (ca). **iStockphoto.com:** Kenneth Canning (c). **22 123RF.com:** David Ronald Head (cra); Oxana Brigadirova / Iarus (bc); Pakhnyushchyy (bc/Raccoon). **Dorling Kindersley:** Twan Leenders (cla); Linda Pitkin (cr). **iStockphoto.com:** Mamarama (cl). **23 123RF.com:** Nancy Botes (cl/Weaver). **Dreamstime.com:** Friedemeier (cl); Patrice Correia (clb). **24 Alamy Stock Photo:** Classic Image (bc). **Getty Images:** Frank Krahmer / Photographer's Choice RF (br). **25 123RF.com:** Eric Isselee (bc). **Alamy Stock Photo:** Zoonar GmbH (bl). **26 Corbis:** (cl). **Dreamstime.com:** Jiang Chi Guan (b). **26-27 123RF.com:** Gino Santa Maria / ginosphotos. **27 Dorling Kindersley:** Banbury Museum (bc). **28 Alamy Stock Photo:** Painting (c). **Bridgeman Images:** Christie's Images (cb). **Getty Images:** DeAgostini (cr); Fine Art Images / Heritage Images (crb). **29 Dorling Kindersley:** Peter Cook (bl). **Fotolia:** Eric Isselee (br). **30 NASA:** (crb). **31 NASA:** (c, br). **34 Dorling Kindersley:** Natural History Museum, London (cb). **35 Dorling Kindersley:** CONACULTA-INAH-MEX (ca). **36 Dreamstime.com:** Mark Eaton (br). **38 Dorling Kindersley:** Neil Fletcher (ca); David J. Patterson (cb). **Getty Images:** Joseph Sohm - Visions of America / Photodisc (cr). **39 Dorling Kindersley:** Alan Murphy (cra). **40 NASA:** JPL-Caltech (bl). **42 Alamy Stock Photo:** JeffG (c); The Granger Collection (cr). **43 Alamy Stock Photo:** Ivy Close Images (tl); Matthias Scholz (crb). **44 Alamy Stock Photo:** A. T. Willett (clb); Art Directors & TRIP (cb). **Dorling Kindersley:** By permission of The British Library (bl, c). **PENGUIN and the Penguin logo are trademarks of Penguin Books Ltd:** (cb/Penguin Book Cover). **46 Dreamstime.com:** Len Green (crb); Mariusz Prusaczyk (cb). **47 Alamy Stock Photo:** Reiner Elsen (b). **Dorling Kindersley:** Durham University Oriental Museum (cr); Royal Pavilion & Museums, Brighton & Hove (c); Museum of London (cra). **48 123RF.com:** Pavel Losevsky (br). **Alamy Stock Photo:** Mark Phillips (b). **51 123RF.com:** Nikolai Grigoriev / ,grynold (br). **54 Alamy Stock Photo:** AfriPics.com (br). **55 123RF.com:** Suranga Weeratunga (bc). **Alamy Stock Photo:** Aurora Photos (br). **56 Getty Images:** Juan Gartner (cr). **58 123RF.com:** Artem Mykhaylichenko / artcasta (bc); Zhang YuanGeng (bl). **Dorling Kindersley:** RGB Research Limited (cr, cr/Gold, fcr). **60 123RF.com:** smileus (br). **Alamy Stock Photo:** FEMA (bl). **iStockphoto.com:** yocamon (c). **63 Dorling Kindersley:** Peter Anderson (cr). **64 Alamy Stock Photo:** Galen Rowell / Mountain Light (br). **65 123RF.com:** Norman Kin Hang Chan (cr). **66 Dorling Kindersley:** The Trustees of the British Museum (cla). **67 Alamy Stock Photo:** Prisma Archivo (cra). **Dorling Kindersley:** Imperial War Museum, London (l). **68 Alamy Stock Photo:** Granger, NYC / Granger Historical Picture Archive (bl). **Daniel Schechter:** (c). **69 123RF.com:** Liliia Rudchenko (c). **Dorling Kindersley:** The Science Museum, London (bc). **Getty Images:** Andrew Burton (br). **70 Dreamstime.com:** Chalermphon Kumchai / iPhone is a trademark of Apple Inc., registered in the U.S. and other countries (br). **71 123RF.com:** Antonio Gravante (cb/Traffic light); cristi180884 (cla); golubovy (cb). **iStockphoto.com:** 3alexd (br); Alexandra Draghici (c); eskymaks (cra); cnythzl (cb/Playstation). **72 123RF.com:** Jagga (bc). **Dorling Kindersley:** Royal Armouries, Leeds (cr). **Getty Images:** Toby Roxburgh / Nature Picture Library (bc/Sprats). **75 Dorling Kindersley:** American Museum of Natural History (bl); Durham University Oriental Museum (c); University of Pennsylvania Museum of Archaeology and Anthropology (cra, br). **76 Alamy Stock Photo:** Bernardo Galmarini (cb/ Tango). **Dreamstime.com:** Carlosphotos (cb); Milanvachal (cla). **Getty Images:** Ken Welsh / Design Pics (ca/Religious Dance); Werner Lang (cra). **77 Dorling Kindersley:** NASA (br). **Science Photo Library:** Pekka Parviainen (clb). **80 Dorling Kindersley:** Andy Crawford / Senckenberg Nature Museum (cl). **81 Dorling Kindersley:** Jerry Young (clb, cb). **Getty Images:** Karl-Josef Hildenbrand / AFP (br). **82 Dorling Kindersley:** Royal Pavilion & Museums, Brighton & Hove (crb, br). **Dreamstime.com:** Thomas Barrat (cb). **83 NASA:** (br). **84 123RF.com:** Ammit (bc). **85 Alamy Stock Photo:** Kevin Schafer (bc). **87 123RF.com:** jezper (clb); Pornkamol Sirimongkolpanich (c). **88 Dreamstime.com:** Tassaphon Vongkittipong (cb). **89 123RF.com:** tebnad (b). **Dorling Kindersley:** The Science Museum, London (tc). **90 Dorling Kindersley:** Holts Gems (cr); RGB Research Limited (clb). **Getty Images:** Christopher Cooper (bc). **91 123RF.com:** quangpraha (cla); Songsak Paname (bl). **Alamy Stock Photo:** Mopic (br); Olaf Doering (cra). **Dorling Kindersley:** The Science Museum, London (fbl). **iStockphoto.com:** anyaivanova (cl). **92 Alamy Stock Photo:** Stephen Dorey ABIPP (clb). **Dreamstime.com:** Tr3gi (crb). **94 Alamy Stock Photo:** Rod McLean (bl). **95 Dreamstime.com:** Isselee (bc). **96 123RF.com:** sabphoto (c). **Dorling Kindersley:** Holts Gems (bc). **97 Alamy Stock Photo:** dpa picture alliance (br); Westend61 GmbH (bc); Jim West (bc/Citrus). **98 Dreamstime.com:** Christian Delbert (b); Orientaly (ca); Yali Shi (cb). **100 Alamy Stock Photo:** 50th Street Films / Courtesy Everett Collection (bc); AF archive (ca, clb, br); Pictorial Press Ltd (ca/The Eagle Huntress); United Archives GmbH (cra). **101 Alamy Stock Photo:** Juniors Bildarchiv GmbH (crb). **102 123RF.com:** Yueh-Hung Shih (br). **103 123RF.com:** Praphan Jampala (bl). **Getty Images:** Photodisc / Frank Krahmer (fbr). **104 Dreamstime.com:** Vtupinamba (c). **106 123RF.com:** Jose Manuel Gelpi Diaz / gelpi (br). **107 Alamy Stock Photo:** Zoonar GmbH (bc/Eagle). **Dorling Kindersley:** Greg and Yvonne Dean (ca, crb); Jerry Young (fcrb). **Dreamstime.com:** Michael Sheehan (cra, bc). **110 123RF.com:** Chuyu (br). **Alamy Stock Photo:** WidStock (cra). **111 Dorling Kindersley:** Andy Crawford / State Museum of Nature, Stuttgart (c). **113 Fotolia:** Dario Sabljak (cla/Frame). **Getty Images:** Bettmann (ca); Leemage / Corbis (b); Fine Art Images / Heritage Images (cla). **115 123RF.com:** Maria Dryfhout (crb/Weed). **Dreamstime.com:** Flynt (cr); Linnette Engler (crb). **116 ESA / Hubble:** NASA (bc). **NASA:** ESA, Hubble Heritage Team (STScI / AURA) (br); JPL-Caltech / ESA / Harvard-Smithsonian CfA (c). **117 Dreamstime.com:** Ulkass (cra). **118 Dorling Kindersley:** Holts Gems (cra, c, cl, fcl, cr, fclb, clb, cb/Iolite, fcrb/Emerald, crb, br); Natural History Museum (ca, ca/Ruby); Natural History Museum, London (c/Ruby, clb/Corundum); Holts (bc). **119 Alamy Stock Photo:** Colin McPherson (bc). **120 123RF.com:** skylightpictures (bl). **120-121 NASA:** NOAA GOES Project, Dennis Chesters. **121 Dorling Kindersley:** Museum of London (cla, ca, cra). **122 Alamy Stock Photo:** Julian Cartwright (cb/Crib Goch). **Dreamstime.com:** Whiskybottle (crb). **Getty Images:** Geography Photos / Universal Images Group (cb); Mint Images - Frans Lanting (c). **123 Alamy Stock Photo:** D. Hurst (br). **125 Dreamstime.com:** Budda (c). **126 123RF.com:** Dmitry Maslov (cra). **Alamy Stock Photo:** Design Pics Inc (cla). **Dreamstime.com:** Fenkie Sumolang (crb); Himanshu Saraf (ca); Salparadis (clb); Maciej Czekajewski (cb). **iStockphoto.com:** Coleong (cl); Lujing (cb/China). **129 123RF.com:** Remus Cucu (cra). **Alamy Stock Photo:** Design Pics Inc (bl). **Dorling Kindersley:** Tim Shepard, Oxford Scientific Films (c). **130 Dorling Kindersley:** Natural History Museum, London (cl). **131 Dorling Kindersley:** Board of Trustees of the Royal Armouries (c); Durham University Oriental Museum (clb). **132 Alamy Stock Photo:** Deco (cra). **Dorling Kindersley:** University of Pennsylvania Museum of Archaeology and Anthropology (bc). **133 Getty Images:** Bettmann (crb). **136 Dorling Kindersley:** The Science Museum, London (cb). **136-137 Dorling Kindersley:** The National Railway Museum, York / Science Museum Group. **137 123RF.com:** cobalt (br). **Dorling Kindersley:** The Shuttleworth Collection, Bedfordshire (t). **139 Dorling Kindersley:** Liberty's Owl, Raptor and Reptile Centre, Hampshire, UK (clb). **140 Alamy Stock Photo:** Alena Brozova (cb); Skyscan Photolibrary (crb). **Dorling Kindersley:** Museum of London (cl). **Getty Images:** VisitBritain / Britain on View (crb/Ironbridge). **141 NASA:** JPL / DLR (bc/Europa, fbr); NASA / JPL / University of Arizona (bc); JPL (br). **142 Dorling Kindersley:** Board of Trustees of the Royal Armouries (c). **143 Dreamstime.com:** Dexigner (br). **Getty Images:** De Agostini (l). **145 akg-images:** Erich Lessing (br). **146 123RF.com:** czardases (br). **147 123RF.com:** Peter Hermes Furian (c); Gunnar Pippel / gunnar3000 (cr). **Dreamstime.com:** Zepherwind (br). **148 Dreamstime.com:** Maresol (br). **150 ROBOVOLC Project:** (br). **152 Dorling Kindersley:** University of Pennsylvania Museum of Archaeology and Anthropology (bl). **153 123RF.com:** Anatolii Tsekhmister / tsekhmister (bl). **Alamy Stock Photo:** ITAR-TASS Photo Agency (tr). **Dreamstime.com:** Laura Cobb (crb). **Fotolia:** xstockerx (cb). **154 123RF.com:** smileus (bl). **155 Alamy Stock Photo:** Heritage Image Partnership Ltd (cl); Wavebreakmedia Ltd VFA1503 (br). **156 NASA:** JPL-Caltech / University of Arizona (fbr, br). **157 123RF.com:** Aliaksei Skreidzeleu (br); PhotosIndia.com LLC (cl). **Dreamstime.com:** Marco Ciannarella (cr). **158 Dorling Kindersley:** CONACULTA-INAH-MEX (c). **159 Alamy Stock Photo:** Science History Images (bl). **Fotolia:** dundanim (br). **160 123RF.com:** Laurent Davoust (bc). **Depositphotos Inc:** Spaces (br). **Dorling Kindersley:** The Science Museum, London (cl). **Science Photo Library:** Jean-Loup Charmet (cr). **161 Alamy Stock Photo:** Konstantin Shaklein (clb). **NASA:** Johns Hopkins University Applied Physics Laboratory / Carnegie Institution of Washington (c, bc). **162 Dorling Kindersley:** Holts Gems (crb). **Dreamstime.com:** Rudy Umans (c); Somyot Pattana (cb). **163 Dreamstime.com:** Isselee (clb). **164 Dorling Kindersley:** Colin Keates / Natural History Museum, London (ca, cla). **Getty Images:** Raquel Lonas / Moment Open (b). **165 Alamy Stock Photo:** Cultura RM (cl). **Getty Images:** Science Photo Library - Steve Gschmeissner (br). **Science Photo Library:** National Institues of Health (cr). **166 123RF.com:** Alberto Loyo (cb); Roy Longmuir / Brochman (crb); Sergey Krasnoshchokov (bc). **Corbis:** Don Hammond / Design Pics (c). **167 ESO:** José Francisco Salgado (josefrancisco.org) (br). **NASA:** JPL-Caltech (c). **168 Dorling Kindersley:** Natural History Museum, London (br). **169 123RF.com:** Blaj Gabriel / justmeyo (br); Matt Trommer / Eintracht (cb/Euro). **Dorling Kindersley:** Stephen Oliver (clb); University of Pennsylvania Museum of Archaeology and Anthropology (c, cb/Egyptian silver coin); The University of Aberdeen (c/Silver coin, clb/Gold coin). **Dreamstime.com:** Andreylobachev (bc/Japanese coin); Miragik (cb/One Indian Rupee); Asafta (cb/1 danish kroner, bl, bc). **170 Getty Images:** DLILLC / Corbis / VCG (br). **171 NASA:** (cr); JPL-Caltech (br). **172 Alamy Stock Photo:** Funky Stock - Paul Williams (b). **iStockphoto.com:** Bkamprath (cr). **174 Alamy Stock Photo:** NatureOnline (br). **175 123RF.com:** Noam Armonn (bl); Sandra Van Der Steen (cl). **176 Getty Images:** Hiroyuki Ito (cl). **177 Dorling Kindersley:** Statens Historiska Museum, Stockholm (tc); National Music Museum (ca). **178 Alamy Stock Photo:** KC Hunter (r). **179 Alamy Stock Photo:** Granger Historical Picture Archive (cb). **Dorling Kindersley:** American Museum of Natural History (cl, br). **180 Alamy Stock Photo:** Pictorial Press Ltd (bl). **Getty Images:** Photodisc / Alex Cao (clb). **180-181 Dorling Kindersley:** National Maritime Museum, London. **181 Alamy Stock Photo:** Aviation Visuals (c); ITAR-TASS Photo Agency (br). **183 NASA:** (br). **186 Dorling Kindersley:** Terry Carter (br). **187 Getty Images:** Ralph White (br). **188 Dorling Kindersley:** Southbank Enterprises (bc). **190 123RF.com:** Yanlev (cb). **Alamy Stock Photo:** A. Astes (bl). **Dorling Kindersley:** Dave King / Science Museum, London (ca). **Dreamstime.com:** Wavebreakmedia Ltd (cr). **Getty Images:** James Looker / PhotoPlus Magazine (crb). **191 123RF.com:** Alfio Scisetti (clb). **Dreamstime.com:** Phanuwatn (br); Scriptx (bc). **192 123RF.com:** Baloncici (ca/Heart rate monitor); Stanislav Khomutovsky (clb/Atom). **Dorling Kindersley:** Science Museum, London (crb). **Dreamstime.com:** Giovanni Gagliardi (clb); Staphy (ca). **Getty Images:** mds0 (bc). **193 Alamy Stock Photo:** Science History Images (br). **Dorling Kindersley:** Andrew Kerr (bl). **195 123RF.com:** citadelle (cr). **Alamy Stock Photo:** Anton Starikov (bc). **196 NASA:** (bc/ Makemake, br, fbr); JHUAPL / SwRI (cl, cr, br/Pluto); JPL-Caltech / UCLA / MPS / DLR / IDA (bc). **198 123RF.com:** Witthaya Phonsawat (c). **Dreamstime.com:** R. Gino Santa Maria / Shutterfree, Llc (ca); Toa555 (cb). **iStockphoto.com:** Marcelo Horn (bc). **Science Photo Library:** Planetary Visions Ltd (br). **199 123RF.com:** Anatol Adutskevich (fcr). **Alamy Stock Photo:** Einar Muoni (clb); Westend61 GmbH (cb); Ikonacolor (cb/Ring); Olekcii Mach (crb). **Dorling Kindersley:** Bolton Library and Museum Services (cla); University of Pennsylvania Museum of Archaeology and Anthropology (ca); Natural History Museum, London (cb/Platinum); Royal International Air Tattoo 2011 (br). **iStockphoto.com:** AlexandrMoroz (cb/Watch); Sergeevspb (cl); AlexStepanov (cr). **200 Dorling Kindersley:** Natural History Museum, London (c). **200-201 Dorling Kindersley:** Tap Service Archaeological Receipts Fund, Hellenic Republic Ministry Of Culture. **201 Dorling Kindersley:** Andy Crawford (tc); University of Pennsylvania Museum of Archaeology and Anthropology (tr); Andy Crawford / Bob Gathany (crb). **202 Dorling Kindersley:** Hunterian Museum University of Glasgow (bc). **iStockphoto.com:** Elnavegante (clb); LauraDin (cla); Lisa5201 (cr). **203 123RF.com:** Citadelle (cl). **Dreamstime.com:** Alexxl66 (bc). **205 123RF.com:** Weerapat Kiatdumrong (br). **Dreamstime.com:** Empire331 (cl); Photka (cra, cr); Stihl024 (bl). **206-207 Dreamstime.com:** Hungchungchih. **207 Dreamstime.com:** Jeremy Richards (tc); Muslim Kapasi (br). **208 123RF.com:** Ievgenii Fesenko (crb). **Dorling Kindersley:** Museum of the Order of St John, London (cb). **209 123RF.com:** Sborisov (ca). **Alamy Stock Photo:** Heritage Image Partnership Ltd (c). **210 Dorling Kindersley:** Jerry Young (cr). **212 123RF.com:** Vereshchagin Dmitry (br). **Getty Images:** ABK (cl). **NASA:** (bl). **213 123RF.com:** Miroslava Holasova / Moksha (cra). **Dreamstime.com:** Mkojot (crb). **214 Dorling Kindersley:** Colin Keates / Natural History Museum, London (fbl, bl). **215 Alamy Stock Photo:** Phil Degginger (cb). **Dorling Kindersley:** Andy Crawford (crb). **Getty Images:** Erik Simonsen (c). **NASA:** (clb). **216 NASA:** JPL / University of Arizona / University of Idaho (bl). **217 Dorling Kindersley:** The Science Museum, London (bc). **218 Dorling Kindersley:** The Science Museum, London (bc). **218-219 Alamy Stock Photo:** Reuters (t). **219 Alamy Stock Photo:** Granger Historical Picture Archive (tr); The Natural History Museum (b). **221 Alamy Stock Photo:** Reuters (crb). **Getty Images:** Gary Vestal (cl, c, c/ Black oak tree, cr). **223 Alamy Stock Photo:** Mark Conlin (br). **Dorling Kindersley:** Brian Pitkin (cb). **224 iStockphoto.com:** Narvikk (c). **Science Photo Library:** Alexis Rosenfeld (br). **227 Alamy Stock Photo:** (ca). **Dreamstime.com:** Lidian Neeleman (br); Vinicius Tupinamba (c). **230 Alamy Stock Photo:** Chronicle (clb); North Wind Picture Archives (c). **233 NASA:** JPL-Caltech / T. Pyle (br). **234 123RF.com:** Sergii Kolesnyk (cr). **Dreamstime.com:** Elena Elisseeva (crb); Maxwell De Araujo Rodrigues (crb/Blacksmith). **237 NASA:** (crb); Sandra Joseph and Kevin O'Connell (l); JPL-Caltech (cr). **239 Dreamstime.com:** Ilja Mašík (br). **Getty Images:** Photographer's Choice RF / Burazin (bl). **240-241 Dorling Kindersley:** Stephen Oliver (cb). **Fotolia:** Gudellaphoto (c). **241 Dreamstime.com:** Grosremy (tr). **Getty Images:** Burazin / Photographer's Choice RF (cl). **242 ESA / Hubble:** NASA (bc). **NASA:** JPL-Caltech / STScI / CXC / SAO (br). **243 Alamy Stock Photo:** Hemis (bl). **Dorling Kindersley:** Museum of London (cla). **244 123RF.com:** Fedor Selivanov / swisshippo (cra). **Dreamstime.com:** Libor Píška (bl). **245 123RF.com:** Luciano Mortula / masterlu (r). **NASA:** (tl). **246 Corbis:** Warren Faidley (cra, crb). **NASA:** (l). **247 123RF.com:** Stanislav Moroz (bl). **NASA:** JPL-Caltech / ESA (br). **250 Dorling Kindersley:** The Science Museum, London (cb). **251 Dorling Kindersley:** Glasgow City Council (Museums) (bc). **252 123RF.com:** only4denn (cra); Steven Coling (cl). **Alamy Stock Photo:** D. Hurst (crb). **Dreamstime.com:** Petro (bc). **253 Alamy Stock Photo:** Interfoto (br). **254 Alamy Stock Photo:** Christopher Nicholson (cr); Ian G Dagnall (cl). **255 Dreamstime.com:** Aleksandar Hubenov (bc). **256 Alamy Stock Photo:** D. Hurst (cr). **258 Dorling Kindersley:** University of Pennsylvania Museum of Archaeology and Anthropology (clb). **258-259 123RF.com:** Iakov Filimonov. **259 Alamy Stock Photo:** Pictorial Press Ltd (tr). **Dorling Kindersley:** R. Florio (tl). **260 123RF.com:** Steve AllenUK (clb). **Alamy Stock Photo:** JTB MEDIA CREATION, Inc. (c). **Dorling Kindersley:** The National Railway Museum, York / Science Museum Group (clb/Aerolite). **Dreamstime.com:** Uatp1 (br). **261 123RF.com:** Sergii Kolesnyk (c). **262 Dorling Kindersley:** Durham University Oriental Museum (bl). **Getty Images:** DEA / A. Dagli Orti (cl). **263 NASA:** ESA and the HST Frontier Fields team (STScI) / Judy Schmidt (cr); JPL-Caltech (c); NOAA / GOES Project (clb); Reto Stöckli, NASA Earth Observatory, based on Quickbird data copyright Digitalglobe (bl). **264 NASA:** (bl). **265 NASA:** (br); JPL (cl). **268 Alamy Stock Photo:** Greg Vaughn (l). **269 Alamy Stock Photo:** Science History Images (br). **271 123RF.com:** Jaroslav Machacek (ca); Nattachart Jerdnapapunt (c); Pere Sanz (cb). **272 Dreamstime.com:** Koscusko (ca). **Getty Images:** DEA PICTURE LIBRARY / De Agostini (clb). **273 123RF.com:** Chris Elwell (cla). **Dorling Kindersley:** Blists Hill and Jackfield Tile Museum, Ironbridge, Shropshire (crb). **Dreamstime.com:** Volodymyr Kyrylyuk (tc). **275 NASA:** (br). **276 Getty Images:** Hulton Archive (c). **277 Dorling Kindersley:** Fleet Air Arm Museum, Richard Stewart (crb/ USS Hornet); RAF Museum, Cosford (cra); The Tank Museum (crb). **Getty Images:** Keystone-France (cl). **278 Dorling Kindersley:** CONACULTA-INAH-MEX (c); Vikings of Middle England (cla). **278-279 Dorling Kindersley:** Royal Armouries, Leeds (c). **279 Bridgem an Images:** Wyllie, William Lionel (1851-1931) (tc). **281 123RF.com:** M R Fakhrurrozi (b); Peter Titmuss (c). **286 Dorling Kindersley:** Dan Crisp (bc)

Cover images: Front: **Dorling Kindersley:** Rob Reichenfeld cb, The National Railway Museum bc; **Science Photo Library:** Natural History Museum, London cb/ (Butterfly); Back: **Alamy Stock Photo:** Ian Dagnall cb/ (Helicopter); **Dorling Kindersley:** Bryan Bowles cb, Ruth Jenkinson / Holts Gems clb; **Getty Images:** Werner Lang cb

Key: a=above; c=center; b=below; l=left; r=right; t=top.

All other images © Dorling Kindersley
For further information see: www.dkimages.com